# MONTANA FLY FISHING AND CAMPING GUIDE

David Archer

www.glaciertoyellowstone.com

First edition 1999, *Montana Fishing and Camping Guide- Glacier to Yellowstone*

Revised 2002, *Montana Fly Fishing and Camping Guide*
ISBN 0-9670806-1-4

I welcome readers to post their fishing stories and anecdotes on my web site,
www.glaciertoyellowstone.com.

Published by David Archer, glaciertoyellowstone.com
5311 Leaning Tree, Florence, Montana 59833

E-mail: dave@glaciertoyellowstone.com

Cover photo by Bob Edgar
Book layout by Ariane C. Smith, vinepress.com/ariane
Fly photographs by Jan Herzog

Maps by Cartographics LLC
112 E. Crestline Drive
Missoula, MT 59803
www.montanamaps.com

Printed in the United States
ISBN 0-9670806-1-4

# ACKNOWLEDGMENTS

I would like to acknowledge Dick Konizeski's book, *The Montanans' Fishing Guide*, which I purchased over 20 years ago, when I moved from Wyoming to Montana. Although initially overwhelmed by the comprehensiveness of the book (Mary's Frog Pond), the book has served me well, and it has also inspired me to make the journey across Montana a little easier for new arrivals and visitors who want to fish and camp in this great state.

I would like to thank my wife Pauline for her support and encouragement as I trudged off to new waters year after year. Best of all, she never once questioned my need for another fishing boat to build and test. She has enriched my life, and I am thankful for her love and support.

I would especially like to thank my son Darin who has prodded and cajoled me to revise this book. He is my computer guru and the architect and designer of our web site, glaciertoyellowstone.com. When I was overwhelmed with the scope of the project and the prospect of digitally designing the book, he came to my rescue with a book designer, Ariane Smith, who scanned all of the photographs and arranged the text and icons. I would also like to thank my son Brandon for his support and help in the the designing of the cover.

Good maps enhance any guidebook so I would like to thank Kevin McCann of Cartographic, LLC in Missoula for his beautiful maps (www.montanamaps.com).

Finally, I would like to pay tribute to some great animal friends who have accompanied me on my journeys up and down the highways, on the rivers and in the backcountry. Thank you, Shadow, Max, Buddy and Banjo.

**Warning:** As much as possible, I have worked diligently to convey the most accurate and up-to-date information. With each passing season, however, Mother Nature shapes and molds her environment. Additionally, the stewards and protectors of these great lands add changes to protect and enhance our national treasures. Be sure to check with the proper agencies or authorities to determine access and restrictions to Montana fishing waters. Fishing regulations and restrictions are subject to change every year. Keep in mind that any trip into unfamiliar mountains or watersheds may offer hazards and dangers. The information covered in this book may be subject to errors, inaccuracies or changes since publication. Readers need to exercise safe fishing, floating and camping practices and not rely solely on the information contained in this book.

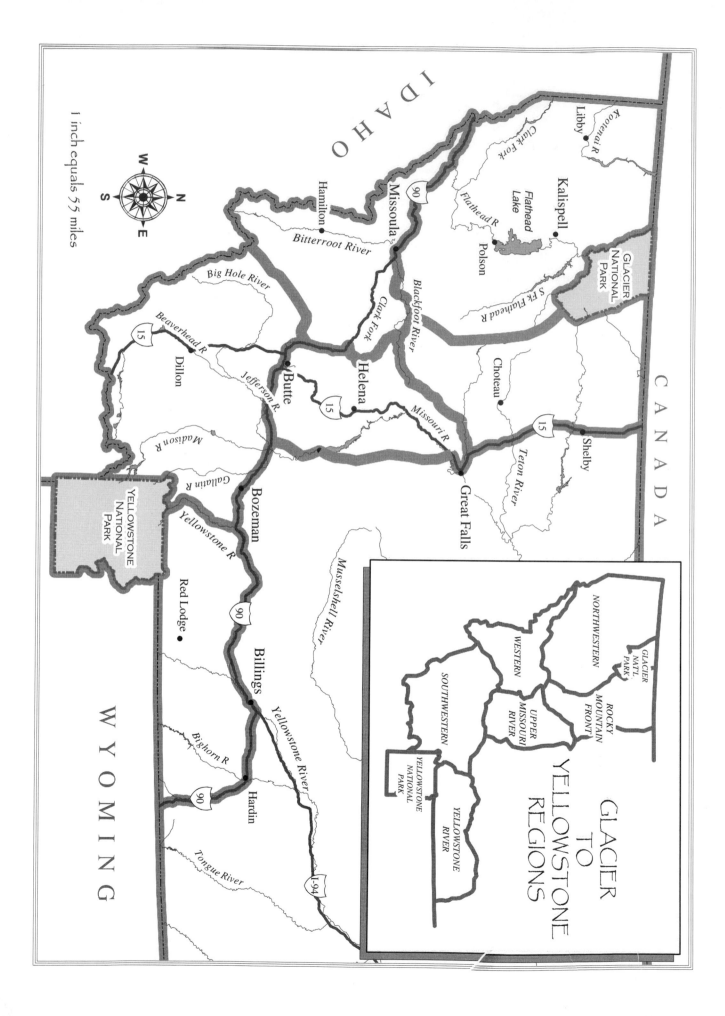

# TABLE OF CONTENTS

# ICON GUIDE

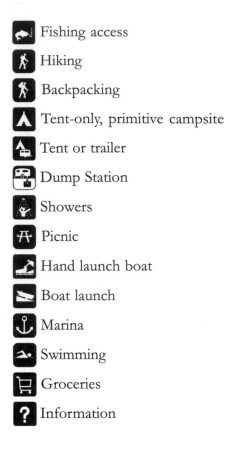

Fishing access

Hiking

Backpacking

Tent-only, primitive campsite

Tent or trailer

Dump Station

Showers

Picnic

Hand launch boat

Boat launch

Marina

Swimming

Groceries

Information

# INTRODUCTION: FLY PATTERNS AND HATCHES

I always drop by a fly shop if I am away from my home waters. The price of bugs is generally the same, but the information is invaluable. Shop owners frequently buy regional and specialty flies from their guides.

Keep in mind that each day shop outfitters send out their guides with the simple goal of getting their clients into fish, and everyday information is traded back and forth on what works, where it works and when it works. Shop owners and clerks readily pass on this information to first-time customers for half a dozen flies or less! Naturally, every shop has their killer flies that they use to expand the sale, but I don't believe that I have ever been

Pale Morning Dun                    Photo by Jan Herzog

duped. Fly shops in Montana have a very short season. In order to survive, they depend on customer loyalty, which in turn depends on their credibility. Regarding published hatch charts, take them with a grain of salt. Although I personally admire the dedication and perseverance that it takes to compile a hatch chart, the vagaries of Mother Nature generally render them in the category of "You should have been here last week." The following hatch information is a compilation from a number of sources

and is provided only to offer an overview. The best source of information will be from the local fly shops. Regardless of where you buy your flies, stay out of the bargain basement. Not all flies are tied equally.

For years I would shake my head in puzzlement when a client would open up his fly box and pull out a cheap and poorly-tied fly. Rather than upset a client's out-of-state purchasing acumen for Montana trout flies, I would just resort to some swaps if

I knew I was dealing with a tightfisted bargain hunter. Look for stiff neck hackles that will keep the fly high and dry. The next simple test is to look at the body to see if it is slender and proportionate. Finally, a good dry fly should have a three-point landing. When the fly is resting in the palm of your hand, the hackle and the tail should be aligned so that the bottom of the hook is barely resting on your palm. If the tail is too short, the fly will not land as well, nor will it offer the same profile to trout.

It is the fly that triggers the strike. The one topic guaranteed to generate instant conversation among fly anglers is the mention of fly patterns. No other facet of fly fishing evokes so much enthusiasm and reverence. Through the years many surveys have asked prominent fly fishers to share their favorite fly patterns. Lefty Kreh, in an article in *Field and Stream*, published February 1972, polled 12 expert fly fishers. The following list of dry flies, nymph flies and streamer flies represents a composite of the most frequently-used flies for each category among these 12 experts.

Dry Flies: Light Cahill, Adams, Royal Wulff, Irresistible, Quill Gordon, Humpy
Nymphs: Trueblood Otter Shrimp, Quill Gordon, Ed Burk, Yellow Stone Fly, Muskrat, Woolly Worm
Streamers: Black Nose Dace, Spruce Fly, Muddler Minnow, Gray Ghost, Black Marabou, White Marabou

Dan Abrams, in a similar type survey published in *Sports Afield*, October 1975, polled 30 notable fly fishers regarding their top four fly patterns. Seven of the 30 were prominent Rocky Mountain fly fishers. A generalized list of the most popular patterns produced the following: Adams, Royal Wulff, Humpy, Muddler Minnow and Gold-ribbed Hare's Ear Nymph. Add the Woolly Bugger and a Light Cahill in varying sizes and I would be content for quite some time. Well, of course, I would need to add a hopper pattern and a PMD and maybe a....

One of the great joys of fly fishing is sharing what works. If you are a beginner and meet a friendly fly fisher, pull out your fly box and ask,

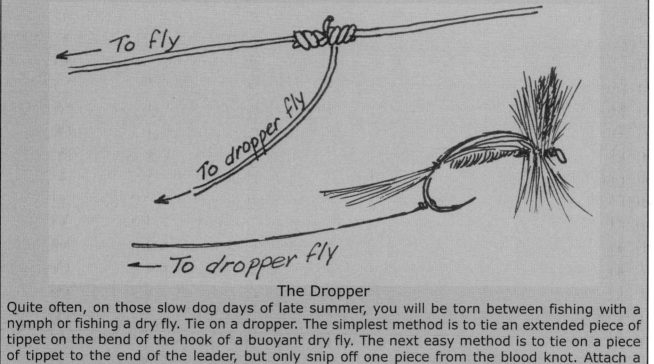

**The Dropper**
Quite often, on those slow dog days of late summer, you will be torn between fishing with a nymph or fishing a dry fly. Tie on a dropper. The simplest method is to tie an extended piece of tippet on the bend of the hook of a buoyant dry fly. The next easy method is to tie on a piece of tippet to the end of the leader, but only snip off one piece from the blood knot. Attach a nymph to the extra piece of line extending from the blood knot.

"Which one should I use?" I fondly recall many occasions when someone took me under their guidance and shared their secret fly for the day. Through the years my own collection of fly patterns grew in direct proportion to my fly fishing budget. Like most of the fly fishers I know, I can never have enough patterns. I have a number of match-the-hatch patterns for those special days, and I have my reliable stand-by attractor patterns and generic patterns that I started out with 35 years ago.

I have prioritized the following recommendations for the young beginner who has an empty fly box and a thin wallet. If you would like to begin tying your own flies, I highly recommend Jack Dennis's manual, *Western Trout Fly Tying Manual.* For a more in-depth approach to matching hatches, I recommend *The Complete Book of Western Hatches* by Rick Hafele and Dave Hughs.

For those of you who are new to the sport of fly fishing and have never fished in Montana, I offer 20 patterns that will cover about 90% of the fishing from Glacier to Yellowstone. Be observant of what the trout are feeding on and use a small aquarium net to scoop up the bugs and look at them closely. Purchase a fly box with a foam backing and sort your dry mayfly patterns by color and size. For example, I start out with light, cream-colored Cahills and progressively move across in increasingly darker shades to pale yellow, bright yellow, yellow-green, green, olive green and into the green-browns and finally mahogany and rust colors. I set up a separate row of gray and tan mayfly patterns. Personally, I am less concerned with Latin identification as I am with finding the right sized imitation in as close to the natural color as possible. Organizing my fly box in this manner helps me to locate a pattern quickly. It also reminds me what colors I am missing or what sizes I am missing. The following 20 patterns are the ones that "I never leave home without."

## Dry Fly Patterns

### 1. **Royal Wulff:** Sizes 10–16

The Royal Wulff is the definitive attractor pattern. Created by the famed Lee Wulff, it imitates nothing, and yet it offers to the trout an equivalent of

Royal Wulff                    Photo by Jan Herzog

an exquisite Julia Child masterpiece. Derisively called the "Dude Fly" because of its white calf-tail wing, this extravaganza brings the fish up! Best of all, it is a fly the caster never fails to see. To digress for the beginner, keep in mind that you have to set the hook, as the trout will spit the fly out on its dive back into the water. Most beginners miss the take because by the time they react, the fish is safely on its way. Wear Polaroid sunglasses so that you can begin to train your eyes for underwater movement. Early detection allows you to react more quickly.

Presentation: Classic, upstream dead drift.

## 2. Humpy (Goofus Bug): Sizes 10–16

The Humpy's origin, according to Jack Dennis, is shrouded in controversy. Whether the fly originated in Jackson, Wyoming, or elsewhere is really unimportant. What is important to the beginner is that this fly works, and it is an indispensable pattern to have in your fly box. Although it is an attractor pattern, it may imitate a large caddis or stonefly in larger sizes. The fly is ideal for fast-flowing waters because of its inherent buoyancy. The Royal Humpy is especially easy to track in fast water. When sparsely tied, the Humpy works amazingly well on slow waters and can be used to imitate a Little Yellow Stonefly. The great advantage of this fly for the beginner is that it is almost unsinkable, and it offers great visibility in fast water for both the fisherman and the trout. It is, however, a most challenging pattern to tie. The best directions for tying this pattern may be found in *The Second Fly-Tyers Almanac* by Robert H. Boyle and Dave Whitlock.

Presentation: Classic, upstream dead drift. However, since this pattern closely resembles a caddis fly and floats so well, try drifting the fly downstream under willows or overhanging branches. As the fly drifts to the targeted area, lift the rod tip up to create an erratic skipping motion on top of the water, and then lower the rod tip quickly to allow the fly to drift once again on top of the water. Await the strike!

Humpy

Renegade                          Photos by Jan Herzog

## 3. Renegade

It would appear that the Renegade attractor pattern has faded in popularity over the last 20 years, but it is a great fly for late evening fishing, as the white hackle in the front helps to see the fly on darkened waters. The second advantage is that the dual hackle design keeps the fly afloat when it is difficult to see after sundown. If you are new to the sport of fly fishing, be sure you have a good supply and a range of sizes for the Royal Wulff, the Humpy, the Renegade, the Adams and the Elk Hair Caddis.

**4. Adams/Parachute Adams:** Sizes 12–22

The ubiquitous Adams is probably the most widely-used dry fly pattern on the North American continent. It imitates any number of gray mayflies. I highly recommend acquiring as many Adams in various sizes as possible. Because of the difficult visibility with this pattern, I have switched over exclusively to Parachute Adams for sizes 16–22. Although this is a generic type pattern, a size 20 Parachute Adams performs quite well during a Trico or Baetis hatch on slow-moving water with a nine-foot leader and 6X tippet.

The Trico spinner imitation has a small black body with divided white poly wings in the spinner position. During the heat of summer, get out on a Rocky Mountain river between 7 and 9 AM (varies) for the Tricorithodes or Trico hatch followed by the spinner fall. Although one of the smallest of mayfly species, nonetheless, this is a staple for feeding trout primarily because of the preponderant numbers during the spinner fall. Generally found in slower waters, the trout settle into a sipping, rhythmic rise form. Do not be deceived by the small rings and the dark noses – big fish! Fish in the morning during those dog days of August. I'm sure you will be delighted with the experience regardless of how many fish break off and get away. Because I have trouble seeing a small Trico, I often add on a small Trico as a trailer behind a small Parachute Adams.

Presentation: Classic, upstream dead drift.

Gray Drakes (Heptagenia and Siphlonurus) typically hatch throughout the summer starting in early June. Sizes 10–18.

Tricorythodes typically hatch late in the summer, usually at the beginning of August. Sizes 20–26.

**5. Light Cahill or Light Variant:** Sizes 12–18

A light cream color Heptagenia mayfly imitation is another must have pattern. The Light Cahill pattern may also be used on slower waters and lakes to imitate Callibaetis. The Callibaetis dun body is olive-brown, however, so you may want to darken a few of your Light Cahills with a magic marker.

The Light Cahill can be used to imitate Ephemerella or Heptagenia mayflies, but be sure to closely inspect the size and color of the insect, and then match it with your color coded fly selection.

Parachute Adams

Light Cahill                    Photos by Jan Herzog

6. **PMD – Pale Morning Dun** (photo on page 1)
Pale Morning Duns are probably the most prolific and reliable hatch from Glacier to Yellowstone. These Ephemerella drake patterns should be part of your must-have patterns in sizes 16–22. PMDs hatch from June through October. Lighter in color from their cousins the Green Drakes, their bodies range from olive green to pale yellow and tan. The wings are generally slate gray to yellow. PMD cripples should be part of your collection. Nymph patterns such as the Zug Bug, Gray Nymph and the Hare's Ear generally work well. The darker green patterns will work well during a Baetis hatch as well.

Elk-Hair Caddis

Blue-Wing Olive                    Photos by Jan Herzog

The famous Green Drake hatches (Ephemerella grandis) are typically from mid-June through mid-July. If you are in an area with a Green Drake hatch, be sure to stock up on a number of these drake patterns at the nearest fly shop. The hatch is generally not heavy, but if they are out, the trout are looking for them. Reports from guides returning to the shop will determine if you should buy traditional drake patterns or Compara Duns or Green Paradrakes. All of the above patterns range in color from pale yellow to green to olive brown. Stock up.

7. **Elk Hair Caddis:** Sizes 10–18
Unlike the graceful rise and gliding fall of the mayfly, a caddis hatch looks like a burst of kindergartners swarming over a playground. An accompanying soundtrack for a mayfly would be a Viennese waltz. Conversely, the caddis dance would be a rap soundtrack by Snoop Dogg. Generally, the caddis will hatch in the evening. The most popular body colors are brown, olive, green, gray and tan.

Caddis flies are not easily missed, and in the pupa and winged stages they are an important part of the trout's diet. Look for them in the quiet pocket water under willow branches or overhangs, especially in the evening. You may also want to select a few patterns for the emergent phase such as a sparkle pupa. For larger caddis imitations use a Humpy or an X-Caddis. Use a Goddard Caddis for fast, heavy water.

One of the guides I worked with collected the caddis cases and tied them on a Mustad hook with a peacock thorax. He fished them on a dead drift, and I was impressed! Beginning with the Grannom Caddis hatch in May, caddis emerge throughout the summer and fall. The most consistently popular pattern is the Elk Hair Caddis.
Presentation: Classic, upstream dead drift or erratic action produced by rod tip action.

8. **Blue-Wing Olive:** Sizes 16–22
The Baetis (Blue-Wing Olive) is an important pattern in Montana, as Baetis hatch from May through October. They are generally smaller than a PMD. The body color for a Baetis pattern is olive brown with gray wings and light gray hackle. It is not uncommon for trout to be sipping the smaller Baetis during a hatch of PMDs.

9. **Salmon Fly**
Montana's favorite hatch calls for big bugs that hold up under heavy water conditions. They need to stay high and dry. The Salmon Fly pattern is constantly being reinvented and improved. During a Salmon Fly hatch, local shops have these flies displayed in tubs and buckets. The Salmon Fly hatch generally emerges late May and is essentially over by mid July. Water temperatures need to be in the low 50s.

10. **Stimulator**
The Stimulator represents a pattern for stoneflies in orange and yellow. When the trout quit hitting the big Salmon Fly patterns, they tend to strike at smaller stimulators long after the Salmon Fly hatch is over. The Stimulator is best used during a Golden Stonefly hatch.

### Streamers and Wet Flies

11. **Muddler Minnow:** Sizes 4–8
Popularized by Dan Bailey of Livingston, Montana, the Muddler Minnow should always be in your fly box. I have met fly fishers who fish almost exclusively with Muddler Minnow patterns. Along with its offshoot, the Marabou Muddler, this pattern has probably taken more large fish than any other fly. The Muddler may also be greased up and used as an effective

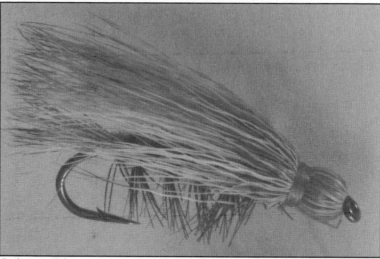
Salmon Fly

Stimulator

Muddler Minnow                    Photos by Jan Herzog

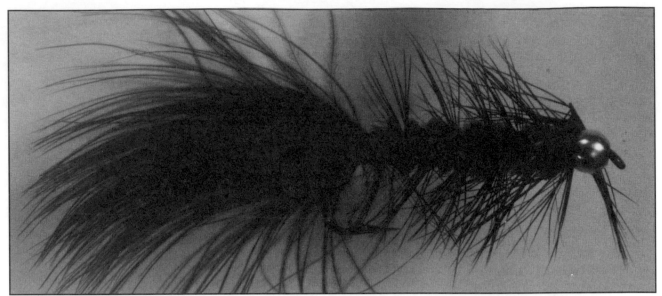

Woolly Bugger

Yuk Bug

hopper pattern, and I have used it both dry and wet on the same cast with interesting results.

Presentation: Fish the Muddler slightly upstream or downstream in a quartering action. Retrieve the Muddler by simultaneously pumping the rod tip and stripping in the line in quick, little jerks which imitates the darting action of a sculpin minnow. Allow for pauses, and add weight if necessary.

make short casts around all the rocks and boulders. Be sure the fly is actually sinking to the bottom. Add lead to your leader if necessary. Use a short 2X or 3X leader. Make short casts and keep the rod tip high so that you keep the Bugger bouncing along the bottom. Lift the rod tip when you feel a bump. Do not assume it is just a rock. If it is, lower the rod tip and let the bugger sink again.

12. **Woolly Bugger:** Sizes 4–8
This pattern is a must for late spring and early summer when the water is high and off-color and the hatches are sporadic. If you are fishing from shore,

13. **Yuk Bug and Girdle Bug:** Sizes 6–12
I love this bug! I have caught so many beautiful fish during early summer when the water is still high but clear. I float along until I find a logjam or flooded

backwater eddy. I usually select a size 10 Yuk Bug. The Yuk Bug has a dark body wrapped with grizzly hackle. Protruding from the body are white rubber legs. I find I generally have to cut back on the length of the rubber legs. I want them to pulse, and I want them to flare at the sides rather than collapsing backwards. I do not use weight. I fish it like a dry fly, allowing it to gradually sink. Most important, I cast from a kneeling position. I am always amazed at how adept large trout are at hiding. As the Yuk Bug sinks into quiet water, the trout will slowly emerge from its hiding spot. I have had large trout appear from under a small tree trunk in shallow water. They never rush to the Yuk. They take their time. It also works well in creeks and small streams. I love this bug!

## Nymphs

### 14. Hare's Ear Nymph: Sizes 12–16

In my opinion, this is the best of the small nymph patterns for spring creeks, beaver ponds and slow, flat stretches of river. When I fish high-elevation lakes, I always bring along the Hare's Ear Nymph and a Zug Bug in smaller sizes. They work wonders. If you have someone along who is not an accomplished fly caster, use a plastic water-filled bubble with as long of a leader as possible. Attach a Hare's Ear or Zug Bug and cast out as far as possible and retrieve with a spinning reel. If the fish are rising to the surface, be sure to cast way over them, as the splashdown from the water-filled bubble will spook the fish in the near vicinity.

### 15. Bead-head Prince Nymph

This is perhaps the most popular nymph in the region! If you don't have any, head to the nearest fly shop. They work great as a dropper off a hopper pattern during the heat of August.

### 16. Pheasant Tail (not pictured)

The Pheasant Tail Nymph is an excellent soft hackle nymph for slow water. The key to this fly is a slender silhouette and a sparely-tied hackle.

Bead-Head Zug Bug

Bead-Head Hare's Ear Nymph

Bead-Head Prince Nymph          Photos by Jan Herzog

## Terrestrials

### 17. Hopper (Joe's, Dave's, Jay's, Dan's):
Sizes 6–12

As you can see from the partial list of Hopper contributors, grasshopper imitations are recorded in the "Who's Who of Terrestrials". Rarely, however, will you find such citations on the bins in a fly shop. For beginners I recommend a clipped deer-hair collar. This feature adds stability and superior floatation. Although the grasshopper is meant to have a low silhouette, without the deer hair the buoyancy is drastically reduced and the caster generally struggles with a sinking pattern.

Presentation: The best source of information on hoppers can be found in the September 1985 issue of *Fly Fisherman*. In this issue Dave Whitlock, in his article "Hoppertunity", discusses hopper behavior, pattern characteristics and Hoppertunity Techniques. Here are a few of his suggestions: Being a terrestrial insect, the grasshopper is on unfamiliar "ground" when he gets blown on the water. No gentle landings here. Make a splash with your hopper. Strip the hopper in with intermittent twitches from rod-tip action. Use a heavy tippet, and use a twist piece of lead to sink the hopper in those promising pools. Cast close to undercut banks and overhangs where trout hide during low water periods. Fish during the heat of the day. Carefully pick your targeted area. Although a smashing hopper on top of the water will trigger a strike, it also quite often spooks fish in the outlying area. Keep moving and practice stealth.

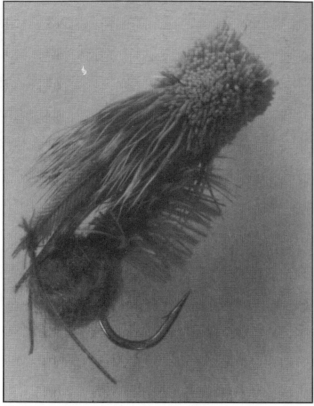

Hopper

### 18. Beetle Patterns
The deer hair patterns dyed black work wonders. Rick Hafele and Dave Hughes in their outstanding book, *The Complete Book of Western Hatches*, point out that the Woolly Worm is also a good pattern to imitate a water beetle in still or slow moving water.

Beetle                    Photos by Jan Herzog

## 19. Ant

Although ant patterns are difficult to see in small sizes, ants are a staple diet for trout during the summer.

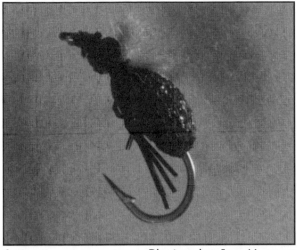

Ant                    Photos by Jan Herzog

## 20. Bead-Head San Juan Worm

I have always had a certain amount of disdain for the San Juan Worm, but I have a growing appreciation for this pattern during the spring and again late in the fall. I favor the bead-head version with the bead in the center.

Well, there you have it – the 20 patterns that I would never leave home without.

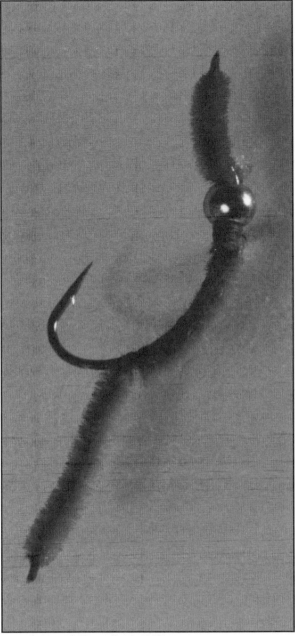

Bead-Head San Juan Worm

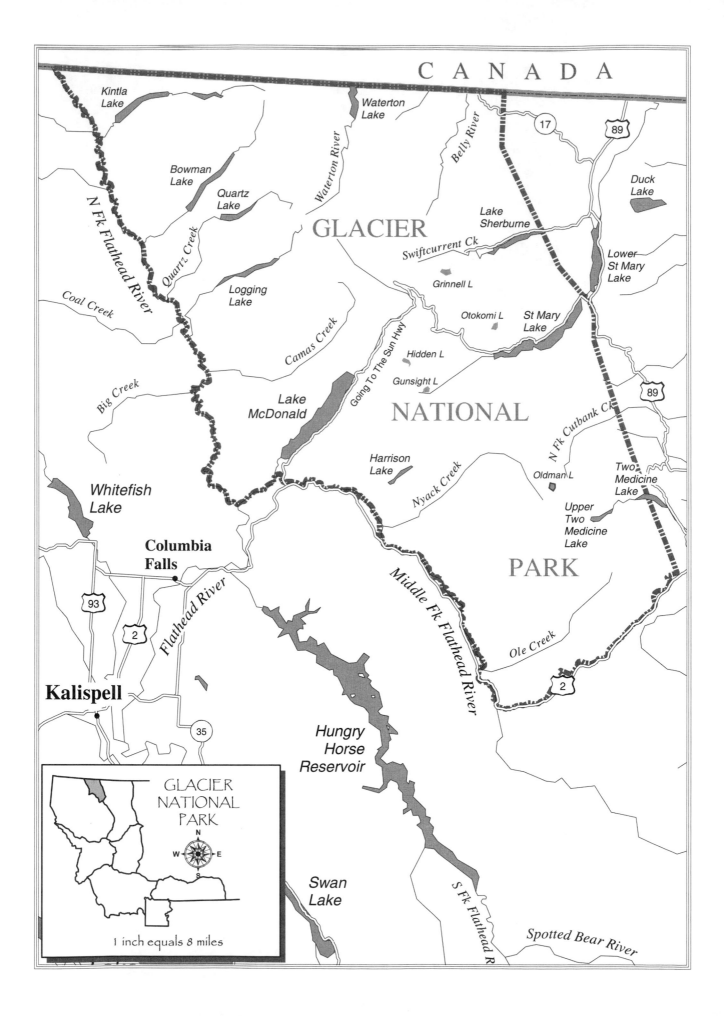

CANADA

Kintla Lake

Waterton Lake

Belly River

Duck Lake

Bowman Lake

Quartz Lake

Waterton River

GLACIER

Lake Sherburne

Swiftcurrent Ck

Lower St Mary Lake

N Fk Flathead River

Quartz Creek

Grinnell L

Coal Creek

Logging Lake

Camas Creek

Otokomi L

St Mary Lake

Big Creek

Going To The Sun Hwy

Hidden L

Gunsight L

NATIONAL

Lake McDonald

Harrison Lake

N Fk Cutbank Ck

Oldman L

Two Medicine Lake

Whitefish Lake

Nyack Creek

Upper Two Medicine Lake

PARK

Columbia Falls

93

2

Flathead River

Middle Fk Flathead River

Ole Creek

Kalispell

35

2

Hungry Horse Reservoir

GLACIER NATIONAL PARK

N
W    E
S

Swan Lake

S Fk Flathead R

Spotted Bear River

1 inch equals 8 miles

# 1
# GLACIER NATIONAL PARK

Looking up at Boulder Pass and Hole in the Wall.
Photo courtesy of Christopher P. Johnson

## Fishing and Camping in Glacier National Park

Covering 1,584 square miles of majestic mountains and icy glaciers, the mountainous wonders of Glacier National Park are viewed by over two million visitors a year. Unlike Yellowstone National Park, which is a mecca for fly fishers from all around the country, Glacier National Park does not host legendary Montana trout fishing rivers and streams like the rivers draining out of Yellowstone National Park. Float fishers, however, will be delighted with the stunning scenery and good fishing that the North Fork and Middle Fork of the Flathead River provides. These

forks serve as the Park boundaries. Glacier does offer good fishing opportunities in over 50 lakes for those fishers who are willing to trek four to six miles or more into the interior lakes. Consider the added pleasure of fishing a bonus to a scenic hike into the wilderness. When fishing high mountain lakes, anglers should prepare themselves for the fickle variance of weather and finicky trout. As with most day-hike fishing trips, the fishing generally picks up towards evening when you are arriving back at your vehicle.

Since the late 1960s, Glacier National Park has not stocked trout, preferring to enhance and protect native species such as cutthroat, lake trout, bull trout and Arctic grayling. Thirty years later, Park anglers enjoy the fruits of a more natural ecology. With this opportunity comes the responsibility for preserving and maintaining these wild trout populations. Please consider adopting the practice of catch-and-

release and using single, barbless hooks. A secondary incentive for this conservation practice is that you further protect yourself from curious bears and their incredible olfactory powers.

Although I have included some backcountry trips with my donkey Buddy, my basic goal in this guidebook is to cover backcountry lakes that may be reached in a day hike. When I decided to expand this book, I resolved to personally fish most of the waters covered in this book. However, sometimes goals are quickly modified with a dose of reality. Glacier National Park has just too many lakes to cover in two or three summers. Many of the lakes covered in this book I did not fish, especially the larger lakes, which are fished best from a boat; some of the lakes I fished for a short time before heading back down the trail. Hard hikes of six or seven miles I passed up, preferring to gather information from other fishing and hiking books on Glacier. For those of you who prefer to backpack and fish the backcountry lakes, I would recommend Russ Schneider's book, *Fishing Glacier National Park* (ISBN: 1-56044-626-9). Another book that I recommend is *Hiker's Guide to Glacier National Park,* which is published by the Glacier Natural History Association in cooperation with the National Park Service (ISBN: 0-915030-24-1).

## Fishing Tips

Most of the Park's smaller lakes are home to brook trout, cutthroat and bull trout. Cutthroat will generally cruise along the shoreline during the day, providing opportunities for the fly fisher. With the approach of dusk, however, the spin fisher will have the advantage by tossing a water-filled bubble far out into the lake and slowly reeling in a small nymph such as a Gold-Ribbed Hare's Ear, a Zug Bug, a bead-

Going-to-the-Sun Road – view of the valley

head Prince or a drowned Elk Hair Caddis. Backpackers with belly boats and flippers will find greater opportunities for those trout cruising just out of range from the shore. If you are a spin fisher, small popular lures such as Mepps, Thomas Cyclone, Rappala and Daredevils are Park standards, as they are for most trout lakes.

If you are new to fly fishing on a lake, I would suggest carrying an assortment of size 16 and 18 dry fly standards such as a yellow Humpy, Parachute Adams, Royal Wulffs, Renegades and Elk Hair Caddis. If you are fishing the outlet of a lake, be sure to have some ant and beetle patterns for late in the summer. Finally, be sure your fly box has a few Girdle Bugs and streamers. One of the best sources for fly fishing high-elevation mountain lakes is Gary LaFontaine's book, *Fly Fishing the Mountain Lakes.* Glacier National Park provides excellent cutthroat fishing in the North Fork of the Flathead River and the Middle Fork of the Flathead River.

Be sure to read the fishing regulations carefully. Keep in mind that your best source of fishing information is often the Park rangers, as Glacier has no stocking programs, and trout populations are adversely impacted by harsh winters. Additionally, trails are often closed due to bear activity or snow conditions. Many of the higher elevation lakes are not reached or fishable until early to mid-July. Be sure to bring bug spray, and for some lakes a mosquito net is essential early in the summer. Regarding the Park's policy on stocking trout, "the National Park Service no longer plants fish in Park waters… The reason is simple. The introduction of exotic game fishes was found to be detrimental to Glacier's native fishes. Predation and competition for space and food adversely affected several native species, and hybridization between indigenous and non-native species of fish also occurred. The native westslope cutthroat trout has been all but eliminated from several lakes, where it was once the dominant species. Today the National Park Service is engaged in fisheries research to determine the extent of damage to native fish populations, and to explore possible means for re-establishing native fishes in some waters where they have been eliminated or replaced by hybrid populations…for the benefit and enjoyment of future generations." –Park newsletter

## Hiking Tips

Fishing in Glacier National Park presents some risks. Of serious concern is preparing for the weather. Summer temperatures may range in the high 80s to low 90s. A common axiom in the mountain communities of Montana is that if you don't like the weather, stick around another 15 minutes! The summer rainfall averages two inches per month. More importantly, daytime temperatures can plummet with the arrival of storm clouds, regardless of how warm the day starts. The eastern border of the Park along the Rocky Mountain Front is always subject to wind blowing up through the canyons across the lakes. It is not uncommon for overnight lows to drop below freezing anywhere in the Park. In August of 1992, a foot of snow fell on the northeastern section of the Park. Dress in layers and always carry raingear.

Another safety concern is contact with bears. The risks of coming in contact with a bear may be minimized with prudent and precautionary behavior. BEAR in mind, of course, that the fickle finger of fate will inevitably point to one of us sooner or later. However, the statistics of bear attacks per Park visitations should provide comfort. Unfortunately, just prior to my first trek into bear country my neighbor kindly loaned me the book *Mark of the Grizzly*. I had already incurred some trepidation when I met a coroner, whose duties include deaths in Glacier National Park. I met the man at a Mule and Donkey Show in Drummond, Montana. He told me he wouldn't think about taking his family into the backcountry of Glacier, preferring instead to ride and hike in the Mission Mountains.

Take the time to read the Park literature on bears. Your chances of being attacked by a bear are about one in a million. The odds are greater that you will be struck by lightning while hiking in the Park. But when there is lightning in the area, I don't stand around smelling the ozone. Read all the Park advisories on avoiding bears. Here are some suggestions taken from the Waterton-Glacier Guide that each Park visitor receives.

"If you surprise a bear, here are a few guidelines to follow that may help:

• Talk quietly or not at all; the time to make loud noise is before you encounter a bear. Try to detour around the bear if possible.

• Do not run! Back away slowly, but stop if it seems to agitate the bear.

• Assume a non-threatening posture. Turn sideways, or bend at the knees to appear smaller.

• Use peripheral vision. Bears appear to interpret direct eye contact as threatening.

• Drop something (not food) to distract the bear. Keep your pack on for protection in case of an attack.

• If a bear attacks and you have pepper spray, use it!

• If the bear makes contact, protect your chest and abdomen by falling to the ground on your stomach, or assuming a fetal position to reduce the severity of the attack. Cover the back of your neck with your hands. Do not move until you are certain the bear has left....

• If you are attacked at night, or if you feel you have been stalked and attacked as prey, try to escape. If you cannot escape, or if the bear follows, use pepper spray, or shout and try to intimidate the bear with a branch or rock. Do whatever it takes to let the bear know you are not easy prey."

Because bears have an incredible sense of smell, Park guidelines remind fishers to use garbage cans to dispose of entrails. "When cleaning fish in the backcountry, puncture the air bladder, and throw entrails deep into water at least 200 feet from the nearest campsite or trail. Do not bury or burn entrails, as they will attract bears."

Finally, be sure to bring along plenty of mosquito repellant, a face net and a raincoat to protect yourself against pests and the elements. —Park newsletter

## Campgrounds in
## Glacier National Park

**Note:** The following information was taken from the *Waterton Glacier Guide*, which is given to each Park visitor. You may request a copy by writing Glacier National Park, West Glacier, MT 59936 or by calling (406) 888-7800. Visit their web site at www.nps.gov/glac for up-to-date information.

"Campgrounds in Glacier provide just over 1,000 campsites. Most are available on a 'first-come, first-served' basis. Fish Creek and St. Mary campgrounds may be reserved ahead through the National Park Service Registration System by calling 800-365-CAMP.

"Campsites are limited to 8 people and 2 vehicles per site. Most campgrounds have drinking water, restrooms with flush toilets, and cold running water. Utility hookups are not available."

- **Apgar:** The campground opens May 7 and closes October 18. There are a total of 196 sites; 25 sites are set aside for RVs. The campground offers flush toilets and a disposal station.
- **Avalanche:** The campground opens June 18 and closes September 7. There are a total of 87 sites; 50 sites have lengths of 26 feet. The campground offers flush toilets but no disposal station.
- **Bowman Lake:** The campground opens May 14 and closes September 15. Bowman offers 48 camping sites, but RVs are not recommended (primitive road).
- **Cut Bank:** The campground opens May 8 and closes September 13. Cut Bank has 19 sites, but RVs are not recommended.
- **Fish Creek:** The campground opens June 1 and closes September 7. Offering 180 sites, three sites provide a maximum length of 35 feet. Flush toilets and a disposal station are provided.
- **Kintla Lake:** The campground opens May 21 and closes September 15. The campground offers 13 sites, but RVs are not recommended.
- **Logging Lake:** The campground opens July 1 and closes September 7. Logging Lake has eight campsites, but RVs are not recommended.

- **Many Glacier:** The campground opens May 28 and closes September 22. Offering 110 campsites, 13 sites have a maximum length of 35 feet. Flush toilets and a disposal are provided.
- **Quartz Creek:** The campground opens July 1 and closes September 7. Quartz Creek has 7 camping sites, but RVs are not recommended.
- **Rising Sun:** The campground opens May 28 and closes September 23. Offering 83 campsites, three sites have a maximum length of 30 feet. Flush toilets and a disposal station are provided.
- **Sprague Creek:** The campground opens May 21 and closes September 27. The campground offers 25 sites, but no towing units are allowed. Flush toilets are provided.
- **St. Mary:** The campground opens May 28 and closes September 13. Offering 148 campsites, 25 sites have a maximum length of 35 feet. Flush toilets and a disposal station are provided.
- **Two Medicine:** The campground opens May 28 and closes September 13. Offering 99 campsites, 13 sites have a maximum length of 32 feet. Flush toilets and a disposal station are provided.

# Glacier National Park's
# Boundary Waters

### Glacier-fed: North Fork and
### Middle Fork of the Flathead River

The combined area of Glacier National Park and the Flathead National Forest will keep any angler busy with over 2,000 miles of streams and more than 900 lakes, most of which provide naturally-reproducing trout. The Flathead River has been designated as a National Wild and Scenic River, which Congress declared "shall be preserved in free-flowing condition, and that they and their immediate environments shall be protected for the benefit and enjoyment of present and future generations...."

The three forks of the Flathead River testify to the raw force of nature and qualify as part of the

National Scenic River Act. Essentially a migratory fishery out of Flathead Lake, the forks of the Flathead River offer unspoiled beauty. With one look at the high water marks and the scrubbed riverbed, a fisher will know immediately why he or she is sharing the river with white-water rafters and kayakers.

Basically the force of spring run-off in glaciated country dooms the forks to a nutrient-deficient environment. This in turn impacts the insect hatches and limits the opportunity for resident trout populations. For the wade angler, all three forks have limited accessibility due to steep canyons and private property on the North Fork and the Middle Fork.

Rafters should have white-water experience before they attempt float fishing any one of the three forks. Some of the coldest river water in the state is found on the South Fork and the North Fork. Rafters need to be properly equipped, experienced and prepared. Although low water levels appear by mid-August, each of the forks offers class II and III spots that can sneak up on rafters intent on catching fish.

The International Scale for River Difficulty grades water based on the characteristics and action of the water as well as how much maneuvering is called for in a given passage. The North Fork, after high water, is generally a Class II water, although some dangerous Class III water may be found between Big Creek and Glacier Rim. The Middle Fork offers Class IV and V whitewater in certain stretches during high water. The South Fork below Spotted Bear is generally rated Class II and III. I highly recommend the guide "Three Forks

of the Flathead River – Floating Guide", published by the Glacier Natural History Association in co-operation with the Flathead National Forest and Glacier National Park. I would also recommend the Montana Afloat river maps, which may be purchased at most of the local fly shops.

At this point I need to add a disclaimer. My descriptions of the forks of the Flathead River are taken from numerous public sources and are not intended as a reliable river guide. I have never floated any section that is rated over class III. Anyone attempting to float these rivers should contact local experts. Finally, float fishers should have a clear understanding of their own boating capabilities and never attempt to float and fish waters beyond their capabilities. Many float fishers have never practiced self-rescue, nor are they trained in rescue skills, CPR or first aid. I am always amazed at how poorly prepared many floaters are in preparing for a fishing trip. In truth, I, too, have been careless in preparing for some outings. Knowing the responsibility that I owe all of my passengers, it always makes me feel a little uneasy when I find I have missed an item or two. Float fishers should always have the following items in their raft or drift boat.

Any family member who has lost a loved one from a boating accident will implore you to insist that every passenger wear an approved life jacket. Keep a lifeline handy at all times as well as a spare oar. Bring along plenty of rope and a first aid kit. A dry bag for extra clothes is essential. Keep this bag where it can be easily grabbed. Add to this bag the necessary provisions for starting a fire, and be sure to throw in some extra batteries for the flash-

Sunken drift boat

light. For years I carried a flare in my dry bag when I floated in the late fall or winter. A flare is a quick fire starter. Beware of the vagaries of weather. Hypothermia is always a present danger in Montana. Even water temperatures in the high 50s can drain one's strength and rob the body of heat loss. A good knife and a fold-up saw are essential. The biggest safety tip is the most obvious and most often overlooked: the oarsman should be completely sober and alert at all times. This means scanning the river ahead 100 yards at a time and pulling over to scout any difficult passage. As the accompanying photograph attests, taking your eyes of the river or helping a buddy land a fish is the primary factor in many river accidents.

I once watched a man excitedly fishing a pod of rising rainbows. He had turned his gaze behind the boat and was attempting to catch one of the sippers behind him. The sweeper, a tall cottonwood tree stretching out into the river, was clearly visible for 200 yards. I yelled at the man, but I was too far back, and my voice did not carry. The tree flipped him out of his small boat and dumped him into the chilly waters in one quick motion. Although I can not claim to have rescued him, he was extremely grateful when I came along and provided him with warm clothes and helped him to aright his boat. I wish I could be smug and arrogant, but I, too, was once a fool and flipped a raft with two anglers. The following is a paraphrased American version of the International Scale for River Difficulty.

### International Scale for River Difficulty

**Class I: Very easy** – Class I water provides small, regular waves with few obstacles. Very little maneuvering is necessary.

**Class II: Novice** – Class II water requires some maneuvering but medium-sized waves are avoidable.

**Class III: Intermediate** – Class III water offers numerous waves, narrow passages and precise maneuvering to avoid large waves, rocks or sweepers. Scouting may be required. Boat fishers with little river experience should not attempt Class III waters.

**Class IV: Advanced** – Class IV challenges kayakers with intense rapids, abrupt bends, narrow passages, and precise maneuvering. Precision maneuvers are required with no options! Scouting is usually required, and self-rescue may be difficult.

**Class V: Expert** – Class V water clearly raises the level of risk for kayakers with long rapids, wild turbulence and extremely congested routes. Complex maneuvering requires scouting.

**Class VI: Extreme–Limits of Navigation** – Nearly impossible and a definite hazard to life.

**Note:** A detailed, spiral-bound series of maps of all three forks may be purchased at the following information centers:

Glacier View Ranger District
774 Railroad Street EN
Columbia Falls, MT 59912
Information: (406) 892-4372

Hungry Horse Ranger District
Box 340
Hungry Horse, MT 59919
Information: (406) 387-5243

## The North Fork of the Flathead River

**General location:** The North Fork of the Flathead River serves as Glacier National Park's western boundary. The North Fork is 22 miles north of Columbia Falls, Montana.

**Maps:** USGS Glacier National Park (ISBN 0-607-32671-9); *Montana Atlas and Gazetteer,* p.83

**Fishing conditions and species:** bull trout, cutthroat, lake trout, rainbow trout, and whitefish

**Special restrictions:** If you fish the west bank, you will need a Montana license. Within the Park you must carry in your possession a copy of the regulations. Cutthroats are protected and must be released.

**Regional Forest Service info:** (406) 387-3800

The North Fork originates in Canada, with the east shore being the border of Glacier National Park. Access for the wade fisher is somewhat limited as the road parallels the river high up the mountain sides in places. Wade fishers are limited to six public access points on the North Fork Road: Canadian Border, Ford, Polebridge, Big Creek, Glacier Rim and Blankenship Bridge. A few undeveloped sites offer access to the river as well. One such access point is at Moose Creek above Polebridge and at the bridge crossing for Coal Creek, which is 5.8 miles north of the Camas Creek Entrance. The Coal Banks offers primitive camping and a primitive boat launch. Keep in mind, however, that access points on the North Fork may also be reached from the Inside North Fork Road inside the Park both above Polebridge and below it. Regardless of which road you select, plan on a bumpy, dusty slow ride north of the Camas Creek Entrance. Big Creek, a few miles from the Camas Creek Entrance, offers the only developed campground on the North Fork. The campground is a fee campground and includes a non-fee picnic site and a boat launch. The campground offers 22 campsites, toilets, water, an RV dump station and a swimming area. Inside the Park, the campgrounds at Quartz Creek and Logging Creek are a distance from the river.

Pick up the North Fork Road inside the Park at the Fish Creek Campground, which is 2.5 miles from the T-intersection at the Apgar Entrance. The Park's North Fork Road is "maintained in primitive condition" and the speed limit is 20 mph. Trailers and large RVs are discouraged from using the road. From Fish Creek Campground to Polebridge is 27 miles; Bowman Lake is 33 miles and Kintla Lake is 43 miles.

Although the North Fork is home to some huge bull trout on their spawning runs between July and October, the majority of the trout will be migratory cutthroats from 8 to 10-inches moving up and down the river between April and August. The North Fork is heavily silted and appears more turquoise in color than the Middle Fork and the South Fork. To reach the North Fork, turn onto Nucleus Street in Columbia Falls. Follow the signs to Glacier National Park, a distance of 22 miles.

Access above the Park entrance is limited due to private property. The first float section is from the border to Ford Access, a distance of 14 miles with a Class II rating. From the Ford Access to Polebridge is 11 river miles and is rated Class II. From Polebridge to Big Creek is 18 miles and is rated as Class II. The next float, from Big Creek to Glacier Rim, is probably the most popular float among the local guides. It is 12 miles and is rated Class II and III. The last float, a short four miles, is from Glacier Rim to Blankenship Bridge and is Class I. The Blankenship Bridge turn-off is before the Glacier Rim Access. The bridge is located just below the

**Fishing conditions and species:** bull trout, cutthroat, lake trout, rainbow trout, and whitefish
**Special restrictions:** If you fish the Montana side, you will need a Montana license. Within the Park you must carry in your possession a copy of the regulations. Cutthroats are protected and must be released.

The only campground in the area is the non-fee campground at Devil Creek. The campground is 38 miles from the entrance to the Park.

## The Middle Fork of the Flathead River
By Steve Smith

Middle Fork of the Flathead River with Glacier National Park on the other bank

confluence of the North Fork and the Middle Fork. On one side of the bridge is a boat launch, and on the other side is a county non-fee campground. Blankenship Bridge may also be reached from Highway 2 above Coram. (Look for mileage marker 148. Take the second left after the marker (148.3). When you reach a hairpin turn, bear left and head down the mountain. From the highway to the bridge is 3.8 miles.)

### The Middle Fork of the Flathead River
**General location:** The Middle Fork of the Flathead River serves as Glacier National Park's southwestern boundary. The Middle Fork is south of the West Entrance on Highway 2.
**Maps:** USGS Glacier National Park (ISBN 0-607-32671-9); *Montana Atlas and Gazetteer,* p 83-84 (ISBN 0-89933-226-9)

When was the last time you fished a river and a grizzly bear swam in front of your boat? Or you came away from the day amazed that fish would live in such fast water, let alone be able to see and rise to your fly as it sped by them? Or you wondered whether you had fished during a whitewater trip or shot some rapids while fishing? And maybe at the end of the day you exclaim, "Holy cow, it has been such a great day, it wouldn't have mattered if we didn't catch a fish at all" (even though you wouldn't really mean that).

The Middle Fork of the Flathead River punches its way through the mountains of northwest Montana. From its beginnings in the Great Bear Wilderness area, the Middle Fork offers a unique blend of scenery, wildlife and fishing in uncrowded and pristine surroundings. From Bear Creek, where the river leaves the Great Bear 45 miles downstream, to Blankenship Bridge, the river separates Glacier National Park and the Bob Marshall Wilderness Complex (of which the Great Bear is a component). Highway 2 and the Burlington Northern Railway run through the canyon cut by the river, though they seldom impose on it.

The Middle Fork is a freestone stream. Freestone streams are not overly rich in nutrients, so the Middle Fork doesn't boast prolific insect hatches or even predictable ones. What it lacks in numbers of insects, it makes up for by supporting one of the most diverse arrays of aquatic insects in the lower 48 states. Understanding this is the key to success on the Middle Fork.

The fish on the Middle Fork, primarily native westslope cutthroat trout and a growing wild rainbow population, thrive in the cool, clear and fast water of the river. They are accustomed to seeing all sorts of insects shooting by them in the current at a high rate of speed.

Envision a native cutthroat lying on the bottom just downstream of a fast riffle waiting for the current to wash feed down to it. The trout snatches up a stonefly nymph, scrambling along the bottom. Next, an emerging mayfly suspended mid-depth floats by and is devoured. Then an adult caddis fly, bobbing along in the choppy water on top, goes flashing by, and the cutthroat goes for it. What the trout may not distinguish in its rush to swallow whatever feed the current delivers is that the caddis fly is a number 12 Elk Hair Caddis on the end of your tippet. The fish, forever famished, doesn't have the luxury of an in-depth analysis on the Middle Fork. Chuck out a high-riding dry fly into choppy water, mend like crazy and pay attention.

Westslope cutthroat trout are indigenous to the river. The higher up the river, the more you will find.

The rainbow trout population is self-sustaining now and is considered wild. The rainbows and cutthroats can interbreed, resulting in the "cuttbow" hybrid. Bull trout also are native to the river. Sadly, sediments from logging roads have destroyed spawning habitats and heavy fishing pressure has combined to dwindle the reserves of this fishery so that it is now illegal to even fish for bull trout. Care must be exercised to properly identify fish caught on the Middle

One of a few easy access points on the Middle Fork of the Flathead River

Fork. Bull trout are often mistaken for brook and lake trout which also inhabit these waters.

The Middle Fork is included in the wild and scenic river system and so is looked after by the U.S. Forest Service. Remember that the north bank of the river is the boundary of Glacier National Park, which has a separate set of regulations concerning camping and other activities.

Access to the river is good, although a four-wheel drive vehicle is handy for some boat launches. Bear Creek is the highest access point along Highway 2. Below that is a rough, sandy access by the bridge at Walton. Paola Creek access is downstream, followed by Cascadilla Creek access, Moccasin Creek access (the beginning of the eight-mile Class III whitewater section and the most heavily used), then the West Glacier access and finally, Blankenship Bridge, where the Middle Fork joins the North Fork of the Flathead River. An excellent map of the entire Flathead River system is available at the Forest Service station in Hungry Horse.

Wade fishing the Middle Fork, while possible, is limited by fast water and deep pools between the runs. The best way to fish it is to cover some water, and for this there is no finer boat than the McKenzie River boat. Whatever craft you choose (don't even think about a canoe), be advised that even outside of the white-water section, the Middle Fork is a fast, powerful, cold and remote river. Blind bends, rock-choked chutes and numerous downed trees make the river pilot's job a demanding and serious one.

The river is frequented by a variety of big game animals, and some of them have fangs and claws. Be aware that this is bear country, and mountain lions have also been sighted along and in the river. Seeing them safely from a McKenzie boat (remember, rafts can pop) is a memorable addition to any fishing trip.

The Middle Fork is a great but relatively unknown river. The combination of the Middle Fork's scenery, wildlife, fishing opportunities and uncrowded conditions rarely is seen in one place all at once. Kindly give plenty of room to other people fishing; there is plenty of it on the Middle Fork.

**Seasons:** The Middle Fork can fish well in April and early May when spawning runs of cutthroat enter the river from Flathead Lake. High water generally occurs mid-May through late June. After July 1, the fishing continues on into October. Local inquiry of river conditions or hazards is recommended.

**Fly selections:** This is easy. Anything will catch fish on the Middle Fork as long as it is well presented. If you are unable to make a good presentation, try dragging a nymph in front of the boat, or let your dry fly draw under the water at the end of your drift. While anathema to the purist, these techniques are godsends to the novice or flustered fishing guide. It ain't pretty, but it works.

**About the Author:** Smith is an advocate of small tippets, large caliber rifles, V-8 engines, and Labrador retrievers. He aspires to one day harpoon a jet ski. He spends the summers rowing fly fishers on the Middle Fork near West Glacier, Montana. He and the other fine fly fishing guides of Glacier Wilderness Guides may be reached at:

Glacier Wilderness Guides
Box 535
West Glacier, MT 59936
(800) 521-7238

# North Fork Drainage • Outside North Fork Road

### Kintla Lake

**General location:** The extreme northwest section of the Park. The lake is 15 miles from the Polebridge Entrance on a dirt road. Plan on a 40-minute drive to the lake.

**Maps:** USGS Glacier National Park (ISBN 0-607-32671-9); *Montana Atlas and Gazetteer,* p.83 (ISBN 0-89933-226-9)

**Fishing conditions and species:** bull trout, cutthroat, kokanee, lake trout, rainbow trout, and whitefish

**Special restrictions:** No motorized boats are allowed on Kintla Lake. (Bowman Lake allows motorized boats with no more than 10 horsepower outboard motors.) Kintla Creek between Kintla Lake and Upper Kintla Lake is closed to fishing, as is Upper Kintla Lake.

Kintla Lake fishes better than Bowman Lake, offering bull trout, westslope cutthroats, lake trout and kokanee, as well as the ubiquitous mountain whitefish. The best fishing is from June through September. Hiking away from the campground provides better fishing. Upper Kintla Lake is closed to fishing, but hiking the Boulder Pass Trail to the Kintla Lake backcountry campsite provides good fishing for those hikers who want to get away from the vehicular hum and drum found at the outlet campground. Bring a lightweight pair of waders. Temperature readings can change quickly, and in most places you will need to wade out a distance to reach the deeper water and allow yourself some back casting room.

Glacier offers advanced reservations, if you want to make plans ahead of time. You may, however, go to the Backcountry Office in Apgar Village at the West Glacier Entrance and sign up for "first-come" walk-in permits, or you may reserve a backcountry site 24 hours in advance for $20. The problem of dropping in and taking what is available is that it is almost impossible to plan a loop hike or even a sequential hike to the next logical stay. I had called ahead and found that the Bowman Campground at Bowman Lake rarely fills up, they had a corral for my donkey, and there was a good chance of getting a backcountry campsite at Lower Quartz Lake. Oh, the questions I should have asked while I had that Park employee on the phone....

Both lakes are reached following the North Fork Road out of Columbia Falls, or by taking the North Fork Road in the Park beginning at Fish Creek Campground. The road outside the Park is considered the best choice, unless you are traveling to Logging Lake or want better access to the North Fork of the Flathead. The road out of Columbia Falls is paved to the Camas Creek Entrance. From Camas Creek to the next Park entrance, Polebridge, is approximately 35 miles of potholes and washboard. Most of the land adjacent to the North Fork of the Flathead is posted, so wade fishers must be content with bridge crossings and the occasional National Forest access. One of the best primitive access points to the river is the Goal Banks, which is 5.8 miles north of the Camas Creek Park Entrance. When I researched the North Fork area, I was pulling an old four-horse trailer that I had converted into an RV Donkey Trailer. For the first time in my life, I became concerned about driving on a bumpy road, as I am sure Buddy did as he sucked in the dust and

braced himself at each jarring hole. When I pulled into Polebridge, a country store and a saloon, I stopped to ask for directions. When I got out of the truck, the trailer was draining 20 gallons of water out the door. My 20-gallon water tank had shifted, snapping a plastic water pipe. To add to the problem, I had part of Buddy's packsaddle on the counter top, and all the jostling had flicked the pump switch. Needless to say, I immediately remembered that I was going to brace and block the water tank. Alas, haste makes waste!

## Bowman Lake

**General location:** The extreme northwest section of the Park

**Maps:** USGS Glacier National Park (ISBN 0-607-32671-9); *Montana Atlas and Gazetteer*, p.83 (ISBN 0-89933-226-9)

**Fishing conditions and species:** bull trout, cutthroat, kokanee, lake trout, rainbow trout, and whitefish

**Special restrictions:** Bowman Lake allows motorized boats with no more than 10 horsepower outboard motors. Bowman Creek above Bowman Lake is closed to fishing.

## Bowman Lake, Akokala Lake and Quartz Lakes

The road from Polebridge to Bowman Lake Campground is a six-mile, winding, narrow, bumpy road. Later I would learn that the literature describes the road as primitive. The Park's goal is to maintain a backcountry campground limited to small trailers and tents. The real reason, one of the volunteer Park rangers surmised, was budget restrictions. If you are pulling a small trailer, plan on a 30-minute drive from Polebridge to the campground. The road from Polebridge to Kintla Lake is 15 miles and it, too, is rough, particularly the last two miles, although the driving time is only 45 minutes. The views, however, make the driving worthwhile. A few years ago a bridge washed out on the Canadian side of the border, so the road from Kintla Lake no longer serves as an entry into Canada. Discussions about reconstruction and financing have yet to be resolved by the Canadian government.

Arriving at Bowman Lake, pulling my monstrous RV conversion, I met the Bowman Lake ranger. She walked me down to the corrals and told me I could camp at the corrals with Buddy, if I thought I could

Buddy crosses the Bowman Lake stock bridge over the outlet.

make the turns. Looking down at this cute, 23-year-old ranger with her blonde braids dangling down from her Smokey-the-Bear hat, I said, "No problem, Little Lady," in my best John Wayne drawl. "Why, there's no trail or road that I can't maneuver this rig."

Sacrificing two little fir trees, the first two sharp turns down the rutted and overgrown road were less than perfect. When I got to the corrals, I knew I was in trouble. The corrals were straight ahead. To the left a few feet away was the outlet creek. The "turn-around" had a stock ramp to the right. It was not a place for a 21-foot trailer. How could I have miscalculated? Backing out through two turns was a nightmare. Later, the pungent smell of a burned clutch lingered as I crawled into my bed, exhausted and shaken.

## Bowman Lake

Although it provides a spectacular backdrop of glacial mountains, Bowman Lake offers only fair fishing at best. The best fishing opportunity is trolling from a boat or searching out deeper spots on the sides of the lake. Fishing is said to be good if you are willing to hike to the head of the lake, or camp at the designated backcountry campsite, Bowman Lake HD, a distance of 7.1 miles. The foot of the lake is very shallow. The outlet, Bowman Creek, offers decent fishing for 7- to 12-inch cutthroats.

### Akokala Lake

Akokala Lake provides another fishing option and backcountry camping site. The trailhead begins right in the Bowman Lake Campground. The steep 5.8-mile hike is often plagued with blowdowns, but the rangers clear them as soon as they can. The 23-acre lake provides good fishing for small cutthroats. The best fishing, however, may be found in the three Quartz Lakes above Bowman Lake.

## Lower Quartz Lake

The next day Buddy and I headed up the trail to Lower Quartz Lake. The loop to all three lakes covers 12.7 miles. The trailhead begins just east of the picnic site on Bowman Lake. Looking up the lake at the imposing Numa Peak to the west and Rainbow Peak to the east, Cerulean Ridge appears much less intimidating to hike. Crossing over the outlet bridge, the trail passes a ranger cabin about a half-mile from the campground. Shortly after the cabin, the trail forks. The trail to the right leads to Lower

Quartz Lake, a distance of 3.6 miles. Taking the left fork leads the hiker up Cerulean Ridge through a heavily-forested trail towards the crest. From the crest hikers may observe the natural reforestation after the 1988 Red Bench Fire. From the fork to Quartz Lake covers a distance of 6.6 miles, offering spectacular views. The backcountry Quartz Lake Campground offers glacial beauty and a small beach. From Quartz Lake Campground to Lower Quartz Campground is approximately three miles, passing by the smaller Middle Quartz Lake.

Taking the right fork to Lower Quartz Lake, a popular day hike, the trail climbs steadily up many switchbacks to Quartz Ridge, where hikers can see Quartz Lake, nestled at the base of Vulture Peak and Square Peak. The trail is quite steep, but it is shaded almost the entire length. Huffing and puffing up the mountainside, I was forced to take a breather when Buddy's pack slowly worked itself off to the side and then plopped on the ground. While I was struggling to readjust everything, I heard the rhythmic synchronization of two hikers in locomotion. "Hey, bear!" the engineer shouted out. "Hey, bear," the fireman repeated three steps later. Two college girls steamed up the switchbacks with full packs, while Buddy and I marveled at their progress. When they were two switchbacks below me, I yelled out, "Just give me a second and I'll get out of your way. I'm almost finished," as I adjusted the sleeping bag riding on top of Buddy's sawbuck.

Not a wheel slipped in this locomotive, nor was there the slightest pause as the engineer's forearms shot out in a piston-like motion and the train steamed up the trail from one switchback to another. "Hey, bear," said the engineer, and exactly three paces later the fireman answered, "Hey, bear!" If someone above us looked down upon Buddy's twitching ears, they could have marked the locomotive's ascent. Rounding the switchback near us, the engineer frowned as she broke her cadence.

"Does he kick?" yelled out the engineer.

"No," I replied, and before I knew it, they had passed, forfeiting any opportunity to say hello, or where are you heading?

"Hey, bear!" shouted the engineer as they disappeared around the bend. I took hold of the lead rope, clicked my tongue (the command for go), looked at the switchbacks in front of me, and, like the little steam engine, said, "I think I can. I think I can. I think I can."

If you bring in stock, be sure to pack in your animal's food, as there are no spots to graze. Be cautious in crossing the small bridges over spring seepage; some of them are quite rotten. The area is thick with underbrush and trees right down to the water's edge. All of the backcountry sites have a hanging pole and an outhouse. Lower Quartz provided a three-week-old sports section and the classifieds of the *Missoulian* for those whose daily constitution requires a more sedate regimen.

I fished the outlet creek first, which flushes a surprising volume of water from the lake down to the North Fork. Every fly fisher regales with nostalgia those stories of fish caught on every cast. I have added another such story to my 45 years of trout fishing. Unfortunately, nary a single fish measured over 5 inches! I fished 300 yards in beautiful water. If I didn't catch a fish on each cast, I flipped one across the riffle or missed one, sometimes two. It reminded me of my personal best day with a client, Sam Laurence, the founder of Budget Rental Cars. Sam caught 97 trout in one day floating the Bitterroot River with me as his guide. In those days my outfitter required his guides to keep a mechanical counter. Of the 97 trout Sam caught that day, not one exceeded 9 inches, and most measured 5 to 7 inches. Guinness should have a record for most dinks in a day! That evening, however, I caught a number of fat cutthroats wading out in the lake. Although none of them were big, a number of them were around 12 inches.

After sipping hot chocolate the following morning, and watching the steam slowly rise and dissipate above the emerald reflection of Quartz Ridge, I readjusted my attitude after a night of painfully swollen knees. Buddy minded his manners and proudly crossed the outlet with nary a prodding, swearing or cajoling. With just a few months training, he packed like a veteran.

## Inside North Fork Road

The road is primitive and poorly maintained. Pick up the road at Fish Creek Campground, which is just a couple of miles from the West Glacier En-

Lower Quartz Lake

trance. From Fish Creek Campground, Polebridge is 27 miles, Bowman Lake is 33 miles, and Kintla Lake is 43 miles. The speed limit is 20 mph, and you will find yourself rarely over that limit. It took me a full hour to reach Logging Lake Campground.

### Camas Creek: 6.7 miles

**Crossing:** Camas Creek holds small cutthroats; however, one of the rangers I spoke with said that a half-mile upstream there are some large beaver ponds, which provide good fishing for larger cutthroats. From Anaconda Creek to Logging Lake is closed to hiking or entry as some gray wolves have set up a den and need isolation to raise their young.

### Logging Lake: 18.6 miles

**General location:** Above the West Glacier Entrance on the Inside North Fork Road
**Access:** From the Logging Creek Ranger Station, take the Logging Lake trail 4.4 miles to the lake.
**Maps:** USGS Glacier National Park (ISBN 0-607-32671-9); *Montana Atlas and Gazetteer*, p.83
**Fish species:** bull trout, cutthroat, lake trout, and whitefish

**Special restrictions:** Logging Creek between Logging Lake and Grace Lake is closed to fishing.

Logging Lake offers fair fishing for cutthroats, but like most of the lakes in the North Fork drainage, fishing from the shore is difficult. Serious fly fishers will pack in a float tube to reach the deeper waters. From the trailhead to the lake is 4.4 miles. The first backcountry campsite is five miles. The hike is rated easy.

**19.3 miles:** Access to the North Fork of the Flathead River

**20.5 miles:** Quartz Creek Campground

**21.1 miles: Winona Lake (Mud Lake)**
The lake offers fair fishing for small cutthroats in a mosquito-infested haven.

**27 miles: Polebridge, Montana**
Be sure to stop at the Polebridge Mercantile for freshly baked goodies!

# West Glacier Entrance: Going-to-the-Sun Road

One of the most famous roads in the Rocky Mountains is the Going-to-the-Sun Road in Glacier National Park. The road is reached shortly after entering the Park at the West Glacier Entrance. Above Lake McDonald, you will drive past McDonald Creek. It is beautiful, but it is generally bereft of trout with the exception of a few migratory fish. Lake McDonald Lodge and the trailhead to Snyder Lake is a distance of nine miles; the Avalanche Lake Trailhead is 14.7 miles; Packer's Roost (Mineral Creek) is 20.8 miles, and St. Mary's Park Entrance is 48 miles.

## McDonald Creek

**General location:** Just inside the West Glacier Entrance from Lake McDonald to the Middle Fork of the Flathead River

**Access:** The creek, as the outlet of Lake McDonald, may be easily accessed at Apgar, or just after entering the Park, turn left at the Glacier Institute sign, and then turn right towards the horse rentals and follow the signs to the Quarter-Circle Bridge.

**Maps:** USGS Glacier National Park (ISBN 0-607-32671-9); *Montana Atlas and Gazetteer*, p.83 (ISBN 0-89933-226-9)

**Fishing species:** brook trout, bull trout, cutthroat, lake trout, rainbow trout, whitefish

**Special restrictions:** "Catch-and-release fishing only with single hooks: Fish caught in Lower McDonald Creek (from the Quarter Circle Bridge and upstream, extending into Lake McDonald for a radius of 300 feet) must be handled carefully and released immediately to the stream or lake. No fish of any species may be in possession at any time along this stream/lake." –Park handout

McDonald Creek, draining McDonald Lake and entering the Middle Fork of the Flathead River, receives a great deal of fishing pressure because of its accessibility and scenic allure. To protect the cutthroat populations, the Park established catch-and-release fishing restrictions using single hooks between Lake McDonald and the Quarter-Circle Bridge. Slow, clear water provides a challenge for those fly fishers who enjoy delicate casting with long leaders and small tippets.

McDonald Creek above the lake, with the exception of the inlet, holds few fish and is a waste of time fishing unless you take the Going-to-the-Sun Road to the Packer's Roost area, which is approximately 20.8 miles. Even in this area the fishing is rated fair to poor.

## Lake McDonald

**General location:** McDonald Lake is just inside the West Glacier Entrance and first viewed from the Apgar Village Center. The Going-to-the-Sun Road follows the southern shoreline, while the northern shoreline is traversed by trail from the Fish Creek Campground for 6.5 miles on the Lake McDonald Trail, where it meets the northern end of the lake at the end of the North Lake McDonald Road. Campers who wish to camp at a backcountry site along this trail may camp 4.5 miles from Fish Creek Campground at the McDonald Lake site, which offers two camping sites close to the lake.

**Boat access:** Apgar Visitor Center and Lake McDonald Lodge

**Maps:** USGS Glacier National Park (ISBN 0-607-32671-9); *Montana Atlas and Gazetteer*, p.83

**Fishing conditions and species:** According to all the published reports, Lake McDonald offers poor fishing, which is due in part to a nutrient-deficient offering from McDonald Creek. The lake is deep, and it requires trolling from a boat with standard hardware for brook trout, bull trout, cutthroat, lake trout and whitefish.

**Rogers Lake and Trout Lake**

**Directions:** Turn left at the top end of McDonald Lake one-and-a-half miles above the lodge. Once you pass some private summer homes the road is quite primitive. The trailhead is a mile from the highway, but it does not offer any parking, except along the side of the road on a steep embankment above the lake. I had to drive another mile on a dark and

and fish those areas for easy-to-catch smaller cutthroats from 6 to 8-inches. I used small bead-head nymphs. (Back to the Going-to-the Sun Highway.)

Trout Lake

narrow road until I could find a place to turn my truck around. Trout Lake is 3.7 miles from the trailhead. The trail is difficult as it climbs straight up two miles to the crest, and then it drops straight down 1.7 miles to Trout Lake. Two hiking fanatics left an hour before me and met me at the crest on their way back. They bragged about hiking to the lake in two hours and eight minutes. It took me three hours, which included a long break at the top, as I was exhausted and cursing the 90-degree heat. Both lakes have populations of cutthroats, but Trout Lake is restricted to fly fishing only and is considered the better of the two. A log jam blocks the lake outlet. If the fishing is slow in the lake, fish the shallow water behind the log jam. Look for dark depressions

**Snyder Creek and Snyder Lakes: 9 miles**
**General location:** Across the trailhead from Lake McDonald Lodge

**Trailhead access:** Snyder Creek is accessible from the Sperry Trailhead above Lake McDonald Lodge, but it is an overgrown, brushy creek holding small cutthroats and brook trout. The trail to Snyder Lake begins near the Going-to-the-Sun Road; follow the trail past the riding stables. After about a mile and a half, the trail to Snyder Lake continues past the Mt. Brown Lookout trail. Snyder Lake, nestled in a small valley, offers three backcountry campsites.

**Hiking conditions:** For the most part the 4.4 mile hike to Snyder Lake is a moderate hike through heavy vegetation and forests of stately cedars, larch and Douglas fir. Early in the season the trail can be wet and muddy.

**Fishing species:** Snyder Lake offers good fishing for small cutthroats in Lower Snyder Lake and the stream between the two lakes. Upper Snyder Lake is fishless.

**Fish Lake**

Accessed from the Snyder Creek Trail, Fish Lake is really a small, shallow pond, which offers poor fishing for small cutthroat trout. Fish Lake is a little more than two miles from the trailhead.

## Avalanche Lake: 14.7 miles

**General location:** Near Avalanche Lake Campground on the Going-to-the-Sun Road, Avalanche Lake attracts a large number of day hikers to one of the Park's mountain jewels. The hike offers spectacular forest green and a destination lake at only 2.9 miles.

**Trailhead access:** The trail begins at Avalanche Campground. Be sure to take the Avalanche Lake Trail rather than Avalanche Trail. The Avalanche Lake Trail closely follows Avalanche Creek, which provides photo opportunities of carved rock, moss and moistened ferns from the mist and spray. At the head of the lake, Monument Falls provides a picturesque backdrop. The lake's opaque color stems from the glacial silt of Sperry Glacier.

**Hiking conditions:** The hike is a fairly easy climb and then ascent to the lake.

Suspension bridge over Mineral Creek

**Fishing conditions and species:** Day hikes of less than three miles tend to bring about heavier fishing pressure. Avalanche Lake draws large groups of both hikers and fishers. Nonetheless, the lake fishes well for small cutthroats. The best fishing, naturally, is far from the maddening crowd, which for some is out in the middle of the lake in a belly-boat.

## Mineral Creek

**General location:** Off of the Going-to-the-Sun Road on a spur road to Packer's Roost

**Maps:** USGS Glacier National Park; *Montana Atlas and Gazetteer,* p.83

**Fishing species:** westslope cutthroat trout

Easily accessed from the Going-to-the-Sun Road, Mineral Creek will not make my list of favorite little creeks. The creek is not prolific in its offerings of westslope cutthroats. Just looking at the carved and sculpted rocks, it is a wonder the creek doesn't have a higher fish mortality during spring run-off. Mineral Creek's cutthroats are found not in the open pools but in the nooks and crannies where they remain protected year round. It receives little fishing pressure, and nymphs seem to work best. But the creek is worth visiting just for its scenic beauty. The hike is along level ground, and it takes only an hour to reach the suspension bridge.

**Directions:** Drive 5.9 miles past the Avalanche Creek bridge. Turn left onto an unmarked dirt road. If you are coming from the Logan Pass Visitor Center, the access road is 1.3 miles from the tunnel. Follow the dirt road to the Packer's Roost Trailhead. Take the Flattop Mountain Trail about two miles to the suspension bridge over Mineral Creek. You may also follow Mineral Creek a half-mile to upper McDonald Creek, but the fishing there is said to be poor.

## Hidden Lake

**General location:** Below the Logan Pass Visitor Center on the Going-to-the-Sun Road
**Maps:** USGS Glacier National Park; *Montana Atlas and Gazetteer*, p.84

Two fishermen below the highway bridge on the Saint Mary River

**Fishing species:** Yellowstone cutthroat trout
**Special restrictions:** Fish caught in Hidden Lake and the outlet must be released. Hidden Lake is closed to fishing during spawning season.

Driving the Going-to-the-Sun Road to the Logan Pass Visitor Center is similar in popularity to driving to Yellowstone's Old Faithful. In truth, I join the masses each time on the boardwalk-guided tour, as it is breathtaking in beauty and offers great photo opps for mountain goats and people. Be advised, however, that the parking lot at Logan Pass Visitor Center often fills during July and August. Plan on arriving early in the day if you want to take the three-mile hike down to Hidden Lake, one of the highest lakes at 6,375 feet elevation. It is a moderately difficult trail that receives a great number of visitors and anglers each year. For that reason, the lake is restricted to catch-and-release. The lake does provide some good opportunities for casting to large Yellowstone cutthroat trout. Bear in mind that this is grizzly country.

## Gunsight Lake: 6 miles

For those hardy hikers looking for a high-elevation, wind-swept lake, Gunsight Lake reportedly offers good fishing for nice-sized rainbows. The outlet creek also offers fun fishing for smaller rainbows. The lake offers eight camping sites so the fishing pressure late in the summer can be fairly heavy at the foot of the lake. The trailhead begins at the Jackson Glacier Overlook below Logan Pass on the Going-to-the-Sun Road. Follow the Piegan Pass Trail one mile down to Deadwood Falls. Continue following the Piegan Pass Trail another mile to its junction with the Gunsight Pass Trail. Take the Gunsight Pass Trail another four miles to the lake.

## Otokomi Lake

**General location:** On the Going-to-the-Sun Road at the Rising Sun Motor Inn, 18 miles west of the Saint Mary Visitor Center

The trailhead begins in the parking lot of the Rising Sun Motor Inn; follow Rose Creek 5.1 miles to Otokomi Lake. If you do not have strong, youthful legs, consider this hike difficult. The trail provides a strenuous hike up through many switchbacks through stands of lodgepole pine and fir as well as meadows and open areas, which provide a food source for bears. The lake is said to provide fair to good fishing for cutthroats.

# Eastern Entrance: Saint Mary

### Saint Mary Lake, Saint Mary River

Like most large lakes, Saint Mary Lake is best fished from a boat. Typically, the best fishing is at the inlet, which is a boggy and difficult bushwhack from Going-to-the-Sun Road. The Saint Mary River above the lake contains mostly whitefish. Below the lake, the river is home to a variety of trout species as well as the voracious pike. A short section of the river at the lake's outlet to the bridge is popular.

### Red Eagle Lake

Although Red Eagle Creek is generally considered to be bereft of fish due the scouring effects of spring run-off, Red Eagle Lake has a reputation for both scenic beauty and big trout. The trail is basically an easy hike, but the one-way trip is 7.8 miles. Four campsites are offered at both the head and the foot of the lake. You will locate the trailhead just south of the Saint Mary Lake Entrance. Just before the Entrance Station, turn south (left) on a paved road. Follow this road for about a half-mile, and then bear right to the parking area near an old ranger station. The trail offers spectacular scenery of snow-capped mountains and surrounding meadows with little elevation gain. Considered to be one of the more prolific lakes for large trout, Red Eagle Lake provides fishing for rainbows, cutthroats and hybrids. These trout are educated trout. Belly boats increase an angler's chance to land one of these beauties.

# Eastern Entrance: Two Medicine

Take Two Medicine Road from Highway 49 to the entrance station. If you plan on fishing Lower Two Medicine Lake in the lower reaches, be sure to acquire a Blackfoot Indian Reservation fishing permit.

### Two Medicine Lake

Glacier Park Boat Company offers boat excursions at Many Glacier, Rising Sun, Two Medicine and Lake McDonald.

Two Medicine Lake and its adjacent lake, **Pray Lake**, are less than 10 miles from the entrance station. The Two Medicine Trail follows the northern shoreline to No Name Lake or Upper Two Medicine Lake, a distance of 4.4 miles. Two Medicine Lake and Pray Lake hold good-sized brook trout and rainbow trout. Two Medicine Lake is a large lake, and high winds should be a concern for those fishing from a cartop boat or a belly boat. Both lakes hold good-sized brook trout for experienced lake fishers.

### Upper Two Medicine Lake

Follow the trail 4.4 miles or cut your distance in half by taking the boat tour to the upper boat landing on Two Medicine Lake. Glacier Park Company offers cruises at 9:00, 10:30, 1:00, 3:00 and 5:00, which provides plenty of time to fish and meet an afternoon departure. Upper Two Medicine Lake offers fair fishing for small brook trout. The trailhead starts in the campground. **No Name Lake** Trail is an optional hike, when you depart off the boat. No Name Lake is a small lake offering fair fishing for brook trout and rainbow trout.

Many Glacier Hotel

### 🎣 🥾 Oldman Lake

Oldman Lake has a reputation for nurturing large Yellowstone cutthroat trout and bull trout. (Bull trout must be released.) The trail from Two Medicine Campground to the lake is nearly seven miles, which in my mind precludes listing it as a day hike.

## Eastern Entrance: Many Glacier

Resembling the European Alps with its stunning vistas and four glaciers, Many Glacier Valley attracted visitors via the Great Northern Railway when Many Glacier Hotel opened in 1914, just four years after the formation of the Park. Branching out from the hotel, hikers, then and now, have a network of trails to choose from for their day's outing. The hotel offers trail rides, and tour boats run between the hotel and the upper end of Lake Josephine. Just outside the Park entrance, the town of Babb also offers visitor services and accommodations.

The Many Glacier Valley offers visitors the opportunity to view wildlife such as the powerful grizzly bear and the agile mountain goat and bighorn sheep. Fishing opportunities include the valley lakes as well as the backcountry lakes. However, some of the lakes, such as Upper Grinnell Lake, Iceberg Lake, Swiftcurrent Ridge Lake, Poia Lake and Cracker Lake, are barren or closed to fishing.

A short distance from Swiftcurrent Lake, at the end of the road, is the trailhead to Red Rock Lake. The hike to Red Rock Lake is three miles. It provides fishing for brook trout. A third trail from Many Glacier leads to Fishercap Lake, Iceberg Lake and Ptarmigan Lake. Fishercap Lake is a five-mile hike from Swiftcurrent Campground and provides fishing for brook trout and rainbows. Pass up the barren Iceberg Lake and plan on a hard five-mile hike to fish **Ptarmigan Lake**.

**Lake Sherrburne**

Lake Sherrburne is actually a reservoir and provides inconsistent fishing for pike and the occasional brook trout.

**Swiftcurrent Lake**

Attracting large numbers of people at both the hotel and the campground, Swiftcurrent Lake receives the most fishing pressure of the area lakes. The lake is home to brook trout and kokanee and the fishing is described as fair. Beginning a half-mile west of the hotel at a picnic site, Swiftcurrent Lake Trail #167 provides a self-guided nature trail that circles the lake. Crossing the footbridge over Grinnel Creek, Trail #180 branches off to take the hiker to Trail #171, which follows the southern shoreline of Lake Josephine.

Swiftcurrent Lake

**Lake Josephine**

Less than a mile hike from Swiftcurrent Lake, Lake Josephine provides fair fishing for brook trout and kokanee. Hikers may choose the South Shore Lake Josephine Trail starting at the hotel or the footpath along the north side of Swiftcurrent Lake to the upper Swiftcurrent boat dock and then westward to Lake Josephine.

**Grinnell Lake**

Lying above Lake Josephine, Grinnell Lake may be reached following the south shore of Lake Josephine or the northern shore. However, the fishing is said to be poor as a result of receding glacial flow from Grinnell Glacier.

**Fishercap Lake**

Just past the parking lot for the Swiftcurrent Motor Inn, Fishercap Lake is easy to reach but disappointing as a fishery, offering up small brook trout in a shallow lake. The inlet stream and the outlet stream offer better opportunities for faster action, albeit small fish. Fishercap Lake is the trailhead for Red Rock Lake and Bullhead Lake.

**Red Rock Lake**

Because of its two-mile hike from the parking lot of the Swiftcurrent Motor Inn, Red Rock Lake gets pounded with hardware and bait. It is said to be fair fishing for brook trout. The final lake in this chain of lakes is **Bullhead Lake**, which is only 3.3 miles from the parking lot. Again, the lake is reported as fair fishing for brook trout.

# Belly River: Belly River Drainage

### Elizabeth Lake, Cosley Lake, Glenns Lake, Mokowanis Lake

**General location:** The Belly River drains the northeast section of the Park. The river flows north into Canada. The closest community is Babb, which is nine miles north of the Saint Mary Entrance. Over-

Author crossing the Belly River with Buddy and Banjo. Photo courtesy of Dennis Cohoe

night camping requires a permit. Elizabeth Lake is the most popular backcountry destination both for its beauty and fishing opportunities. For this reason hikers are restricted to only one night at Elizabeth Lake.

**Trailhead access:** The trailhead is easy to locate as it is next to the Chief Mountain Custom Office on the border. The parking lot is large and includes a hitching rail and designated parking for stock trailers. Take Highway 89 from Saint Mary. About four miles north of the community of Babb, turn left on Route 17, the **Chief Mountain International Highway.**

**Hiking conditions:** From the parking lot high up

on a ridgeline, the trail drops straight down a couple of miles to the Belly River. All of the trails to the above lakes are rated easy to moderate, with the exception of the two-mile drop to the Belly River. Except for the trail that follows the Belly River to the Ranger Station Campground, most of the time hikers are in and out of shade, which along with numerous little creek crossings makes the hikes very pleasant in warmer weather. The scenery is breathtaking.

**Fishing species:** The drainage contains rainbow trout, brook trout, lake trout, arctic grayling and whitefish.

### Belly River

The Belly River flows through a lush, narrow valley until it reaches the Ranger Station and Gable Creek Campground. The jagged, snowcapped pinnacles provide a panoramic sweep of the valley's promise as the trail winds in and out of spruce, lodgepole and quaking aspen. Grass and wildflowers sway knee-high, providing abundant forage for elk, deer and other wildlife. Just above the Belly River Ranger Station, the river splits with one fork leading to Elizabeth Lake and the other fork leading to Cosley Lake. As it is glacier-fed, this little river rips up the streambed during spring run-off. In spite of the abundant insect presence during the summer, the river's cold rushing waters do not provide the best habitat. Fishing is reported to be fair, although it is good in its diversity of species offerings.

When the river drops in late summer in time for hopper fishing, the meadow sections reportedly fish well. I must confess that I did not fish it. I was just too pooped to fish when I reached Gable Creek Campground. Every backcountry angler I queried said the same thing: a day hike down to the Belly River would provide incredible scenery, absolute solitude and fair to good fishing for rainbow trout, brook trout and arctic grayling. From the trailhead to the Belly River Ranger Station and campground is 6.1 miles and offers a number of campsites as well as a stock area. Into this garden of paradise, pesky flies and mosquitoes greet hikers. Be prepared. Bring plenty of repellant during early summer. I found that a mosquito net over my head was perfect for those short trail naps!

![hiking icons]

### Cosley Lake, Glenns Lake and Mokowanis River

Traveling 6.1 miles to the Belly River Ranger Station and Gable

Belly River trail

Creek Campground, the trail splits. From the ranger station to Elizabeth Lake is 3.5 miles. From this point to Cosley Lake is two miles, plus another six-tenths to the campground, a total of 8.7 miles from the trailhead. Just behind the campground, the trail crosses the Belly River via a one-person suspension bridge. A ford is marked just below the bridge. The trail climbs up the slope, eventually following the Mokowanis River. Just before the trail crests, hikers are treated with a view of the Gros Ventre Falls plunging 100 feet into a cauldron of foam and a deep green pool. Cosley Lake is beautiful, and campers are treated to their own beachfront campsites. Directly across the lake is the colorful and rugged Cosley Ridge. At the head of the lake

towards Mokowanis Lake, Mount Merritt and Pyramid Peak provide huge patches of snow, along with cascading falls for picture-perfect photographs of Glacier grandeur.

Although Cosley Lake has a few trout, it is basically barren with the exception of some lake trout patrolling the bottom. The outlet of Cosley Lake and the Mokowanis River above the falls were equally disappointing. I talked to one Park biologist who was studying the lynx population, and he told me that all of the lakes connecting the Mokowanis River were either near barren or disappointing in fish counts and frequency of catches. The inlet to Cosley Lake provides the best fishing, but it has now been closed to protect nesting eagles. Glenns Lake, just above Cosley Lake, is also rated poor fishing. Mokowanis Lake, the last lake in this string of lakes, offers fair to good fishing for small brook trout. So, what does a hiker who is eager to catch some high-elevation trout do? Simple solution! From the foot of Cosley Lake, hikers may cross the outlet at the cable crossing and hike 3.7 miles to Elizabeth Lake.

Along the way you will be treated to another spectacular photo opportunity, Dawn Mist Falls.

## 🦬 🚶 Elizabeth Lake

In addition to the Big Hole River and a few other spots in Montana, Elizabeth Lake is one of just a few places in the lower 48 states where anglers can catch both rainbow trout and arctic grayling, and big ones at that! The lake is quite large, and most anglers concentrate at the foot of the lake and the inlet. The trout and the grayling cruise along the shelf where the clear, shallow water meets the impenetrable green-blue line of water, which is produced by glacial silt.

Grayling and trout reaching 14 to 16 inches and larger ones are not uncommon. In addition to the mayfly hatch, I saw lots of caddis and stoneflies enticing lots of fish midday, in spite of the heavy winds. Look for some protected coves along the eastern side of the lake. The western side of the lake may be reached from a suspension bridge. Looking down into the water from the bridge, anglers will observe four or five really large rainbows sipping on midges. They, of course, are quite aware of human presence as well and are very wary, not to mention irritated that they have to constantly slide over to the other side of the pool each time an excited angler discovers them. (Yes, I couldn't resist and made a couple of foolish casts from the swinging bridge. They nonchalantly ignored my offerings.)

Cosley Lake campground site

Cosley Lake outlet

Pauline and I packed up our two donkeys and met her son Dennis on the way up to the Park. I had secured a reservation early in the spring for one night at Gable Creek and two nights at Cosley Lake. Although I had asked for Elizabeth Lake, I was pleased to get so close to this most popular fishing lake. For the most part the donkeys behaved quite well. Because we had not stayed the night at Saint Mary or Babb, we reached the trailhead late, despite hitting the road at 6 AM. This kept me from fishing the Belly River section by the campground that evening. If you are not a healthy, strong backpacker, I most certainly recommend staying the first night at Gable Creek Campground, which is only 6.1 miles from the trailhead. In retrospect, I would prefer to stay two nights at Gable Creek Campground and do a day hike to Elizabeth if I couldn't get a campsite the second day at Elizabeth Lake.

When Dennis and I reached Elizabeth Lake from our campground at Cosley Lake, the wind was blowing hard, producing small, choppy waves. Wading out into shallow water about 20 yards, I faced squarely into the wind. Having recently had arthroscopic shoulder surgery, I gave up after a few futile casts and retreated to a piece of shade. I was too tired to brood over our bad luck on facing hot dry winds, which thrashed the surface of the lake. Dennis looked at me sympathetically and went off

exploring. (I am sure he made a silent vow not to be so out of shape at 55.) Dennis disdains all forms of fishing elitism and prefers to carry a two-foot Snoopy rod and reel. About a half-hour later he came back

Dawn Mist Falls. Photo courtesy of Dennis Cohoe

and said, "Sorry to disturb your nap, Dave, but I think you had better grab your rod and follow me. I found a spot where there are tons of fish. They follow my lure all the way in until they see me, but I can't get them to hit."

I was instantly awake to the possibilities. Sore shoulders and blistered feet vanished. Dennis led me over to the first cove on the eastern shoreline, a quarter of a mile in sight of the campground at the outlet. Before I had even made my first cast, Dennis pointed out the cruisers swimming along the line where shallow water meets the deep blue. I had already had a Goddard Caddis on my line with a bead-head dropper. Within two or three casts I had caught a very large grayling on the nymph.

I quickly changed Dennis's Snoopy rig and put

on a bead-head Prince nymph with two strike indicators and a swivel to add a little weight. Dennis began making 20-foot casts and caught both rainbows and grayling. After catching a number of fish, I offered Dennis my fly rod, as he had never used one before. His second cast along the shoreline threw a size 16 yellow Wulff pattern into the shallow water. The 16-inch rainbow shot right out of the shallows no more than six feet from the shore-

Footbridge across the outlet of Elizabeth Lake

line and snatched Dennis' offering. After Dennis released this beauty, my generosity and sharing quickly dissolved when I saw the size of his fish. I deftly snatched back my fly rod and went on to catch a lot of small and large fish before we had to head back down the trail. Dennis did quite well with his Snoopy outfit until the reel broke. The last fish he landed he brought in hand-over-hand. His only comment: "They don't make Snoopy rods like they used to."

## Saga: I Don't Mess with Moose

About a half-mile up the creek from the Mill Creek Trailhead, the Forest Service sign warned of an aggressive bear in the area. I had heard that the bear had been feeding on a dead moose. I decided to take my chances with the aggressive bear. If it had been a warning of an aggressive moose, however, I would have hastily left the area.

When I taught in Jackson, Wyoming, over 20 years ago, I once had a student walk in late to my first period class with a note from his mother. I had assumed he was a town kid, as he wore a baseball hat, a satin jacket promoting a local business and Nike shoes. His attire was not exactly the attire I attributed to a ranch kid. Later I found out that the kids in school with the cowboy attire lived out on five- to-10-acre "spreads" west of town.

The note read: "Dear Mr. Archer, Bill is late to class this morning because he was trapped under his truck by a mean-tempered cow moose."

"You're kidding," I said. "Nah," the teenager drawled. "The worst part was when I dashed out to warm up the truck. I forgot to put on my coat. The moose charged, I dove under my truck, and she kept me there for about 20 minutes until my mom came out and shooed it away."

For the rest of the class period in my sophomore English class, harrowing moose stories prevailed. Years later while floating on Rock Creek, I had a bull moose charge into the creek right after we silently floated past him. After some quiet reflection, my clients and I concurred that his stopping point would have been right in the middle of my raft had he decided to charge when we were abreast of him. And then a few years later I experienced my brush-with-death moose story.

If you have seen the movie *The Ghost and the Darkness* about two man-eating lions, you will recall the line when the white hunter says to the young engineer after he has had a close encounter with a lion: "You got knocked down. Now you got to stand up and decide what you're going to do about it." I got knocked down too, but I don't want a rematch!

Unlike the brave engineer, moose will forever intimidate me. Pauline and my sons and I were camped out at the second hogback on Rock Creek during Memorial Day weekend. I was fishing alone on an island with Shadow, my black Labrador. When I came to a spot on the creek that was too deep to wade, I pulled myself up on the grass bank and pushed my way through the dense willow thicket. The creek was still to my left as I entered a small opening. I walked a couple of paces, and suddenly a cow moose struggled up from her bed, scattering dust like a cowpoke's pickup truck on a Saturday night.

I froze. Shadow froze. The moose pawed the ground. I let out a startled whoop and took off running. I saw an opening in the brush and jumped into the creek. I heard the snorts and grunts from the moose directly behind me. At any moment I was expecting a hoof to split me in two. The creek was only a foot deep when I landed. Unlike the pro-

tagonist in the adolescent novel *Hatchet*, the water's depth was not going to help me.

Across the narrow creek I observed a rock cliff with no trees. Down I went on the slippery rocks. I heard a terrible commotion in the brush. I turned around just in time to see the pawing moose chasing my Lab in circles around a thin willow bush. Poor Shadow. Her tail was tucked under her belly, her ears were drooped, and she was running around

Author landing a fat grayling on Elizabeth Lake. Photo courtesy of Dennis Cohoe

the willow in a sideways motion with her head turned towards the moose in askance. Shocked silent, she never let out a bark. Finally, the cow charged off, and Shadow meekly joined me at my side in the creek. She had silently stood her ground and saved my life as I ran away.

My sons accused me of story embellishment, but Shadow and I know. The following year, two anglers barely escaped a charging moose in the same area. Their dog stood his ground and was injured. Later that same summer, a cow moose killed a man as he crossed the street in a small town in the state of Washington.

I don't mess with moose.

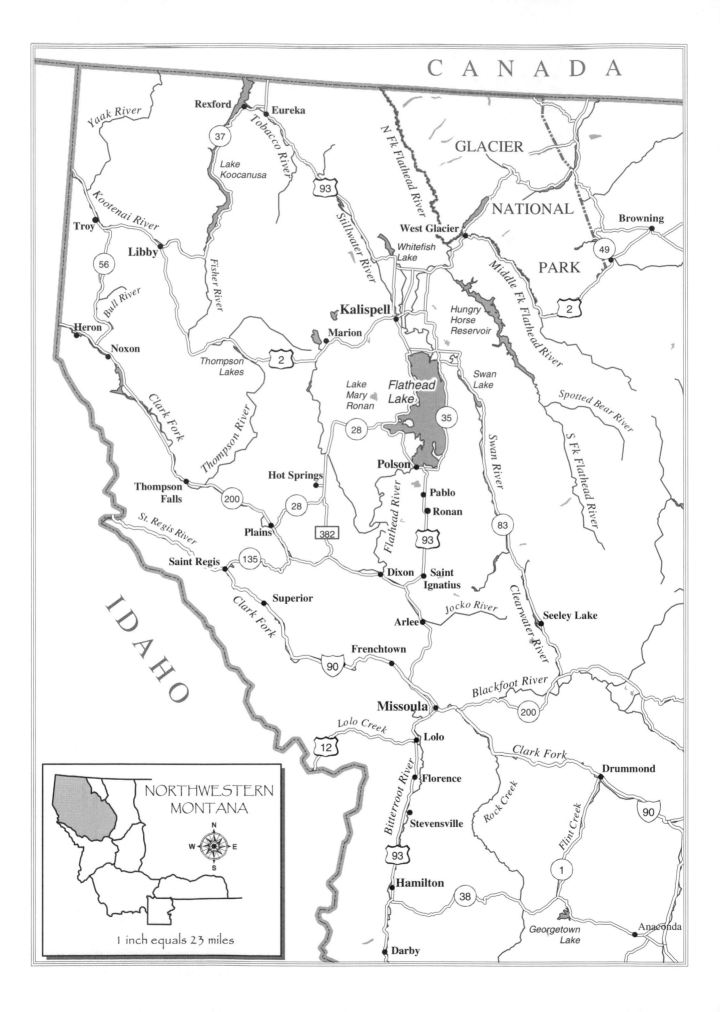

CANADA

GLACIER

NATIONAL

PARK

IDAHO

NORTHWESTERN
MONTANA

1 inch equals 23 miles

Yaak River

Rexford

Eureka

37

Tobacco River

Lake
Koocanusa

93

Kootenai River

Troy

Libby

56

Bull River

Fisher River

Heron

Noxon

Thompson Lakes

2

Marion

Kalispell

Stillwater River

N Fk Flathead River

West Glacier

Whitefish
Lake

Browning

49

2

Middle Fk Flathead River

S Fk Flathead River

Spotted Bear River

Hungry
Horse
Reservoir

Lake
Mary
Ronan

Flathead
Lake

Swan Lake

35

28

Swan River

83

Clark Fork

Thompson River

Hot Springs

Polson

Pablo

Ronan

Thompson
Falls

200

28

Plains

382

Flathead River

93

St. Regis River

Saint Regis

135

Clark Fork

Superior

Dixon

Saint
Ignatius

Arlee

Jocko River

Clearwater River

Seeley Lake

Frenchtown

90

Blackfoot River

200

Missoula

Lolo Creek

Lolo

12

Florence

Bitterroot River

Stevensville

93

Hamilton

38

Darby

Clark Fork

Drummond

90

Rock Creek

Flint Creek

1

Georgetown
Lake

Anaconda

# 2

# NORTHWESTERN MONTANA

# Highway 200 – The Idaho Border to the Junction with Highway 93 North of Missoula

**MM 0:** Idaho Border.

**MM 3.7:** Heron, Montana.

**MM 10.5** Junction with Montana State Highway 56 to Troy, Montana. (See Highway 56.)

 **MM 11: Bull River Campground**
26 campsites, two pull-throughs, water, flush toilets, fully-developed boat launch, fee area.

 **MM 14:** Gas and store.

**MM 15.5:** Noxon, Montana.

**MM 18.5:** Noxon Rapids Dam.

**MM 26.7: North Shore Campground**
12 campsites, water, toilets, fully-developed boat launch, fee area.

**MM 27:** Cabinet Ranger Station.

**MM 28: Vermillion River**
The lower section of the river is slow fishing, but above the falls about 11 miles from the highway, the river (creek) provides good fishing for creek-size cutthroats and brookies. If you arrive in the fall, cross your fingers that you will find and entice a big brown up from the Clark Fork.

**MM 29-30:** Trout Creek, Montana.

**MM 41:** Gas and country store.

**MM 47:** Fishing access and boat launch.

**MM 49.5: Thompson Falls State Park**
17 campsites, 55-foot trailer space.

Lower Thompson River

**MM 50-52:** Thompson Falls, Montana.

**MM 56: Thompson River, Junction with Thompson River Road**
Thompson River Road follows the river and intersects with Highway 2 to Libby or Kalispell.

The Thompson River flows from the Thompson Lake chain to the Clark Fork River. Considered one of the best streams in the area, the Thompson River is pounded by catch-and-eat fishermen who have easy access to the river along Thompson River Road #56 and the private logging road on the east side of the river. Road #56 parallels the river for almost 40 miles. If you plan on camping and fishing, Copper King Campground (USFS) offers a nice campground right on the river four miles from the junction with Highway 200. Offering five sites, the campground

has no drinking water. Above the campground the road begins a single-lane dirt and gravel road with a number of intersecting logging roads. The Thompson River is worth the dusty ride, as the stream and road wind up through wooded mountainsides and canyons to the meadow section. A free-flowing stream, the Thompson River produces healthy populations of 10- to 12-inch rainbows, along with some hefty browns and bull trout in the lower section. Small cutthroats and brook trout are the staple in the upper river.

The Thompson River kicks off in the spring with a healthy Salmon Fly hatch and an abundance of Grannom caddis. Late summer brings out the hoppers, drakes and Baetis hatches all the way into the

fall. The Thompson is just fun to fish. For the most part, fly fishers need only present an attractor pattern on a short cast to hungry trout!

The river is easily fished with lightweight spinning rods and fly rods. It offers a little bit of everyone's favorite type of water, from small riffles and pools to long glides and deep pockets in the canyon section. During late summer and early fall, large stonefly nymphs such as the Bitch Creek and Woolly Buggers are the choice patterns of fly fishers searching for the early browns and bulls heading up from the Clark Fork to spawn.

**MM 63:** Big Horn Sheep Viewing Area.

**MM 75:** Plains, Montana.

**MM 77:** Junction with Highway 28 to Elmo, Montana, and Highway 93.

**MM 81.7:** Paradise, Montana.

**MM 85:** Junction with Highway 135 to St. Regis, Montana, and Interstate 90.

**MM 96:** Junction with Highway 382 cutoff north to Hot Springs, Montana.

### MM 109: Dixon, Montana

Dixon has a boat launch on the Flathead River, which is popular with local pike fishermen. Floating down to the Perma Bridge is almost 17 miles so plan on a long day. This would be a great stretch for a canoeist or family float. However, don't forget to purchase a tribal use permit.

**MM 110.2:** Junction with Route 212 to the National Bison Range, Charlo, Montana, and the Ninepipe Wildlife Refuge on Highway 93.

**MM 116:** Bridge over the Jocko River (Flathead Indian Reservation).

Junction with Highway 93.

# Highway 56 to Troy

**MM 0:** Junction with Highway 56 a few miles west of Noxon, Montana.

 **MM 7.8: Bridge over the Bull River**
Fishing and boat launching.

**Bull River**
**Warning:** The last four miles of the Bull River run down through a canyon to meet the Clark Fork. During spring this section offers some nasty whitewater, and during the summer the same stretch calls for dragging your raft or canoe over a lot of shallow, rocky stretches. With the exception of a few lurking bull trout, the Bull River hosts 8- to 12-inch rainbows and cutthroats. Mostly the river meanders through bottomland that is posted. The river is narrow, slow, clear and deceptively deep in places. Once summer arrives, the trout have less cover and tend to hide in or around grassy tendrils along the bottom of the stream, as well as those shady banks afforded by willow and tag alder. Floating access is at the bridges.

**MM 8.9: East Fork Bull River, St. Paul Lake Trailhead**
At 1.3 miles the road forks left to the north fork and the St. Paul Lake trailhead, which is six miles from the highway. St. Paul Lake is a three-mile hike. Although it lacks in scenery, the lake fishes well for 10- to 14-

inch cutthroats. Below the trailhead the creek is small and offers good fishing for typical creek-sized trout. You have to look for a pullout and scramble down to the creek. Plan on heavy brush and pocket water. At 1.3 mileage turn right and go one mile to a historic ranger station and a great spot to fish the lower creek.

 **MM 11.6:** Pullout access and boat launching access.

**MM 13.8:** Fishing access.

 **MM 15:** Fishing access and canoe launch.

**MM 16: South Fork Bull River** Too small to be worthwhile.

**MM 16.8: Ross Creek Cedar Picnic Site and Bad Medicine Campground**

17 campsites, water, toilets, fully-developed boat launch, fee area.

**MM 21: Dorr Skeel Campground (Bull Lake)**

Kootenai River

Seven campsites, toilets, fully-developed boat launch, non-fee.

### Side Trip – Spar Lake

**MM 29.4: Spar Lake Campground, Chase Cutoff** Spar Lake may also be accessed from Highway 2 near Troy.

**MM 16.5: Lake Creek Road** Affording little access due to private property, Lake Creek surely has some bragging rights for the prettiest creek in the area.

Nonetheless, bridge crossing and a few non-posted spots provide a sampling of this beautiful creek. I came upon one couple who fished right from the side of the road. The wife had just killed a 16-inch rainbow dragging a night crawler through a small hole next to the road. The Lake Creek Road is actually a loop that connects Highway 56 with Spar Lake via Chase Cutoff. The upper road is gravel all the way with a few washboard sections. From the highway to the lake is 17.4 miles.

**Spar Lake Campground**
Eight campsites, water, toilets, non-fee.

**MM 32.4: Savage Lake**
A relatively small lake of about 100 acres, Savage Lake is surrounded by summer homes with only one public access right off the highway. Belly boaters have fun on this lake for both cold- and warm-water species.

**MM 35: Junction with Highway 2** Go west to Troy or east to Libby.

## Highway 2 – The Idaho Border to Libby

### The Kootenai River

The Kootenai River, from Libby Dam 17 miles downriver to Libby, is another great tailwater fishery for Montana. After years of pressure from an glers, biologists and local concerned citizens, the days of wild water fluctuations have come to an end. Posing danger to fishers and floaters, the erratic rise and fall of the river also posed a threat to the insect larva stranded high and dry by the whims of a dam Army Corps engineer. With current standards for water drawdown, insect larva have a chance to retreat into deeper receding water. With consistent yearly insect survival, the Kootenai River gets better every year.

Sitting in the Kootenai Angler, I overheard Dave Blackburn's exuberant announcement to a local fisherman that Green Drakes had appeared in the river, possibly washed down from the Fisher River. Being one of the first fly fishing guide service on the Kootenai River, Dave and his guides are intimately acquainted with all the nuances and fluctuations of this tailwater fishery. In his 1998 newsletter (e-mail kangler@libby.org), Dave talks about the genetic verification of native redband trout in the Kootenai River. Indigenous to the Columbia River drainage, redband trout are noted for having larger spots and a darker background. Dave reports that they are both acrobatic and strong fighters. In addition to a healthy population of trout averaging 2,400 per mile below the dam, one advantage to this large tailwater marvel is the extended season.

Dave reports that the cold waters of March and April provide fishing opportunities for rainbows during the spawning period. Although the water can be off-colored, anglers can experience some good nymphing and streamer fishing. During May and June the water begins to warm, precipitating the emergence of caddis and the Western March Brown. Dry fly fishing heats up, and by far the most important hatch is the PMDs ranging in size 14 to 16 in the early summer to size 18 in the latter part of summer. July and August may bring the heat to the fishermen, but the warmer water activates fish feeding on both dry flies and hoppers. The fall brings foliage change and clarity to the river. With lots of mid-day hatches, trout are eager to store up fat re-

serves for the winter. According to Dave, however, winter is a long time coming on the Kootenai River. The Kootenai season is extended with warm water releases in the 50s, and the fish are still active all the way into December.

Wade fishing is best from 8,000 cubic feet per

A view from Libby Dam

second to 12,000 cfs. It is next to impossible during high water releases of over 15,000 cfs. When the water rises, guides and float fishermen move to the side channels for the larger trout. Popular float trips originate at the dam with the final take-out in the town of Libby. The 17-mile section can be broken up into a number of potential float trips, depending how much time one would like to spend on the water. Below Libby are the deadly Kootenai Falls.

Powerboat operators fishing below the Libby Bridge should first confer with a local expert. Although the world record rainbow at 33 pounds, one ounce, was caught at the outlet of the dam, the average catch of the day will be around 10 to 14-inches with plenty of 18+-inch trout to challenge any angler.

Yaak River

Overlooked for years by the fly fishing public who ply the waters of the Madison and Missouri, people in the know are looking to the northwest. A tour of the Clark Fork drainage rivers and then a sampling of the Kootenai provides excellent trout fishing.

## Lake Koocanusa

Straddling the border with 48 miles in Montana and 42 miles in British Columbia, Lake Koocanusa was formed with the creation of the Libby Dam in 1971. Alice Beers of Rexford, Montana, coined the name for the lake. The name combines the first part of Kootenai, the second part "can" from Canada and the last three letters for "USA". The lake is immense and offers very marginal shore fishing. The principal draw is the prodigious numbers of kokanee salmon ranging from 11 to 14-inches. Large kamloop rainbows lure boat fishers from all around the region. Boaters will find plenty of water to fish with over 46,000 surface acres. Campground and boat launches are spread evenly around the lake.

### Highway 2 Mileage Markers

**MM 1.9: Fishing access to the Kootenai River**
The access is right next to a residence. Drive one mile to a parking place, but do not drive the last two-tenths of a mile to the old bridge – it is steep at the bottom and there is little room to turn around. The road is bumpy and unmaintained and leads to a closed bridge. Upriver from the bridge is a long bank with shallow water. Park up from the bridge and follow the trail down to the river. This could be a good evening spot in the early summer or fall.

**MM 3: Junction with Route 508 to Yaak, Montana** Two dueling bars face each other across the street.

### Side Trip – Highway 2: Route 508 • The Yaak River

Yaak River

The Yaak River is a fair-sized tributary of the Kootenai River, which enters at the Yaak Campground. The Yaak River splits the campground, which provides good access to both rivers as well as a boat launch. It has two distinct types of water. Below the falls by the Yaak Falls Campground (non-fee), the river quickly drops in elevation, which provides lots of holding water down through a steep canyon gorge. A haven to some big bull trout, the canyon is difficult to access, and much of it is posted. After a long hike down the canyon during a heat spell, I caught a few fish in the 12-inch range, but most of the ones I caught were 8 to 10, which is more typical of the river in general. Good water may be found above the falls, but a good portion of it flattens out and heats up during summer. Above and below the town of Yaak, the river looks like a slough, and most of it runs through private property. This valley section is home to a lot of small brookies, rainbows and a few small cutthroats. The Yaak Falls Campground offers seven campsites, toilets, and is a non-fee area. It offers a great swimming hole, if you are hot and driving through the area. At mile marker 27 the Yaak picks up some speed.

###  Seventeen Mile Creek

A few miles above the Yaak Falls Campground, Seventeen Mile Creek Road is closed and gated due to flood damage. It is also a wildlife sanctuary. The lower stretch of the creek can be accessed at the first right turn, which provides an access by the bridge. The area is posted, so stay in the creek. Take Seventeen Mile Creek 4.5 miles to the gate and hike into a great little creek. This would be a good creek to ride in on a mountain bike, as the closed road parallels the creek. The first 4.5 miles of the creek is blocked by private property.

###  MM 15.6: Red Top Recreation

Five primitive camping sites.

**MM 20.9:** Bridge access to the south fork.

### MM 24.1: Whitetail Campground

12 campsites, water, toilets, fee area, right on the river.

### MM 26.8: Pete Creek Campground

12 campsites, water, toilets, fee area.

### MM 6.2: Yaak Campground, Boat Launch

44 campsites, pull-throughs, water, toilets, fee area.

### MM 7.8: Fishing access

The turn-around offers a jeep trail which follows the river downstream.

### MM 10: Fishing access, boat launch

Follow Forest Drive and then Beachward Trail a half-mile to a nice boat launch.

### MM 10: Kilbrennan Lake: 9.2 miles

Kilbrennan Lake is a 59-acre lake, and is deep in the middle. At the far end of the lake is a non-fee campground and a boat launch. The lake is full of perch and bullhead, but boat fishermen can catch good numbers of brook trout on the side of the lake opposite the road. Locals tend to fill up this campground Thursday through Sunday. Seven campsites, toilets, non-fee.

**MM 11.8:** Bridge crossing.

### MM 14: Troy, Montana; Kootenai River boat launch

Turn on Third Street and drive four-tenths of a mile, and then turn left on Riverside Drive another four-tenths of a mile to the launch.

### MM 15: Callahan Creek Road

Callahan Creek is not accessible in its lower reaches near Troy, as the road climbs up the mountain for a number of miles. To fish this creek, you will need to drive all the way back to the bridge by the south fork and north fork. From this point you can fish the main stem of the creek or the forks. The creek is boulder-strewn, however, so walking is tough for the young and old. Fish for small cutthroats. The road is paved all the way with the exception of the last mile and a half. From the highway to the bridge is 7.5 miles.

🚶 **MM 21: Kootenai Falls Scenic Trail**

🐟 **MM 22.2:** Fishing access along the railroad track.

🐟 **MM 23:** Fishing access (rapids).

**MM 30:** Libby, Montana.

# Highway 37 – Libby to Eureka

## Side Trip –
## Route 567 from Libby to Yaak

🐟 **Route 68 and Pipe Creek**

Follow California Street out of Libby and cross the Kootenai River (boat launch just by the bridge). California Street changes to Route 567. Take Route 567 (also called Pipe Creek Road) to Yaak, a distance of 37 miles. Pipe Creek gets fairly small during the summer. Nonetheless, it offers good fishing for small trout. The East Fork of Pipe Creek is a tiny, brushy creek holding small brookies.

🐟 **Rainbow Lake**

One lake that is worth fishing is Rainbow Lake at mileage marker 22. Rainbow Lake is reached on Road #4712. It is a bit bumpy and narrow, and a second-gear pull in places. A little over 30 acres, the lake is a small circular lake with a grassy-lined shoreline. You cannot drive to the lake. From the small parking area, you have to follow a trail three minutes down to the lake. This is a great lake for a canoe or belly boat. It offers fair catches of cutthroats.

🐟 **Vinal Lake (Road 746 MM 32.3)**

Vinal Lake is about eight miles on Road 746 that forks north. You will need to hike a half-mile to the lake. Easily fished from the shoreline, this 18-acre lake fishes well for 12-inch rainbows. Continuing on Route 68 to Yaak, the road follows the South Fork of the Yaak River. The south fork is very small and posted.

## Return to Highway 37
**Highway 37 from Libby to Eureka, via Lake Koocanusa**

Highway 37 passes the Libby Dam via Lake Koocanusa 66 miles to Eureka and then into Canada on Highway 93 to Banff and Jasper National Parks in British Columbia. Parallel to this highway is a paved road on the other side of the lake that intersects with the highway at the Koocanusa Bridge, a distance of 45 miles. Take California Street to the bridge crossing and the city boat launch.

❓ **MM 1: Ranger Station** Information.

**MM 13: Canoe Gulch Ranger Station** USFS information on camping and boating facilities.

🐟🛶 **MM 8.9:** Boat launch on the Kootenai River.

🐟 **MM 14: Junction with the Fisher River and the Fisher River Road #763**
Fisher River is more like a creek and has fair fishing.

## Side Trip – The Fisher River

🐟🏕 **Fisher River, Shortcut to Highway 2 connecting Kalispell and Libby**

The Fisher River access is at mileage marker 14 on Highway 37 a few miles below the Libby Dam. The Fisher River is only fair fishing for small rainbows and whitefish. The road is paved and runs 24 miles to meet Highway 2. The road is narrow in places. Primitive campsites may be found throughout the Fisher River drainage.

## Return to Highway 37

**MM 13: Dunn Creek Recreation Campground**
US Army Corps of Engineers (non-fee) Alexander Creek Campground, Dunn Creek Flats Campground, Blackwell Flats Campground.

 **MM 15: Libby Dam**
The dam road can be crossed to Souse Gulch adjacent to the dam, which provides picnicking as well as a boat launch. You may follow this road downstream to Blackwell Flats Campground. Both Blackwell and Dunn Creek Flats provide boat launches. Along Lake Koocanusa are a series of campgrounds and marinas. Lake Koocanusa is a popular lake for boaters.

**MM 23.8: Koocanusa Resort**
Public boat launch.

**Rocky Gorge Campground**
120 campsites, water, toilets, fully-developed boat launch, fee area.

**MM 48.8: Peck Gulch**
75 camping sites, picnicking, boat launch, water, toilets, fee area.

**MM 61.5: Rexford, Montana; Rexford Bench Complex**
Campground with 54 campsites, water, flush toilets, fee area, boating site with 33 campsites, water, flush toilets, fully-developed boat launch, fee area.
**Kamloops Terrace:** 50 campsites, water, flush toilets, fee area.

**MM 64: Tobacco River access**

**MM 64.8: Eureka airport, Tetrault Lake, Sophie Lake, fishing access on Lake Koocanusa**
Tetrault is periodically stocked with Arlee rainbows and is a popular lake with the locals. Bill Myra of Green Mountain Sports reported that the lake was scheduled for poisoning sometime in 1998 so that the lake could be managed as a trophy trout lake.
**Sophie Lake**
Sophie Lake offers a full range of fish species. This 200-acre lake has recently been stocked with kamloop rainbows.

**MM 66.8:** Junction with Highway 93, a mile from Eureka.

## Highway 2 – Libby to Kalispell

**MM 30:** Libby, Montana.

**MM 44: Howard Lake Loop**
The loop follows Libby Creek and Howard Lake and exits again on Highway 2 at MM 56.8. A small 34-acre lake 14 miles from the highway, Howard Lake is a popular fishing lake for rainbows from 8 to 14 inches. The lake has a popular campground with nine campsites, water, toilets, small boat launch, and it is a fee area. Libby Creek follows the highway a number of miles outside of Libby, but it offers only fair fishing. The Howard Lake outlet creek is a tiny creek holding small rainbows.

**MM 56.8: Howard Lake Loop** Taking the Silver Butte Road #148 will both lead you to another fork of the Fisher River, which provides creek-type fishing as well as a junction with Highway 200 near Trout Creek. The road is narrow and winding.

**MM 63.4: Pleasant Valley Campground** Pleasant Valley Fisher River Section.

**MM 65.8: Lyons Spring Campground** St. Regis Company.

**MM 69: McKillop Road #535** This paved road leads north to the main stem of the Fisher River and exits out on Highway 37 14 miles above Libby and just a few miles from the Libby Dam. The road is 32 miles long; the first eight miles are narrow and wind high up on the side of the mountains. Called the McKillop Road, it intersects with Fisher River Road #763.

## Thompson Chain of Lakes

**MM 69 to MM 86:** The Thompson Chain of Lakes, stretching along Highway 2 for 17 miles between Libby and Kalispell, quite possibly offers more fishing variety than any other stretch of highway in Montana. Nineteen lakes ranging in size from three acres to 1,300 acres, the chain boosts both warm-water game fish and cold-water trout. The area offers 60 campsites.

Perch, pumpkinseeds, largemouth bass and northern pike cruise through Crystal, Horseshoe, Lavon, Little Loon, Little McGregor, Loon, Lower Thompson, Middle Thompson and Upper Thompson Lakes. Rainbows, eastern brook and cutthroats can be located together or isolated in Banana, Bootjack, Cad, Cibid, Leon, Lilly Pad, Little Loon, Little McGregor, Loon, Lower Thompson, Middle Thompson, Myron, Rainbow, Topless and Upper Thompson Lakes.

Compressed into a 17-mile stretch, sprinkle in kokanee salmon and browns and anglers have enough variety and challenges to last a lifetime. Best of all, some of the lakes hold huge lake trout in the 10- to 20-pound range; however, with the illegal introduction of pike to some of the lakes, trout and bass numbers have declined in some of the lakes. What follows is a listing of the lakes starting with Loon Lake and progressing towards McGregor Lake, which is 28 miles from Kalispell.

Camping is allowed only in the 60 designated campsites spread throughout the chain of lakes.

### MM 70: Loon Lake
238 acres, 114 feet maximum depth. Contains yellow perch, rainbow, largemouth bass, Eastern brook trout. Day use only. Concrete boat launch.

### Little Loon Lake
South of Loon Lake. 11.6 acres, 38 feet maximum depth. Contains cutthroat, largemouth bass, and small mouth bass. Dirt ramp.

### Leon Lake
Southwesterly tip of Loon Lake. 22 acres, 22 feet maximum depth. Contains yellow perch, cutthroats. Dirt ramp.

### Horseshoe Lake
159 acres, 133 feet maximum depth. Contains pumpkinseed, largemouth bass, whitefish. Concrete boat ramp.

### Cibid Lake
11 acres, 60 feet maximum depth. Contains rainbows. Day use only.

### Banana Lake
Across the highway from Horseshoe Lake. Contains rainbows and cutthroats. Day use only.

### Topless Lake
Clustered along with Lilly Pad Lake, Bootjack Lake and Lavon Lake between Horseshoe Lake and Crystal Lake, Topless Lake is 9.2 acres and holds cutthroat. Lilly Pad Lake is a three-acre lake holding brook trout and largemouth bass. Bootjack Lake is a 12-acre lake holding cutthroats and rainbows. The lake is mostly on private land, but there is public access if you can find it.

## Lavon Lake

17 acres, 91 feet. Contains yellow perch, kokanee salmon, rainbow, largemouth bass. Day use only.

## Crystal Lake

178 acres, 154 feet. Contains yellow perch, kokanee salmon, rainbow, largemouth bass. Dirt ramp.

**MM 74: Rainbow Lake** A small lake nestled up against Upper Thompson Lake at the northern end, Rainbow Lake is 20 acres and has no public access.

## Upper Thompson

375 acres, 50 feet. Contains yellow perch, northern pike, largemouth bass, pumpkinseeds, rainbows, small mouth bass. Concrete boat ramp.

## MM 77: Middle Thompson Lake

Contains yellow perch, northern pike, largemouth bass, pumpkinseeds, rainbows and small mouth bass. **Logan State Park Campground:** Logan has 39 campsites and trailer spaces up to 40 feet. Gravel ramp.

## Lower Thompson Lake

Contains yellow perch, rainbow, largemouth bass, pumpkinseeds, kokanee salmon, northern pike, brown trout. Concrete boat launch.

## Little McGregor Lake

North side of the highway. 40 acres. Contains brook trout, cutthroat, yellow perch, large mouth bass. Dirt ramp.

## MM 85: McGregor Lake

1,328 acres. Contains lake trout, rainbow, yellow perch, whitefish. McGregor Lake Campground has 15 campsites accommodating trailer space up to 32 feet. Dirt ramp.

## MM 100.7: Little Bitterroot Lake

Almost three miles long and a half-mile wide, the lake is a recreational lake with summer homes and boating activities. Nonetheless, the lake fishes well for perch, kokanee salmon and nice-size rainbows.

## MM 105: Ashley Lake

Another large recreation lake, Ashley Lake offers good fishing for kokanee salmon and nice-sized rainbows.

## MM 110: Smith Lake

A marshy, shallow 300 acre lake, Smith Lake has one state access site to launch a boat. The lake fishes well for perch and bass.

**MM 120:** Kalispell, Montana.

# Highway 93 North – Missoula to Kalispell

Highway 93 continues west of Missoula from Exit 96 on Interstate 90. From the Interstate 90 exit, it is 17 miles to Arlee, 27 miles to the junction with Highway 200 and 112 miles to Kalispell. Highway 93 from Missoula to the Canadian border covers almost 188 miles through some of the most beautiful country in western Montana. Exiting Interstate 90 onto Highway 93 north, the highway cuts across the Flathead Indian Reservation towards Flathead Lake.

The majestic Mission Mountains rise straight up from the valley floor as the highway passes through the towns of Arlee, St. Ignatius and Polson. A few miles north of Polson, visitors will come to a crest and be struck by the size and beauty of Flathead Lake, the largest natural lake west of the Great Lakes. Highway 93 follows the east shore of the lake to Kalispell, or travelers may choose Highway 35 to Bigfork and then reconnect with Highway 93 at the head of the lake.

From Kalispell, travelers to Glacier National Park may route themselves on Highway 93 to Whitefish, take the mid-way Highway 2 or pick up Highway 35 which turns into Route 206 to Columbia Falls.

## Flathead Indian Reservation

Established July 16, 1885, as part of the Hellgate Treaty, the Salish and Kootenai tribes were forced to move to the Flathead Indian Reservation. Encompassing 1.2 million acres, the reservation has as its northern boundary Flathead Lake, which is almost 27 miles long and 16 miles wide at its widest point. To the east the reservation is bordered by the towering Mission Mountains. Across the rolling pothole country to the west, the reservation is bordered by the Cabinet Mountains. Although originally including portions of the Bitterroot Valley, those lands were lost in subsequent revisions of the treaty, which was typical of Indian treaties in general. Fishing on the reservation requires a special tribal stamp and a recreation permit. The reservation offers excellent angling opportunities for warmwater species such as perch, bass and pike as well as all the major trout species.

The reservation offers alpine lakes, streams, ponds and reservoirs. Tribal wildlife managers continually work to upgrade the quality of riparian habitat for enhancement of native salmonids. The Jocko River is testimony to their efforts, providing good fishing for browns, cutthroats and rainbows. Local fishermen boast that Kicking Horse and Ninepipe Reservoir offer some of the best largemouth bass fishing in the region. And there is always the prospect of landing a 20-pound pike on the lower Flathead River or hiking into the Mission Mountains for native westslope cutthroats, brook trout and rainbows. The Flathead Reservation offers over a million acres of fishing opportunities. Stop in at Ronan Sports and Western in Ronan for fishing information on the reservation.

The southern half of Flathead Lake is part of the reservation. During the past 15 years a number of changes have impacted the lake, most notably the introduction of mysis shrimp, which precipitated the decline of the kokanee salmon. Preyed upon by lake trout, native cutthroats, bull trout and kokanee salmon have declined steadily during the past two decades.

Many local experts believe that a growing balance between species is possible and does not necessitate over-harvesting the lake trout. The average lake trout is 20 inches, and 20 pounds is not uncommon. The best fishing is from October to December, when lake trout are spawning in the shallows along the lake. Fishing guides boast of large catches of these prodigious lunkers with jig-type lures.

## Flathead Lake

A number of launch sites are available at private marinas as well as the three state parks. Contrary to popular belief, many areas are safe for fishing out of a small boat, if boaters are observant of the weather and don't venture too far from the shoreline. The Flathead Lake fishery has changed dramatically with the invasion of the mysis shrimp in the early 1980s. Introduced in the '60s and '70s opossum shrimp were planted by fisheries management across the western United States and Canada to increase the growth of kokanee salmon. Unfortunately, their proclivity for avoiding light and their habit of resting in deep water adversely impacted both the populations of cutthroat and kokanee. Mysis awake from their lairs at depths of 100 feet and rise to the surface at night to feed on zooplankton, the same food source preferred by kokanee.

By first light they have safely settled again on the bottom, quite out of reach of their intended prey, the kokanee. The zooplankton populations crashed. Unfortunately, the beneficiary of the mysis shrimp is the lake trout, who grow fat on both shrimp and kokanee. Today large populations of lake trout may be caught throughout the lake. Lake trout (mackinaw or "macs") are primarily fish predators with whitefish as their main course.

"They prefer colder water and are usually found near the bottom, although they can be found at all depths when the water is cold. Generally fish 30 to 100 feet deep for smaller (2-5 lb.) lakers and over 100 feet deep for larger lake trout, but expect lots of mixing of sizes. Generally, look for areas that will concentrate bait fish such as points, sloping areas of large rubble, or flats adjacent to drop-offs or steep slopes. Expansive flats may not hold many fish. A fish finder helps locate likely spots and may locate schools of bait fish or lake trout, but lake trout can hold so tight to the bottom most fish finders won't show them.

"Lake trout prefer dim light so the best fishing is dawn to mid-morning.... Lake trout up to five pounds eat lots of shrimp and can be delicious fried, baked barbecued, or smoked....

"Vertical jigging...has really revolutionized lake trout fishing since it is simple, productive, and requires little gear. A medium-weight spinning or bait casting outfit with 10-lb. test monofilament will work. Drop the lure to the bottom, reel up about a foot and jig the lure up sharply one to three feet, and then let it free-fall back. Jig every 10 to 20 seconds. Set the hook hard when you feel a tap or a jerk. Often the fish will hit as the lure is dropping so if the line stays slack reel up and strike....

"Lake trout can be readily caught from shore in May-June and October-November when the water is cool and they're in shallow to look for food...or to spawn in the fall. Generally look for steep to moderately sloping bottoms with lots of rubble.... Count down before starting your retrieve so the lure is near the bottom. Use silver/red or gold/red lures. You'll lose lures so use inexpensive ones. Most lakers will be two to four pounds, but you may catch a larger one, particularly in the fall....

"A good contour map of Flathead Lake showing access points is available locally.... For more information on fishing, seasons and limits, and licenses, contact local sporting good stores or Fish, Wildlife and Parks (406) 752-5501 or the Confederated Salish and Kootenai Tribe (406) 675-2700." –Montana Fish, Wildlife and Parks publication, 1999

Visitors to Flathead Lake who are pulling a large boat behind their rig may want to consider combining a fishing trip with a tour of Wild Horse Island State Park. Access to the island is best from Flathead State Park at Big Arm, located about 35 miles south of Kalispell and 13 miles north of Polson along Highway 93. Wild Horse Island encompasses 2,163 acres of primitive management. Just a few shoreline parcels are still owned by private landowners. No camping is allowed, and boaters are cautioned to beach their boats at one of the five public landing sites. Yes, in addition to more than 100 species of birds and mammals, the island's tradition of wild horses is still kept alive by the Bureau of Land Management.

For more information contact:
Montana State Parks
490 N Meridian Road
Kalispell, Montana 59901-3854
(406) 752-5501
For information on booking a guided fishing tour on Flathead Lake, contact:
Montana Charter Boat Association
375 Jensen Road
Columbia Falls, Montana 59912
(800) 735-9244

## Mileage Markers for Highway 93 North — Missoula to Kalispell

### MM 16.7: Jocko River Road

Jocko Road winds up the headwaters of the Jocko River over the divide and down into the Seeley Lake area past Lake Placid. A tribal fishing permit is required on tribal lands.

**MM 17:** Arlee, Montana.

**MM 19:** Crossing the Jocko River.

**MM 27:** Ravalli, Montana.

**MM 27.5: Junction with Highway 200 to Thompson Falls** See Highway 200, page 47.

**MM 32.5:** St. Ignatius, Montana.

 **MM 39:** McDonald Lake.

 **MM 40.4: Ninepipe Reservoir**

**MM 42:** Charlo, Montana; National Bison Range.

 **MM 42: Kicking Horse Reservoir**
Dirt road to the right. Excellent bass fishing.

 **MM 44:** Picnic site with shaded tables, toilets.

**MM 46:** Ronan, Montana.

**MM 52.5:** Pablo National Wildlife Refuge.

**MM 59:** Junction Highway 35 to Bigfork, Kalispell.

**MM 59.5:** Polson, Montana; Polson Recreation Park.

 **MM 61:** Riverside Park, city boat launch.

**MM 71.5: Walstad Memorial State Recreation Area**
Fishing access, boat launch, picnic area.

**MM 73:** Big Arm Resort and Marina.

**MM 74.4:** Big Arm Campground and Picnic Area.

 **MM 77: Elmo** Store, gas.

**MM 77.3:** Junction with Highway 28 to Hot Springs, Montana.

**MM 82.8: Lake Mary Ronan State Park**
Lake Mary Ronan is a large recreational lake encompassing almost 1,500 acres. It provides good fishing for kokanee, rainbow and bass. 27 campsites, 35-foot trailer spaces, water, fee area.

**MM 85:** Northern boundary for the Flathead Indian Reservation.

**MM 92.8: Westshore State Campground, boat launch**
26 campsites, water, toilets, fee area.

**MM 97.5:** Lakeside, Montana.

**MM 102.5:** Somers Fishing Access, boat launch and picnic site.

**MM 103:** Somers, Montana.

**MM 104.2:** Junction with Highway 82 to Bigfork, Montana.

**MM 110:** Kalispell, Montana, Information Center

**MM 112:** Kalispell, Montana.

**MM 113:** Junction with Highway 2 to Whitefish and Glacier National Park.

**MM 125: Whitefish, Montana; Columbia Falls, Montana; and Glacier National Park** The cutoff to Glacier National Park from Whitefish is 24 miles.

# Highway 93 –
# Whitefish to the Canadian Border

 **Stillwater River**

The Stillwater is just that – still. The mid-section often abuts Highway 93, and access points are found at bridge crossings, pullouts and dirt roads. Slow water and willow-lined stream banks provide good populations of brook trout, rainbows and cutthroats. Some sections are floatable.

**MM 129: Whitefish Lake State Park**

1.1 miles from Highway 93 in the town of Whitefish. Shaded and beautiful, the campground is close to a golf course as well!

**MM 132: Tally Lake** See MM 139.

**MM 135: Beaver Lake:** Four miles
**Little Beaver Lake, Murray Lake, Rainbow Lake, Woods Lake, Dollar Lake**

Beaver Lake is a beautiful lake with just a small turn-around provided by the state. The lake is bordered by private property. The access site has one picnic site. Canoeists will have to slide their canoes down an embankment to the lake. Beaver Lake is a popular lake for rainbows. Coming into the area, you will find a sign showing the location of all of the little lakes. The roads are bumpy and narrow, and some of them, like the road to Little Beaver Lake, definitely need the high clearance of a truck. Little Beaver Lake has one public access spot to launch a boat, but you will probably need a 4X4 vehicle, especially in the early summer.

I personally would pass up Little Beaver Lake, as the last two-tenths of a mile is on a rutted, boggy road, and when I pulled up to the lake there were already two families camped in a one-family site. I walked down to Dollar Lake and met a teenage boy

and his friend who said the lake has always fished well for them, but some of the lakes have been over-populated with Flathead minnows and as such are scheduled for rehabilitation. I would stick with Beaver Lake if you have a car-topper boat, a canoe or a belly boat.

**MM 139: Tally Lake Campground, Sheppard Creek, Sylvia Lake Campground**

Take the Star Meadow road about 10 miles to the turn-off to Tally Lake. Tally Lake is a large 1,300-acre lake, and it is the deepest lake in Montana at 492 feet. Tally Lake is a recreation lake and popular with water skiers. The campground is on the north shore and has 39 campsites, water, toilets, and boat launch as well as an RV dump station and a swimming area. Fee area.

If you continue to Star Meadows, consult the Flathead National Forest Visitor's Map for mileage. **Sheppard Lake and Sylvia Lake**

On the way to Sylvia Lake, you will pass Sheppard Creek, a brushy little creek holding typical creek-size trout. Sylvia Lake is a 20-acre lake, and it is stocked with grayling.

**MM 144.2: Good Creek, Martin Lake, access to the Stillwater River**

The road to Good Creek is an easy drive to a good creek. At four-tenths of a mile, you will cross a bridge over the Stillwater River, which provides fishing access. At 3.2 miles there is a turn-off road to Martin Lake, which is a fair fishing lake for smaller rainbows. The pavement ends at 6.1 miles, and there is a turn-off to Star Meadows at 15 miles and Sylvia Lake at 23 miles.

At 8.6 miles Good Creek is not visible, but the distance to the creek is less than a mile. At mile 9.3 you will have your first sighting of the creek. Further up the road the creek meanders through thick willow and tag alder. The creek holds lots of small brook trout and cutthroats.

## MM 145.6: Upper Whitefish Lake and Red Meadow Lake

Both lakes can be driven to on a fairly good dirt road. The first lake, Upper Whitefish Lake, is 13.5 miles.

Upper Whitefish Lake is in the Stillwater State Forest and offers a campground and fishing for small cutthroats. Red Meadow Lake is about six miles further and offers camping on a picturesque 19-acre lake, which provides fair fishing for cutthroats and grayling.

## MM 151.5: Upper Stillwater Lake and Lagoni Lake

Upper Stillwater Lake is unseen from the highway, but it is only 1.3 miles away. This 630-acre lake offers a campground and fair fishing for brook trout, pike, perch and the occasional cutthroat. Above Upper Stillwater Lake is Lagoni Lake, a small 20-acre lake offering the same type of fishing.

## MM 158.8: Bull Lake and Stryker Lake (Fish Lake)

Both lakes lie side-by-side just a few miles from the community of Stryker and offer good fishing for cutthroat and brook trout. These are native trout, but be sure you have a Montana State Land Permit before you fish!

 **MM 159.8: Picnic spot on South Dickey Lake**
Day use only.

**MM 161: Dickey Lake**
Dickey Lake is a summer recreation lake with a potpourri of species offerings, none of which get very big.

## MM 163.3: Dickey Lake Campground

25 campsites, 50-foot trailer spaces, toilets, water, boat launch, fee area.

**MM 165.1:** Murphy Lake Ranger Station

## MM 165.8: Murphy Lake

Murphy Lake is a popular 163-acre, warm-water fishery for largemouth bass, perch and pike. Murphy Lake also offers camping.

## MM 170.2: Grave Creek and Campground, Blue Sky Creek, Weasel Lake, Therriault Lakes (Little and Big) and the Ten Lakes Scenic Area

For fishermen and campers in the Eureka area, this is your access! Grave Creek has the largest volume of water of any creek in the area. Just a few miles from the highway, Grave Creek Campground offers a number of campsites right on the creek, but the campground is not practical for larger RVs or trailers. In fact, I found only three sites suitable for smaller trailers. The short access road into the campground makes a tight turn, and the road is bumpy. Grave Creek, a tributary of the Tobacco River, is a good fishing creek for 10- to 12-inch rainbows and cutthroats. The bottom section is private, and there is a small area of private land near the campground, but above the campground is National Forest land with a number of miles of creek to fish.

Above Grave Creek is Blue Sky Creek, a tributary of Grave Creek. The creek is small and the small fish are plentiful, but the creek is closed to protect spawning runs of cutthroats and bulls as of July 31. Before you reach Therriault Lakes, the road goes by Weasel Lake. Weasel Lake is a pretty little lake with small fish.

Therriault Lakes are about 28 miles from the highway. Both lakes offer camping and good fishing for 10- to 12-inch cutthroats. The big lake is 55 acres, and the smaller lake 26 acres. Little Therriault Lake is the trailhead for the Ten Lakes Scenic Area.

When I spoke to Bill Myra, owner of Green Mountain Sports Center in Eureka, Bill became passionate in describing the Ten Lakes Area. Having spoken about my home waters with the same enthusiasm, I know I will have to spend a couple of days exploring the region on my next trip. Bill said to plan on a full day hike to these high-elevation lakes, where you can expect great beauty and feisty 10- to 12-inch native trout. Some of the lakes are barren, so you might want to check in with Bill to plan your hike.

**MM 174: Glen Lake** Glen Lake is surrounded by residences, and the fishing is fair to poor.

**MM 178:** Eureka, Montana.

A view of Hungry Horse Reservoir

**MM 180:** Junction with Highway 37 to Libby via Lake Koocanusa.

# Highway 2 – The Columbia Falls Area

## The Hungry Horse Reservoir – South Fork of the Flathead River

Top off your gas tank if you are heading up the South Fork. Follow Highway 2 to the town of Hungry Horse at mileage marker 143.4. Follow the signs to Hungry Horse Dam. Cross the dam and follow the West Side South Fork Road. The mileage markers start at the dam. Spotted Bear Campground, a few miles above the inlet to Hungry Horse Lake, is 55 miles from the dam, and most of it is dirt road. If you are pulling a trailer, plan on cruising at 35 mph. Draining the Bob Marshall Wilderness, the South Fork is the crown jewel of northwestern Montana. From the Spotted Bear Campground, access is by trail or plane into the designated Wild River section. A good portion of this wilderness encompasses the Jewell Basin Hiking Area. To reach the trailheads to the Jewell Basin, look for Wounded Buck Road, West Fork Clayton Creek Road, Clayton Creek Road, Graves Creek Road or Wheeler Creek Road. For more information on the Jewell Basin Hiking Area, see Highway 83, page 74.

Unlike the other forks of the Flathead River, the South Fork fishery is not a migratory fishery owing to the completion of Hungry Horse Dam in 1952. Expect to catch cutthroats averaging 8 to 10 inches. Bull trout, although plentiful, have been protected since 1993. One of the guides that I spoke to said that some days the river offers many 14- to 16-inch trout, but again, access is limited. The primary floating section that can be reached by road is from Cedar Flats River Access to a launch access just below Spotted Bear Campground. The guides in this country work very hard for their wages. Having guided in western Montana all those years, the toughest launch I can think of consisted of dragging my raft maybe 30 yards to the water. When I got out of my truck at Cedar Flats, I kept thinking,

there must be a mistake! I walked a narrow trail about 50 yards until the trail plunged down a cliff. Standing high up on the ridge, I couldn't even hear the water below. Later I talked to a local guide who told me he has to completely break his raft down, and depending on the willingness of his clients, he could count on a minimum of four trips up and down the steep trail.

From Cedar Flats to the Spotted Bear Access point is eight miles and rated Class II water. Above Cedar Flats is a gorge rated Class V to VI. From Spotted Bear Campground Boat Launch to the next access, Twin Creeks, is 6.5 miles and rated Class III, although I swear there are some Class IV spots, which is probably just a perspective view sitting in my 10-foot, one-man drift boat.

Numerous non-fee primitive campsites may be found during the last few miles along Hungry Horse Lake. In addition to the Spotted Bear Campground, Crossover Campground can be easily found on the east side of the lake a couple of miles below Twin Creeks. When you are headed to the Spotted Bear Ranger Station, you will cross the river on the South Fork Bridge and come to a T-intersection. If you turn left, the road heads back down the lake on the eastside to the town of Hungry Horse. Crossover Campground is a few miles down this road and provides a boat launch to the lake.

### Spotted Bear River

The Spotted Bear Campground, ranger station and river all come together 55 miles from the dam. Spotted Bear River is indeed a river during spring runoff, but by summer it drops to creek size. The river is excellent for 10-to 14-inch cutthroats, but once again access is difficult in all but a few places. From the confluence with the South Fork to Beaver Creek Campground is 9.4 miles, with only the lower stretch accessible for parking your vehicle and walking down to the river. Two miles above the Beaver Creek Campground (non-fee) the road is blocked. The access roads in the upper half are not really access roads! The first three access roads in the lower half of the road will get you right to the river or very close; in between you have to park and hike down the mountain. The hike back up the mountain would be tough for me, but the biggest challenge for me would be on deciding the question, "Do I walk up the road looking for my rig or walk down?"

When I took the first access road that led to a primitive camping site on the river, I ran into what I consider a real "Old Timer". I had just stopped to fish a section of the river and caught three fat cutthroats from 10 to 12 inches. I worked one riffle and one hole, but in truth I had to fish these two spots hard and smart to bring them up from the bottom. I was a bit disappointed, but it was almost 90 degrees, so even the usual greedy little ones were sulking from the heat. As I pulled out, I drove past a primitive campsite and spotted an older man sitting in a lawn chair reading a novel.

I leaned out of my truck window and asked him about the typical size for this section. Pat Hardin smiled. Wearing a white brimmed hat and red suspenders, Pat looked like the friendly grandfather type. His kind eyes and easy smile marked him as a soft touch for grandkids.

"Depends when you're here," he said.

"Well, I just caught three over there and the largest was 12 inches. What kind of size do you generally catch?"

"Depends on when I was here. The first time was 1928. That was 70 years ago."

Without even hesitating I asked, "Could I get out of this truck and talk to you?"

"Grab a chair and join me in this patch of shade," he said.

What a story he had to tell. The next day, wishing I had had the instincts of a newspaper reporter, I regretted not asking all of the questions I would have liked to ask. With some experience as a reporter, I might have probed his story for all the rich details. Pat's parents were ranchers in the Columbia Falls area. Both were avid outdoors people, and both his mom and dad hunted elk in the fall. Pat said they'd hitch up a wagon with a team of horses and head up Hungry Horse Creek, camping and hunting until they both shot their elk.

Pat recalled his first trip up the South Fork to the Spotted Bear Ranger Station in 1928. The rough road paralleled the river, and the going was rough for a Model T Ford. It took them two days to travel the 60 miles from Hungry Horse to the Spotted Bear Ranger Station. They'd stop and fish when they needed to stretch their legs. Pat remembered the excitement of arriving at the ranger station, which at that time was fairly new. He was seven years old on his first visit to the South Fork.

As a little kid he most enjoyed fishing the little feeder creeks, which produced some very nice-sized cutthroats. Fourth of July on the South Fork was tradition for a number of local ranching families. Years later, after the dam was built, Pat noticed a decline in the numbers of fish just above the reservoir to Spotted Bear, although above Spotted Bear the river maintained its richness. As the popularity of floating increased on the South Fork, noticeable declines in numbers and size alarmed Pat and other folks who had fished the South Fork for years. Pat joined a committee and helped to establish the Wilderness Limit, which limits a fisherman to three fish, all less than 12 inches. Pat now feels the South Fork is rebounding.

Just as I was getting up to leave, Pat confided that a good fisherman could still catch them up to 18 inches, if he knew what he was doing. "My old holes on the South Fork and Spotted Bear are just about as good as they ever were." Pat's final comment for me to include in this book was to encourage campers to have a fish fry without any guilt. "Whitefish," he asserted, "are as good eating as a trout, maybe better." The cold waters of the South Fork produce some of the best-eating whitefish in Montana. With incredibly generous limits, Pat suggests filleting them or just skinning them. The flaky white meat just falls off the bones.

## Mileage Distance for the Westside Road

**MM 0:** Hungry Horse Dam.

 **Doris Boat Landing**

Located eight miles from the dam, the Doris Boat Landing is reached by a paved road.

Blackfoot River. Photo courtesy of Bob Edgar

**MM 5: Lost Johnny Campground**

Five campsites, water, toilets, limited space for large trailers or RVs. Fee area.

**MM 5.6: Lost Johnny Point Campground**

21 campsites, water, trailer space for 26-foot camper trailers, concrete launch site to 45-foot drawdown. Fee area.

**MM 8.3: Lid Creek Campground**

23 campsites, toilets, concrete boat ramp serving full pool to 31-foot drawdown. Fee area.

**MM 19: Lakeview Campground**

Five campsites, no water.

**MM 28.9: Graves Bay Campground**

10 campsites, no water.

**Graves Creek**

Graves Creek may be accessed along the road to Handkerchief Lake and above the lake and then by trail into the Jewell Basin. The creek fishes well for 8- to 10-inch cutthroats.

**MM 28.9: Handkerchief Lake Campground**

32 acres. Handkerchief Lake can be reached within a couple hundred yards of the campground. Fishing is good for cutthroats and grayling. This is also one of the access trailheads for the Jewell Basin. (See Highway 83, page 74.)

**MM 55: Spotted Bear Campground**

13 campsites, toilets, water, RV dump facility. Just short of the campground is an access road for launching rafts, although during mid-summer plan on carrying your boat about 40 yards over rocks.

**Beaver Creek Campground**

9.4 miles above the ranger station on Spotted Bear Road. Three sites, outhouses, loading ramp, feed bunks for horses.

## Mileage Distance for the Eastside Road

**MM 0:** Martin City.

### MM 5: Emery Bay Campground
26 campsites, toilets, water, concrete boat ramp serving full pool to 35 foot. Fee area.

### MM 22.2: Murray Bay Campground
18 campsites, water, toilets, boat ramp to drawdown level 20 feet.

### MM 37.4: Devil's Corkscrew Campground
Four campsites, toilets, cement boat ramp.

### MM 42.2: Peters Creek Campground
Six campsites, toilets, no water.

Blackfoot River at Round-Up

### MM 46.8: Cross Over Campground

# Highway 200 – Interstate 90 at Bonner to Lincoln

## The Blackfoot River

During the early '80s I got a call from one of the longest-tenured guides in western Montana. He asked me if I had guided much on the Blackfoot River. I was honest in telling him that I had never floated the Big Blackfoot. "It doesn't matter," he countered. "I need three boats for a scenic float trip. Only one member of the group will fish, and he will be in my boat. You get the women and kids." The next morning I met my party, backed up my trailer close to the ramp and waited my turn to launch my raft down a plank chute. Looking down the 30-foot ramp to the beach and the boulder-strewn river, I took a deep breath.

The outfitter had confidence in me as a rower and guide because we had worked together on the Bitterroot River and Rock Creek, and he knew of my guiding experience in Wyoming. Sauntering up to me as I gazed down the river, he slapped me on the back and said, "Don't screw up. The river is more dangerous now than it was a few weeks ago. Now you have to do a whole lot of dodging and fancy oar work. You're going to earn your pay today."

We had talked about the rock garden on the Green River in Wyoming, which we had both floated through, but I was not prepared for the Big Blackfoot's Rock Garden. Inexperienced rafters should shun the stretch from Roundup to River Bend Campground and from Russell Gates Campground down to Roundup. After the spring runoff is over, the Rock Garden will challenge any oarsman, but particularly the oarsman who must both navigate the river safely as well as align the boat for those passengers who want to cast. The rocks come at you so fast that you can hardly decide which way to

Cottonwood Creek — Mileage Marker 37.9

turn, and once you make the decision of which way to turn, you immediately have to start another maneuver. As each season passed I prided myself on never touching a rock, but on every one of those days in my 50s, I was bone-shoulder weary at the end of the day.

The Blackfoot River has steadily improved as a fishery during the last decade thanks to the concerted efforts of environmentalists, ranchers and local members of Trout Unlimited. Popularized by Norman McLean's novel, *A River Runs Through It*, the Blackfoot's real legacy is that it is host to two of Montana's native salmonids, the westslope cutthroat and the bull trout. Although restrictions exist for purposely fishing for bulls, the river is rich in trophy-size browns and hefty rainbows and cutthroats in the 14- to 17-inch range. Although the river is approximately 130 miles long, the best fishing stretches start at Ovando down to the confluence with the Clark Fork River at Bonner. After spending years on this river, it is only fair to add a disclaimer. Blackfoot River trout sometimes skip a meal!

Spanning 26 miles, the Blackfoot River Recreation Corridor provides both picnicking and camping at 13 locations. Both improved and unimproved camping spots exist all up and down the Blackfoot River. For the camper who wants to fish with younger children, I would recommend the unimproved campground at River Junction on the North Fork of the Blackfoot. Regardless of which one you select, the beauty of the Blackfoot River overwhelms the first-time visitor. Carving its way through the canyon, the river floats by 100-foot cliffs. Ocher in color, the tinted shades and moss-lined shadows make the Blackfoot one of the most scenic rivers in Montana, as well as offering good fishing.

### The Blackfoot River – Mileage Markers

**MM 0:** Exxon Travel Plaza (Milltown) – Exit from Interstate 90 onto Highway 200.

**MM 1:** Access dirt pull-out.

**MM 2: Marco Flats**
Marco Flats is easy to miss. The access road takes a sharp turn and drops to the river.

**MM 6: Angelvine Park** A nice rest stop if you are pulling a trailer.

 **MM 8:** A narrow gravel pullout with no turn-around area for trailers or large rigs. Short trail to river. MM 8+ pull-over with a dropoff to the river.

##  MM 9: Gold Creek

Follow Gold Creek Road seven miles up the mountain to the first unimproved campsite. I do not recommend this road or the campsite for trailers, as the actual camping spots are off the main road, and they are rough and rutted. Surrounded by grassy meadows, the creek is ideal for families who want to rough it, but do check for tics in the late spring and early summer. Keep in mind that this is a "pack it in – pack it out!" area. The area is owned by Plum Creek, and it is sad to see how slovenly some campers have been. If you wish to access the creek lower down, make a right turn just short of the two-mile marker. Follow the road 2.8 miles until you reach a small bridge. Park by the bridge, as the road that follows the creek is blocked a mile up the canyon, and there is no turning around. The canyon is excellent fishing for small cutthroats.

## MM 10: Blackfoot Recreation Corridor

Thanks to the cooperative efforts of land owners and the Department of Fish, Wildlife and Parks, a 26-mile corridor has been made available to the public. Johnsrud Park offers camping, picnicking, swimming and an excellent take-out for floaters who launch at Roundup or at the Nine-Mile Prairie Road campground.

**Floaters warning:** The section of the river from Johnsrud Park to Roundup is interspersed with dangerous rapids. Wade fishers may follow the Blackfoot River on an 18.2-mile dirt road that will swing around and rejoin Highway 200 at Roundup, which is the next highway crossing of the Blackfoot River above Johnsrud Park. The road is narrow at times and very bumpy, and as such it is not safe to pull a camping trailer. Throughout the course of this road, there are numerous day-use access points. The two campgrounds, Ninemile Prairie and River Bend, are best reached just short of mileage marker 27 as you cross the bridge at Roundup. Launching

The author's sons floating the Blackfoot in their dad's Little Dippers

a raft or drift boat at Roundup requires use of a 30-foot ramp down to the water's edge.

**MM 22: Garnet Ghost Town** The last remnants of this bustling ghost town have been preserved in its original state of natural decay. From the highway, take the Garnet Road 11 miles. For more information call (406) 329-3914.

 **MM 26.5: Roundup**

Just as you cross the bridge, you will note a 30-foot ramp for launching rafts on this popular stretch of the Blackfoot. Most rafters take out at River Bend campground or Whitaker Bridge, which is about 9.5 miles.

 **MM 35: Russell Gates Campground**

The campground is off the highway on the river's edge and is a popular floating take-out.

**MM 37.9: Upsata Lake & Cottonwood Creek**

Exit on Woodsworth Road. Turn left 1.4 miles from the highway at the Blackfoot Clearwater Game Range. Drive one mile to the bridge on Cottonwood Creek by the fish and game house and barn. Fish upstream or down, but be prepared to navigate through heavy brush. The creek hosts small cuts and surprisingly hefty browns that hide in those tough-to-fish willow overhangs.

Author landing a rainbow as his new pup surveys the action. Photo courtesy of Bob Edgar

**MM 31: Clearwater River**

The Clearwater River access is a park-like setting and offers good access for anglers. Because of the river's clear water, fishing is excellent in the spring. From this crossing the Clearwater offers a short float trip or canoe trip to the Blackfoot. Floaters will drift under safety fence partitions. This is a popular run for summer tubers.

**Clearwater Junction:** Highway 200 intersects with Highway 83 to Seeley Lake. See Northwest Montana.

Continuing on Highway 200 a couple of miles up from the Cottonwood Creek access, Woodworth Road leads to Upsata Lake. Upsata is a small, shallow lake bordered mostly by private property in pothole country. Periodically stocked, the lake produces fair fishing for smaller rainbows. If you have a canoe strapped on top of your rig, this would be a good choice for some evening casting and paddling. Woodsworth Road turns to the left towards Kozy Corner and then continues to Highway 83 near Salmon Lake.

## MM 39: River Junction Campground and Scotty Brown Bridge

Follow the access road a short distance to the Scotty Brown Bridge. The landowner forbids any launching of watercraft from his property; however, he has provided four parking spaces for wade fishers. Be sure to respect the rights of property owners and stay below the high water mark. River Junction Campground is one of the most beautiful unimproved campgrounds in the area and provides an opportunity to fish both the main stem of the Blackfoot River and the North Fork. The road to the campground is approximately nine miles, and I would not recommend it for trailers.

## MM 40: Monture Creek Campground

Monture Creek Campground is a small campground at the bottom of a ravine just off Highway 200. The campground is mowed, and the campsites sit on the water's edge surrounded by trees and wild roses. Monture Creek is usually fast and clear in the early summer and provides fair fishing down to the mouth of the Blackfoot River for spawning stragglers. By mid-summer the creek warms up and the trout look for small pools to hide in. Look for the access road further down the highway for the 12-mile drive to the headwaters. Although the creek fishes well for small fry, be prepared to scramble and climb through brush and downed timber in its upper reaches.

## Ovando

A short distance up the highway from Monture Creek Campground, the small town of Ovando rests on the hillside overlooking the highway. A cluster of homes, Ovando offers a small store, an inn, a trading post, a brand museum and a post office. (On a knoll just off the highway above Ovando, stop in at Trixie's Bar and Grill for a great hamburger.) From Ovando follow the road 3.5 miles to the Harry Morgan Campground, which is a popular launching place for floaters. The campground offers only a few sites, but when the river clears you will be hard-pressed to find a parking spot amongst the outfitter's rigs. Harry Morgan access is a great wading access for fishing the North Fork of the Blackfoot. Traveling another 5.5 miles up the road will take you to Brown's Lake, which is a good fishing lake, but don't expect much shade in summer. Popular with boat fishermen and belly-boaters, Brown's Lake is stocked with some whopper brood stock. Stocked trout grow fast and fat in this lake. Another 1.5 miles down the road will take you to the last floating access point, Cedar Meadows.

## MM 51.1: North Fork of the Blackfoot Trailhead and Cooper's Lake

Exit onto Kleinschmidt Road and follow the signs 11 miles to the trailhead. The North Fork of the Blackfoot is a popular trailhead for backcountry horsemen and fly fishers. For years I never found the time to actually hike back into the wilderness and fish the North Fork. On July 5, 1998, I finally hiked the trail. Following the wettest June on record, I looked down the canyon at the turquoise, silted river and inwardly prejudged the fishing I would have. Much to my surprise, in a 200-yard section in a steep canyon, I picked up six cutthroats, one of which was a fat 16-incher. Elderly fishers may want to pass up the North Fork, as it is a tough hike down the narrow canyon to the water. During high water, you have to scramble up the canyon wall to a bench every 100 yards when it becomes impassable. At age 53 I was huffing and puffing, and I was damn glad that I could still huff and puff for fat westslope cutthroats. The mountainsides look like the back of a porcupine. Gray, burnt-out lodgepole trees blanket the entire area from the 1988 Canyon Creek Fire that destroyed 247,600 acres before it was contained.

Cooper's Lake is a short distance from the trailhead. Follow Whitetail Ranch Road to the lake.

The lake is a fairly large lake surrounded by cottages. Public access is limited to a few tent sites and a boat launch. Fishing is only fair.

**Highway 200 from Ovando to Lincoln:** Slow winding water and lots of mud, brush and sediment characterize this section of the river. Although it can produce some hefty browns, it generally does not produce good habitat for rainbows and cutthroats.

North Fork of the Blackfoot River

## Popular Float Trips on the Blackfoot River

**• Float Trip 1: Harry Morgan to Russell Gates**
Harry Morgan Campground is a couple of miles outside of the little town of Ovando just off of Highway 200. From here floaters generally float down to the Russell Gates Campground (County Line), which is easily seen from the highway. One may float further down to the confluence with the Clearwater River. Floaters will have to carry their rafts about 20 yards up a gradual bank to the parking area. The section from Russell Gates to the Clearwater Bridge has numerous rapids. The canyon drops quickly in this section, and

casters have to work the pockets and rocks diligently. From the Clearwater Bridge to Roundup, in my opinion, is extremely dangerous and should be avoided by all float fishers.

**• Float Trip 2: Roundup to River Bend Campground or Whitaker's Bridge**
Only expert rowers should float this section as it is extremely dangerous with all the boulder-strewn rapids. A short float would be to River Bend Campground, and a full day's float would be Whitaker's Bridge.

**• Float Trip 3: River Bend Campground or Whitaker's Bridge to Johnsrud Park**

It only takes one nasty drop-off and a sluice of water with huge rocks to make for an unpleasant day. Standing on the water's edge, Thibodeau Rapid doesn't look all that impressive, especially during high water when half of the boulders are submerged and out of sight in the murky water. When the water drops, however, make no mistake. I always have my passengers exit from my boat just upstream on the right side. They can take a well-worn path just below the bottleneck.

Throughout my years of guiding in my raft, I enjoyed this small challenge. During my last year of guiding, I had to maneuver through Thibodeau in a low-profile pram that I had designed and built. Without the cushion of air and the forgiveness of a raft, I was scared. When my last client stepped out of the pram, he turned to me and said, "I'd really like to show off in front of my wife and run it with you."

I replied, "No, I am being very safe and prudent

by allowing no passengers."

What I didn't say was that I had a knot in my stomach, and I wasn't sure how my pram would handle in the fast-water chute. As it turned out, the boat handled well, but I had to do some artful dodging in that short drop-off. Turning around, I marveled at how simple it looked, but I know tales and true stories of river carnage.

## Highway 83 – Seeley-Swan Valleys

Some fishers travel in packs and grudgingly compromise on their fishing itinerary; others travel with loved ones and, to the chagrin of family members, plan their family vacations not by destination resorts but by river tributaries. For the fly fisher who cajoles and pleads and promises the moon to his family in order to just wet a line on another river, the Seeley-Swan promises something for everyone in the family. Nestled between the Mission Mountains Wilderness and the Bob Marshall Wilderness, the Seeley Lake recreation area and the Swan River basin offer summer recreation at its best.

Golfing, swimming, canoeing, jet skiing, water skiing, trail riding and wilderness excursions provide just some of the many activities for the entire family. Oh, but here is the dilemma for dad and his fishing converts – just what type of fish to fish? The small creeks contain cutthroats and brookies, as do the mountain lakes. The Clearwater River holds nice browns, and the Swan River is home to both cutthroats and bull trout. The Seeley Lake chain offers kokanee salmon, rainbows, cutthroats, yellow perch and the notorious pike.

From Summit Lake down to the town of Seeley, and then down to Clearwater Junction, the watershed is a tributary of the Blackfoot River, which in turn is a tributary of the Clark Fork. At Summit Lake, Highway 83 crests on a small divide, which begins the watershed for the Swan River that runs north to Flathead Lake. Throughout this recreational wonderland are numerous forest service camp-grounds, Montana state park campgrounds and many unimproved camping sites on both Plum Creek logging land and in the Lolo and Flathead National Forests. Backpackers will find that the Bob Marshall Wilderness offers over a million acres to explore.

The Bob is 60 miles in length and joins the Scapegoat Wilderness to the south and the Great Bear Wilderness to the north, which reaches all the way up into Glacier National Park. On the eastern side of the valley, the Mission Wilderness encompasses over 70,000 acres of jagged peaks, small glaciers and many mountain lakes and streams. All of this country is easily accessed from Highway 83, and every mile marker beckons the fishermen to a new piece of water.

Joe Bender of High Basin Sports in Seeley recommends ¼-ounce Rooster Tail lures in the rainbow, chartreuse and brown trout colors as well as $^1/_8$- and ¼-ounce Panther Martin lures in all gold or silver. He also recommends the yellow and red pattern and the black and red pattern. Joe said, "This country is where the fly fishers and the night crawler fishermen co-exist in harmony. There is just so much variety to choose from. In addition to the lures and spinners, one popular method of fishing from a canoe is to simply troll with a bobber and a piece of night crawler on a six-foot leader.

For the fly fisher, Joe generally recommends nymphs, unless they are rising to a hatch. He uses a sinking tip with a Prince or a bead-head pattern or an olive or black Wooly Bugger or leech pattern. When fishing for kokanee, Joe recommends a leaded line with cowbells, plus a three-foot leader and a Wedding Ring with a piece of white corn or a night crawler. Expect to catch kokanee from 8 to 13-inches.

Hyperbole and verisimilitude quite often tend to enter into discussions with fishing outfitters and shop owners. Joe is a refreshing anomaly. The evening before I met him I had hiked down to Clearwater Lake. Walking up the trail were three float-tube fishermen. They had fished all day and were quite pleased with the results, whenever the wind had died down. One of the anglers good-naturally boosted of the catch of the day, a 20-inch cutthroat. I told Joe I was a little skeptical. After 15 years as a guide, I am accustomed to some gross misjudgments for length and poundage of trout. Year after year I have had clients innocently proclaim that an 11-inch trout was a 14-incher. And when it comes to poundage, I have always marveled at full pound increments. When I do hear someone split the difference and call the catch a 4½ pounder, my imagination soars with the possibilities.

Joe confirmed that the lake contained many such specimens, but the lake was frustrating at times, as it lacked consistency. "When it's hot, it is one of the best fishing spots in the region, but I have spent a half a day fishing and gone home skunked." The mere word "skunked" is an anathema rarely spoken but in private moments with one's most intimate friends or spouse, and I took an instant liking to Joe. Comfortable with Joe's enthusiasm for the region's fishing and his open candor, I pressed him for his views on Seeley's Loch Ness Godzilla, the notorious pike. Brought in by bucket biologists, the pike introduction is the bane of trout fishers. According to Joe the pike explosion has been a boon to the Seeley area, as it draws in pike fishers from all around the country. "Prior to the pike fishing, Seeley Lake was crap fishing for planted rainbows, sun fish, suckers and a few bass. It was the pits. Last year the largest pike that I know of being caught was 25 pounds and measured 46 inches. Now, that's a fish with an attitude."

What most fishermen come to realize is that, unlike the pike up in Canada who often feed on themselves due to the scarce food supply, Seeley Pike are not aggressive feeders, as they have large numbers of sun fish and trash fish to feed on. Joe recommends one-ounce red and white Dare Devils, big buzz baits, and large-jointed Rappalas. At the very minimum he suggests using 12-pound line. Other popular lures are Rappala Magnums, weedless rubber mice, Jaw Breakers and spinner bait. Joe forewarns those who fish the lily pads, "Plan on actually landing about 10% of the fish you catch."

Fly fishers wishing to fish for pike should use wire leaders and deer-hair mice. If you are fishing from a belly-boat or float tube, be sure to bring along a pair of pliers and gloves. When releasing a pike, turn them belly up so that they become motionless. When I asked Joe what his predictions were regarding the explosion of pike in the basin, he replied, "I think they are here to stay. According to a number of knowledgeable sources, the pike will peak in numbers and then decline. When this happens, they will move into pike zones, which we are seeing already. Once this happens the trout population will stabilize as well. The major detriment to the introduction of pike has been the decline of kokanee salmon, but in spite of this loss, I'm glad they are here."

Joe's store, High Basin Sports, is located on Highway 83 in Seeley Lake.

# Highway 83

**MM 0:** Clearwater Junction to Bigfork.

### MM 1: Harper's Lake and Blanchard Lake

Harper's Lake and Blanchard Lake are right next to each other. Both lakes are ¼ of a mile off the highway and provide access to the Clearwater River and a nice campground, especially for a family who has brought along a canoe. The campground is suitable for trailers and offers shade and an ideal spot for family recreation. Harper's Lake prohibits boats with motors. The lake is planted with trout each year, as well as some retired brood stock. A small 18-acre pothole lake, Harper's Lake is separated from Blanchard Lake by the access road. Blanchard Lake is a misnomer, as it is actually a 10-acre flooded oxbow of the Clearwater River. Blanchard Lake offers a potpourri of small trout, perch, bass, whitefish and rough fish.

**MM 6.5: Salmon Lake State Park** Fee area. Salmon Lake State Park campground has been updated and provides new lavatories with coin-operated showers. The campground has a boat launch and a picnic area as well as an amphitheater where they bring in guest speakers to talk about the wildlife as well as educational seminars sponsored by Montana Fish, Wildlife and Parks. Native Americans also give presentations on their cultural heritage and history. Salmon Lake is a popular lake for all of the trout species and kokanee salmon.

The Clearwater River above Salmon Lake is a popular fishing area for browns. This short section to the Placid Lake turn-off is a challenge, however, as it is braided swampland crowded with willow and tag alder.

**MM 10.1: Placid Lake State Park, Owl Creek, Jocko Lakes** Right after you exit the highway, you will cross the Clearwater River, which has a campsite and a fishing trail both upstream and downstream. About a half-mile further are some nice unimproved Plum Creek campsites on Owl Creek, the outlet creek for Placid Lake. Placid Lake State Park is three miles from the highway and charges a fee. The park has recently been upgraded and improved with coin-operated showers and handicapped-accessible rest rooms with hot and cold water. Placid Lake also has a boat launch. Popular with water skiers, the lake doesn't offer much for quality fishing, although it is loaded with small kokanee.

Owl Creek parallels the road and offers small cutthroats and brookies. Bring plenty of mosquito repellant if you plan on fishing the Clearwater River area where it is joined by Owl Creek.

**Jocko Lakes**

Ignore the signs to Jocko Lakes. The road takes off from the campground entrance. The lakes are high up in the Mission Mountains on the Flathead Indian Reservation. They are closed to fishing. The outlet, the Jocko River, is an excellent high-country stream. However, you will need a tribal permit to fish so you would need to continue driving to Arlee, Montana. From Highway 83 to the fishing area on the Jocko River is approximately 25 miles.

**MM 14: Seeley Lake camping**

 **River Point Campground**

Just after mile-marker 14, look for Boy Scout Road on the left. The road swings around the east side of Seeley Lake and rejoins Highway 83 above the town. River Point Campground is 2.1 miles from the highway and offers 26 campsites, swimming and picnicking. It is a USFS fee campground and provides lots of shade.

**Seeley Lake Campground**

A fee campground right on the lake, Seeley Lake Campground, Lolo National Forest, is 3.3 miles. Shaded by larch, it also offers a nice concrete boat launch and a beach with a roped-in swimming area. Public pay phones are available, but the campground does not offer showers. 29 campsites. Flush toilets. Cold drinking water. Boat launch.

Seeley Lake provides lots of fishing opportunities for perch, stocked rainbows, cutthroats and pike, not to mention some hefty 5- to 10-pound brood stock from the Arlee hatchery. Yellow perch are best caught with a rubber jig with a piece of night crawler. The best pike fishing is found at the outlet of the lake.

**MM 15-16:** Seeley Lake, Montana.

**Seeley Trailhead Campground, Morrell Creek, Morrell Falls, Morrell Lake and Cottonwood Lakes (Road #477)**

Just as you reach the outskirts of the town of Seeley, look for Morrell Creek Road which heads east. Morrell Creek is first crossed two miles from the highway. The creek offers small cutthroats, brookies and the occasional brown spawner in the fall.

**Cottonwood Lakes, Seeley Trailhead Campground**
The campground is one mile from the highway and not to be confused with the lakeside campground. Cottonwood Lakes are 8.4 miles from the campground, although there is only one real lake, which is the middle lake. The other two "lakes" are shallow mud ponds. The middle lake is a narrow 15-acre lake, and it is only fished out of a canoe or small boat. The lake is stocked with Arlee rainbows, and it is a popular lake for cutthroats and brookies. The lake offers a number of unimproved campsites. This is "pack it in – pack it out" country. Morrell Creek Road is actually a loop that comes out at Kozy Korner three miles from Highway 83. Take Woodworth Road just past Salmon Lake State Park.

**MM 17.9:** Seeley Lake Ranger Station.

**MM 19.4: Boy Scout Road** This is the loop road which swings around the west side of the lake and re-connects at mileage marker 14.

**MM 20: Clearwater Lake Loop** Refer to Mileage Marker 28.

**MM 22.5: Lake Inez**
293 acres with a maximum depth of 70 feet. Fishing is similar to Seeley Lake. Lake Inez has USFS non-fee campgrounds running along the shore of the lake right beneath the highway. Some of the sites are squeezed between the water and the access road with the highway up above it.

**MM 24:** Lake Inez Campground access.

**MM 25: West Fork of the Clearwater River, Marshall Lake**
As soon as you turn off the highway, you will cross the Clearwater River. Right alongside the creek and the road are two grassy unimproved campsites. The West Fork of the Clearwater River is a brushy little creek with few fish. The road to Marshall Lake is 6.4 miles and offers a stunning view of the valley. Narrow and bumpy in places, I would recommend pulling only a tent trailer. When I got up to the lake, however, I was surprised to see a 19-foot trailer. When I talked to the camper, he had a harrowing tale about backing up his trailer on a windy cliff-side road when he ran into a gate. Marshall Lake has one campsite and a place to launch a boat, although there are a couple of unimproved campsites on the creek about a hundred yards from the lake. The road forks just above the campsite and follows the side of the mountain up above the lake, where a gate blocks further travel. Vandals had removed the warning sign. The father said that it had taken hours to back the trailer down the narrow, windy road, and his two young sons were terrified.

Marshall Lake froze a number of years ago. All that was left were a few five-inch cuts when I fished it. The creek also froze out and offers poor fishing in the upper reaches. Check to see if the lake has been re-stocked.

**MM 26: Lake Alva**
Approximately 300 acres with a maximum depth of 90 feet. Lake Alva is the most popular fishing lake among the locals. Offering good catches of kokanee, trout and the occasional bull trout, the lake also offers perch and pike. Similar to Lake Inez, Lake Alva has a non-fee USFS campground that runs along the water's edge just short of mile marker 25, but it is more suitable to tents and truck campers.

**Lake Alva Campground**

Lake Alva Campground is a self-serve fee campground with no showers. 41 campsites. Cold drinking water. U.S. Fee Area. During the ice-fishing season, a 27-pound pike was speared in the lake. The campground has an excellent boat launch and a small beach with a roped-off area for swimming.

**MM 27: Rainy Lake**

70-acre shallow lake. Rainy Lake is popular fishing for 12-inch cutthroats. Rainy Lake has the largest population of bull trout and is free of pike.

**MM 28: Clearwater Lake Loop**

The dirt road is surprisingly smooth, and the view of the Bob Marshall Wilderness peaks are stunning. Clearwater Lake is seven miles from the highway. You will find a parking spot with a half-mile trail down to the lake (it seemed much shorter than a half-mile). Don't waste your time trying to fish this lake from the shore. The lake is extremely shallow around its entire length. The lake is rich in leeches and freshwater shrimp with good hatches so the cutthroats are sometimes uncooperative. The lake is best fished from a belly boat or a canoe. The best fishing is in the northwest end of the lake. Joe Bender recommends olive leeches, bead-head nymphs and hoppers in August. The lake offers a number of pack-in camping sites.

**MM 31: Summit Lake** Summit Lake is a small, brushy-lined lake that freezes. It is rarely fished. The few rises that you see are smaller cutthroats moving up or down from Bertha Creek. Bertha Creek is so overgrown it is not worth the effort to fish it. Summit Lake is the dividing line for the Clearwater that drains south to the Blackfoot River and the Swan River drainage that flows north to Flathead Lake.

**MM 34.3: Lindbergh Lake, Bunyon Lake, Meadow Lake, Crystal Lake**

725 acres with a maximum depth of 125 feet. Within a half-mile of exiting Highway 83, the road

> ### Cry of the Loon
> "The cry of the loon is no laughing matter. The common loon is becoming uncommon. Nearly 200 loons take up summer residency in Montana. Of the 60 nesting pairs, only about 30 chicks survive. Loons are very sensitive to human presence. If a loon is forced off her nest, the eggs will cool or predators will eat them. If you see a single bird in the water in May, she is probably off her nest near the shoreline. Leave the area immediately." –USFS

crosses the Swan River. The campground is 4.5 miles from the highway and offers a few camping sites, a picnic area and a boat launch. The lake is surrounded by summer homes. The campground only offers four sites suitable for camping trailers. Halfway up the road is a road to the right leading to **Bunyon Lake**, a distance of seven miles. Bunyon Lake is a high-elevation lake with no camping facilities, unless you are willing to pack your gear down to the lake, a distance of 200 yards. This is not a road for trailers!

Bunyon Lake fishes very well for small cutthroats. For every four 6-inch fish that you catch, you'll land a 10- or 12-incher. This is a beautiful little lake a bit short of 10 acres. It would be the perfect spot to launch a belly-boat and just cruise around catching hungry little cuts. Less than a mile away lies **Meadow Lake.** Meadow Lake is only slightly bigger. Somewhat swampy, the lake is blocked by a gate so you must walk a short distance to the lake for 8- to 12-inch cuts. **Crystal Lake** (186 acres) may be reached from a trail at Meadow Lake, the southern end of Lindbergh Lake, or a trailhead may be taken from Beaver Creek Road, which is just above Summit Lake. A relatively large lake, the lake seems to be declining in both the numbers of fish and the size of the fish.

Floating on the scenic Swan River

### MM 34.3:Glacier Lake

In my sojourn through this country, I didn't get a chance to hike in and fish Glacier Lake. However, when I hiked down to Bunyon Lake, I ran into a family who had just fished Glacier Lake. It was their first choice from all the lakes that they had fished. Although they never caught anything larger than 12 inches, they watched a lone fisherman pulling in some hefty 14-inch cuts, but by the time he headed out, it was time for them to leave as well. Follow the Glacier Creek Road. Plan on an hour's hike to reach the lake.

### MM 35.6: Holland Lake

416 acres with a maximum depth of 150 at the east end of the lake. Holland Lake offers two large USFS fee campgrounds, a boat launch and a roped swimming area. Campsites line the shore with spectacular views of the waterfall at the east end of the lake. Fishing is generally good for cutthroats, rainbow trout, kokanee and a few bull trout. Be prepared for lots of boating activity and jet skis. The outlet creek is good fishing for small trout.

### ? MM 43: Flathead National Forest Work Center

### Swan River

Originating out of Lindbergh Lake, the Swan River rushes 35 miles to Swan Lake. Although not as fertile of a river as other rivers in western Montana, the Swan River, nonetheless, produces good numbers of westslope cutthroat, rainbow, bull trout and mountain whitefish. The great advantage of the Swan is that it is relatively isolated with less fishing pressure. The challenge is two-fold from Mother Nature. The mosquitoes and flies feast on fly fishers who defy the tangled, dense foliage along the shore. The greatest challenge, however, lies waiting for the rafters and canoeists. Good luck!

Rafting the Swan is similar to rafting on Rock Creek. The oarsman must be ever-vigilant, and their fly casters cannot be contemplative or inaccurate in their casting ability. The water is especially swift in the early summer and appears to be one long riffle, punctuated by occasional pools and eddies. The best cover for the trout is under the logjams and downed trees, and it is these obstacles which make the Swan River risky. After a record rainfall for June 1998, I launched my one-man drift boat at Piper Creek and floated down to my campsite at Cedar Creek Campground on the Fatty Creek Road. I had received information on a large logjam, but I didn't listen carefully. Left or right? I went right, and it was the wrong decision as I came around a swift bend and encountered an incredible 20-yard logjam. If I had been floating in a raft, I would have been faced with an extremely difficult decision, as there was no going back upstream due to the fast current. Luckily I found a narrow opening to follow, and I only had to drag my little boat over two logs.

Normally, I am fairly adept at floating while I am tying on a new fly. Not so for the Swan. Because I wanted to fish Jim Lake that evening, I just fished without stopping. What a rush it was for speed, scenery and fishing. I started out with a size 12 Royal Humpy and went 100 yards without catching a fish. Oh, oh, I thought. But then they started coming up to my fly, one after another. I must have caught over 15 rainbows and cuts, all under 9 inches. Due to the speed of the water, I knew I was missing good pocket water and sheltered downfall. Rowing and casting without stopping is not the way to fish the Swan.

I switched to a girdle bug and didn't have another fish on for over an hour. I thought to myself, Okay, you've caught the river's dinks, now let's put on a Muddler and pull in some of those bigger guys. With about a mile to go to my campsite, I tossed out an unweighted Muddler. The deer-hair collar kept the large Muddler floating high and dry. One dink after another rose to hit it even before I had a chance to strip it under the water. When I got off the river, I walked up to Eric Bjorge, who is a river guide and owner of the Two River Gear store in Bigfork.

"Well, all I've caught is dinks today," I said.

"Pretty typical for the first day on the Swan," he replied. "If you want the big guys, you've got to work a nymph."

"What can I expect from this river?" I asked.

"Twenty-four to 30 inchers," he retorted.

"Bull," I said.

"Yeah, bull trout, but I've caught a lot of 18- to

Swan River by Cedar Creek Campground

20-inch rainbows in this river."

Swan River trout average between 8 and 12 inches. In talking to Eric further, he suggested that if you are going to fish the Swan, "go big or go home." The Swan has a long and steady hatch of Isoperla stoneflies so stimulators or large yellow Humpies will work well.

Access is restricted from Lindbergh Lake crossing all the way down to Cold Creek. Many roads cross the river, but for the most part the property is posted and there is no place to park. The following information was excerpted from the pamphlet "Fishing Waters of the Swan Valley", a joint publication sponsored by the United States Forest Service for the Flathead National Forest and the Montana Department of Fish, Wildlife and Parks.

**Upper Section:** "From Lindbergh Lake Road to Condon the upper river is relatively shallow and wadable, containing numerous riffles and runs. Water temperatures warm by mid-summer and smaller brook trout and rainbow trout favor the area. Floating is difficult due to low water, logjams and split channels on the lower end. General stream regulations apply (see fishing regs).

**Middle Section:** "The section from Condon to Piper Creek Road is characterized by smaller flows, a diversity of channel conditions and pools formed behind log jams and fallen trees. Good-sized rainbow trout are common along with bull, cutthroat and brook trout and abundant mountain whitefish. Logjams hamper floating above Cold Creek and skilled rafting is recommended below this point. General stream regulations apply upstream from Piper Creek Bridge (see fishing regs).

**Lower Section:** "From Piper Creek Road to Porcupine Creek Road this section contains the greatest diversity with respect to depth, cover and water volume. Stream banks are fairly open after spring high water and there is some channel splitting. Experienced canoeists and rafters navigate this section, but caution must be exercised due to fallen trees and log jams. Catch-and-release regulations for rainbow and cutthroat trout apply from Swan Lake up to Piper Creek Bridge." –USFS

### MM 46.7: Cold Creek Road Fishing Access for the Swan River plus access to high-elevation lakes

The Swan River access has good parking on both sides of the bridge. Peck Lake is six miles; the trailhead to Cold Lakes is seven miles; Jim Lake is 10 miles.

### Peck Lake

Peck Lake access is six miles from the highway. Watch for the sign, as you will need to make a right turn. Peck Lake can be accessed close to the road. The lake is a shallow, swampy lake with stocked trout.

### Upper and Lower Cold Lakes

Nestled close to the Mission Mountains divide, both lakes are reached within 2.5 miles from the trailhead, and each have healthy populations of cutthroats from 12 to 16-inches. At 2.9 miles from the highway, the road to Cold Lakes and Jim Lakes turns to the right. At 5.9 miles the road forks to the left for the Cold Lakes trailhead. From the turnoff to Cold Lakes continue four miles to **Jim Lake**. The last four miles is a second-gear pull; the road is bumpy and should be attempted only by high-clearance vehicles. The Jim Lakes basin is a photographer's dream. Even in July there were slivers and patches of snow on the mountain rims over looking Jim Lakes. Be forewarned that the narrow and bumpy entrance to the lake is strictly for trucks. The primitive road jack-knifes down to three compact camping sites on the lake. To make the turn I had to back up a few times, and I was tempted to put my truck in four-wheel drive. The lake offers excellent scenery and good fishing. Just after you cross the bridge over the outlet creek, there is a turn-around and parking area for non-four-wheel-drive vehicles. From that point to the lake is only a half-mile.

### MM 50.8: Salmon Prairie Road

Good river access less than a mile from the highway. Most floaters float to Fatty Creek.

**MM 52: Lion Creek Road** Lion Creek is closed to fishing.

**MM 53.6: Piper Creek Road** Access is three-tenths of a mile from the highway, but has limited parking.

## MM 54.5: Van Lake Road #9882

58 acres with a maximum depth of 40 feet. Van Lake is a popular local fishing lake, but you will need a pick-up truck and a small boat, as the shoreline is difficult to fish. After two miles, stay left. The lake has primitive camping sites.

## MM 58.5: Fatty Creek Road

Access to Metcalf Lake, Shay Lake, Fatty Lake and Cedar Lake, Cedar Creek and Fatty Creek. The bridge is three-tenths of a mile from the highway and offers a boat-launching access. Across the river is Cedar Creek Campground, which provides drinking water and toilets. On the far side of the bridge is a bumpy road which leads to a nice picnic area with tables right on the river, about 100 yards down from the bridge. Cedar Creek is crossed right after the campground, but it offers only very small cutthroats. From the highway six-tenths of a mile, you will note a fork to the left. This road will lead to Shay Lake. **Caution:** Shay Lake "road" should be driven to only in a 4X4 rig that has already received abuse through the years, as the road is overgrown in parts. If you have a new paint job, plan on scratches! After 1.4 miles, the main road forks to the left.

## Metcalf Lake

Metcalf Lake is 2.2 miles from the Cedar Creek Campground. Make the first right turn off of Fatty Creek Road, and then make another right turn to the lake. There are no signs for the second right turn except a "Pack it in – pack it out!" sign. The lake may be almost reached by a car with a three-tenths-of-a-mile hike. Only a truck should attempt the last section of the road. The lake is popular with local youth. They have built a high swinging rope above the lake. The lake is shallow except for the small portion by the swing. The lake is being managed for trophy trout.

Fatty Creek is crossed 3.6 miles from the highway. The Fatty Creek Road to the Cedar Lake trailhead is exactly nine miles from the highway. The road is an ear-popping second-gear climb high up in the Mission Mountains. It can be rutted and very bumpy in places. Check with the forest service prior to driving the road with a low-clearance vehicle.

## Cedar Lake

Cedar Lake trailhead has a large turnaround. The lake is about a four-mile hike. Keep in mind that you are in grizzly country, so if you are traveling alone or in a group, pepper spray may be a prudent purchase. Camping at the lake is designated as no-impact camping. Fatty Lake is accessed by a hunter's trail about 1.5 miles before the trailhead. I could not find it. Although it reportedly fishes well, I would recommend the established trail to Cedar Lake, which has a healthy population of cutthroats.

## Return to Highway 83

### MM 63.5: Point Pleasant Campground

The campground offers a boat access, but it is very overgrown and easily missed. This is a beautiful non-fee campground right on the river.

## MM 66.7: Road #10161

Easily missed, this site offers a great access to the river as well as a take-out for rafters. Camping is allowed on a "pack it in – pack it out" basis.

## MM 68.2: Porcupine Creek Road

The Swan River is crossed one mile from the highway. Access is good for wade fishers, but you will have to drag your raft or canoe up a 15-foot bank to the road.

**MM 71-72:** Swan Lake, Montana.

## MM 71.9: Swan Lake Campground

USFS. 36 campsites for trailers, RVs and tents. Fee area. Water available, vault-type toilets, swimming beach, boat ramp.

**MM 82.5: Junction** Montana State Route 209 heads west five miles to the town of Bigfork and Highway 35, which is the westside route along Flathead Lake, beginning at Polson and ending at Kalispell.

## MM 86: Echo Lake

The highway now turns due east. Follow the signs to Echo Lake. The lake is popular for water skiing and summer homes, but it does have fair fishing, nonetheless.

## MM 88.6: Jewell Basin Hiking Area

The Jewell Basin Hiking Area is at the north end of the Swan Mountain Range between Kalispell and Hungry Horse Reservoir. It is 17 miles east of Kalispell and 18 miles southeast of Columbia Falls. To reach the Jewell Basin hiking area, follow State Highway 83 to the Echo Lake Road; follow the Echo Lake Road north approximately two miles to a T-intersection. Turn right. This road leads to a junction with the Jewell Basin Road (#5392). Follow the Jewell Basin Road approximately seven miles to the trailhead and parking area. The last five miles are steep and contain drive-through drainage dips. Caution is advised if traveling with low-clearance vehicles. Trailers are not recommended.

The Jewell Basin Hiking Area is a specially-designated backcountry-use area consisting of 15,349 acres of high mountains. It includes 27 alpine lakes, many picturesque mountain streams, mountain meadows, rocky peaks, sub-alpine timber and a variety of flowers. Elevations within the basin range from 4,240 feet on Graves Creek to 7,542 feet on Big Hawk Mountain. Thirty-five miles of trails connect most of the lakes. The average hiker in good physical condition can travel two to three miles per hour.

Fishing is generally excellent in the lakes and creeks, although like all fishing it is subject to the whims and fickleness of Mother Nature. Camping in the Jewell Basin is on the basis of "no impact". Be cautious, as this is grizzly country. Bears are unpredictable and, in certain circumstances, can be very dangerous. Additional information on how to camp in bear habitat is available at any of the five District Offices or the Forest Supervisor's Office in Kalispell. For additional information contact::

District Ranger
Swan Lake Ranger District
Big Fork, MT 59911
(406) 837-5081

Forest Supervisor
Flathead National Forest
Box 147
Kalispell, MT 59901
(406) 755-5401

**MM 91: Junction with Highway 35** You are two miles to Bigfork or 17 miles to Kalispell.

# Saga: Crick Fishing

Years ago, when I worked out of a local fly shop, I wouldn't hesitate in suggesting a guided instructional trip to one of our local creeks. I fondly recall many days when instruction was immediately reinforced with fish after fish rising to take a swat at my client's Royal Wulff or bushy Humpy. If you are new to the sport of fly fishing, spend as much time as you can on mountain creeks. You will be delighted with the action as well as your accelerated mastery of requisite skills. Having spent 15 years behind the oars as a fly fishing guide, I would also recommend as many days on the river with a guide as you can afford! A good guide will not only help you catch fish, he will instruct you in the nuances of the sport.

The size of a trout is relative to the conditions of its environment. High-elevation canyon creeks do not produce large trout, but they do provide a respite from the summer heat and an intimacy with the water and flora of a mountain stream. Best of all, they produce an abundance of small, hungry trout. And when you catch a 10-incher, it is akin to landing a 16-incher on the river. If you are new to fly fishing, start out on a creek. Besides offering lots of fish, it will teach you many skills in a short amount of time. A creek-fishing trip will teach you that a short cast is all you need. Get right out in the middle of the creek and fish directly upstream on both sides. Make short casts, and control your line. In most cases you merely have to hold your rod tip up and keep the line out of the water!

Regarding your choice of fly patterns, big is better on a creek. Use size 10 and 12 common attractor patterns. If the water is heavy and you have to stay to one side of the creek, use a Girdle Bug or a Yuk Bug. Fish these bugs just as you would a dry fly. Allow them to sink under the surface and watch for the strike. Learn where the fish hide, as it is much the same on the rivers. With lots of action, you will learn to read the water, anticipate the strike, and set the hook.

I always proclaim that I am an expert when it comes to fishing a creek, even though expertise can be acquired with just a few creek experiences in late July or August. One summer I was taking a father and his son out to teach them "crick fishin'". Looking up the trail, I spotted a lone fly fisherman walking down the trail. "I'll bet he had lousy fishing," I whispered to the young boy. "Let's find out." Sure enough the man had caught only a few small cutthroats, and it was obvious he was disappointed.

When he was out of hearing, the father looked at me quizzically, and the young boy asked, "How did you know?"

"Simple," I replied. "He had dry pants and dry sneakers!"

Follow these four rules for successful creek fishing: (1) Get wet! (2) Position yourself in the middle of the creek, and keep moving upstream in the water. (3) Better yet, keep your fly along the seams and in slow pockets at a slower speed. (4) Unless you are using a hopper, present your fly gently on the water.

Once you have caught a dozen fish, the stress of your daily life will slip away as you sit on a rock contemplating what fly you will use next. Resting your feet on the gold, pebbly bottom, you will take in a breath of cool mountain air and think, "This is what it is all about."

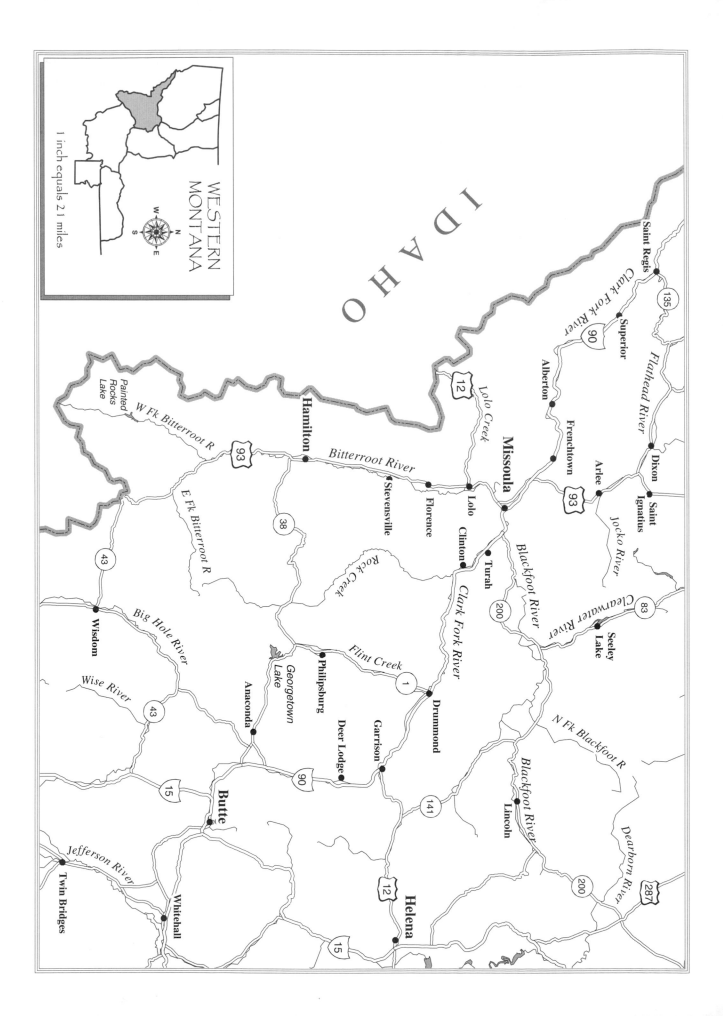

WESTERN
MONTANA

1 inch equals 21 miles

IDAHO

Saint Regis

135

Clark Fork River

90  Superior

Flathead River

Alberton

12

Lolo Creek

Frenchtown

Dixon

Arlee

Saint
Ignatius

93

Jocko River

Missoula

Hamilton

Bitterroot River

W Fk Bitterroot R

Painted
Rocks
Lake

93

Stevensville

Florence

Lolo

Clinton

Turah

200

Blackfoot River

Clearwater River

83

Seeley
Lake

38

E Fk Bitterroot R

Rock Creek

Clark Fork River

43

Wisdom

Big Hole River

Flint Creek

1

Drummond

N Fk Blackfoot R

Wise River

43

Georgetown
Lake

Philipsburg

Deer Lodge

Garrison

Blackfoot River

Lincoln

Anaconda

141

15

Butte

90

200

Jefferson River

Twin Bridges

Whitehall

12

Helena

15

Dearborn River

287

# 3
# WESTERN MONTANA

# Highway 93 –
# The Idaho Border North through the Bitterroot Valley to Missoula

## The Bitterroot River

Crossing over from Idaho to Montana, Highway 93 plunges down the mountain to meet the east and west forks of the Bitterroot River and the beginning of the Bitterroot Valley. Bordered by the Sapphire Mountains to the east and the Bitterroots to the west, the river and highway stretch over 70 miles to join the Clark Fork River near Missoula. Popular with visitors and new arrivals, the Bitterroot Valley is increasingly losing its rural heritage. Giving up prime bottomland and long slopes to developers, the suburban sprawl masks the marvel of the valley. In spite of increasing pressure, the Bitterroot River has few rivals for dry fly fishing and easy access. Its rugged west-slope mountains cradle one of the nation's largest wilderness areas, the Selway-Bitterroot Wilderness. The freestone canyon feeder streams offer some of the best-concentrated crick fishing in Montana. Best of all, the Bitterroot River has not been impacted by whirling disease.

Thanks to the support of local guides and outfitters and Trout Unlimited members, the state has implemented over 50 miles of catch-and-release zones and trophy management areas. Rainbows in the upper sections average 800 to 900 per mile along with an equal number of browns. With increased protective regulations, the cutthroat's population has

Lower section of the Bitterroot

exploded in numbers. Although I confess to be a romantic by nature, I do not disdain science and statistics; after all, I am an educator. However, I am always leery of fish counts in describing a river; I am puzzled by the results of electric fish counts. Often they do not seem reflective of the actual fishing action one has on a particular stretch of river.

Outfitter Dave Odell of Anglers Afloat rewards his clients with a specially-designed coffee cup when they catch a 20-inch trout. These "trophy" coffee cups used to be rewarded for an 18-inch trout. A number of years ago he was giving away so many that he upped the qualifications to 20 inches. He champions the Bitterroot River as a great fly fishing river. He now awards just as many cups for 20-inch catches! The Bitterroot River deserves high praise.

The upper stretch from Hannon Memorial (junction bridge with the West Fork Road just below Connor) to the Como Bridge is by far the most popular floating stretch, and fishermen must prepare to share the river with other floaters. In spite of the increased traffic, this section offers some of the highest fish counts, although there has been a small decline in the number of trophy trout (18+

inches). The upper stretch all the way down to Angler's Roost Campground provides a mixed forest floor, gin-clear water and lots of riffles and runs. This freestone stream slows down to runs and pools behind the city of Hamilton. Punctuated by an occasional riffle, the town section provides lush cover right down to the water's edge.

Below Hamilton the river loses its many braids and flattens out to receive the broad valley floor.

The author's 13-foot Little Dipper. "One can never have enough boats!"

The mid-section of the river historically has suffered from de-watering and warmer temperatures. With the addition of habitat improvement for feeder stream spawning and increased regulations, along with guaranteed minimum stream flows, the middle section of the river has experienced rejuvenation. From Tucker Crossing just south of Victor to the Florence Bridge, catch-and-release regulations have steadfastly increased trout populations in both numbers and size. Years ago I disliked having to guide on this section, even though I lived within a mile. The trout populations were thinner than in the upper river, and the warm water in mid-summer created a crapshoot at best. Today this section is one of my favorite sections year-round.

With the exception of those diehards who refuse to say "when", the season officially kicks off with the Skwala stonefly hatch in mid-March and early April. Bill Bean of the Fishaus in Hamilton figures the hatch is good for a full six weeks if the weather cooperates. "One pattern to use for the Skwala is a bullet-head fly tied with a black egg sack and dark body," he said. "The underwing is dark brown deer hair. The fish seem to look for this hatch to begin their yearly feeding habits, and with the size of this stonefly, they can build bulk fast." Keep in mind, however, that weather patterns at this time of year are unpredictable. During my 15-year tenure as a guide, I was often asked about the weather and the best time to book a trip.

The weather and words such as 'typical' and 'normal' are based on 30-year cycles. Since I began guiding in 1981, I have dropped those words from my vocabulary. During the drought years I would tell people the Bitterroot would be prime during the last week in June through July. September would see a return of water, as irrigators cut back on their watering and the river would cool along with the nights. Correspondingly, the hatches return mid-day and late afternoon. The year 1997 brought record snow accumulations and a very late run-off. Typically, the canyon creeks warm up later and the insect hatches appear later as well.

I recommend waiting until mid or late July for fishing those creeks. The year 1998 had half the normal snow pack, so we eagerly anticipated the Salmon Fly hatch on the West Fork and East Fork. Mother Nature plays nasty tricks on Bitterrooters: June rainfall broke all the records, and all of the rivers in the area experienced high and muddy water throughout the entire month. So I would say, based on a typical year, to plan your fishing whenever you have the chance, come hell or high water.

During April through June the river explodes with mayfly and caddis hatches on warm cloudy days. May and June typically see the Isoperla stonefly, Salmon Fly activity on the forks and the eagerly awaited green, gray and brown drakes. Mid-summer settles into an early-morning appearance of smaller mayflies which necessitates smaller tippets and size 14–18 Pale Morning Duns, Light Cahills and Parachute Adams. Chuck Stranahan of Riverbend Flyfishing in Hamilton recommends the Quigley Cripple during the drake hatches.

To borrow a wonderful phrase from Dave Whitlock, the heat of

The West Fork of the Bitterroot River

August brings forth "hoppertunity time". Terrestrials supplement the finicky appetite of Old Man Brown along with the tiny Tricorythodes mayfly. Bring your raingear with you in August to arm yourself against the LATS (Late Afternoon Thunder Showers). An effective hopper technique for cutthroats is to dress a Muddler and fish it both as a hopper pattern next to the bank as well as a sculpin pattern on the drift.

Bill Bean describes the summer fishing as "a continual opportunity for dry fly action. With the abundance of mayfly hatches, the expert as well as the novice fisherman can do well. If you are not capable of matching the hatch, a well-tied attractor pattern such as a Stimulator will usually do the trick. Opportunities abound for fishermen who prefer

wading, as well as those who prefer floating from a raft or a personal watercraft. Many access sites provide the wading fisherman ample stretches to spend a few hours or the entire day."

Falling cottonwood leaves and the orange splendor of mountainside tamarack signal the arrival of the giant orange caddisfly, as well as progressively larger mayfly hatches such as the size 10 rusty, green Emphermeralla Heccuba mayfly. With school back in session and many of the fly fishers replacing their rods for bows, shotguns, rifles and chainsaws, the river offers up her finest fishing to the solitary fisher.

## The Bitterroot Valley

### MM 12.7: Sula, Montana, East Fork of the Bitterroot River

Sula offers a gas station, private campground and country store. Just past this facility is the East Fork Road. After you cross the bridge, turn right (east) on East Fork Road. From here, the wilderness trailhead for the East Fork is 17 miles. The last four miles are dirt road. Plan on hiking up the trail at least an hour to get to better fishing in the bea-

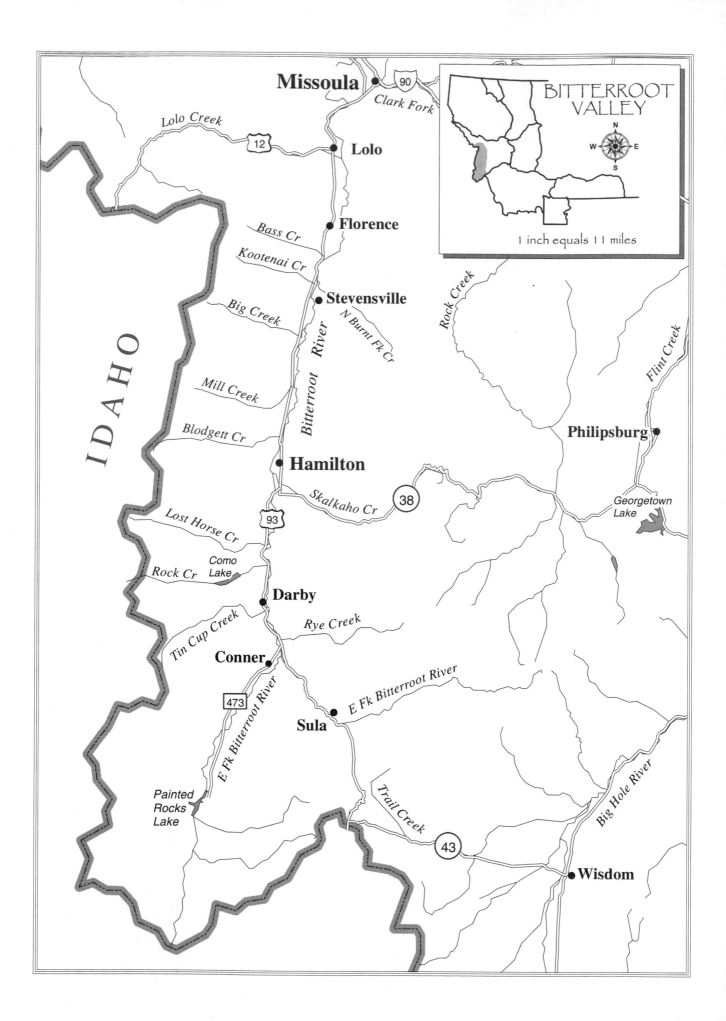

ver ponds. The East Fork is a beautiful crick. In addition to the great scenery, the creek is loaded with small cutthroats in the 6- to 9-inch range with an occasional 12- to 14-inch "lunker". The East Fork along the highway is also fun fishing for smaller trout, although early in June some big fish are caught during the Salmon Fly hatch. From the highway Jenny Creek Campground is 10 miles and offers four camp units with toilet facilities. Fee area. Martin Creek Campground is 16 miles and offers seven camp units with water and toilet facilities.

## MM 15.9: Spring Gulch Campground

11 camping units. Water, garbage disposal, accessible toilet. Fee area.

## MM 15.9: Warm Springs Campground

One mile to the west off the highway. 14 camp units and picnic area. Water, toilet, and garbage facilities. Fee area. 50- to 55-foot level spots for large trailers.

## MM 15.9: Crazy Creek Campground

Just past the Warm Springs Campground. Seven upper camp units for general camping; five lower units for campers with horses. Water and toilet facilities. Fee area.

## MM 23: Connor Turn-off, Painted Rocks Reservoir, West Fork of the Bitterroot, Connor

A few miles south of Hannon Memorial, you will see a sign to Connor. When you cross the bridge by the Connor store, you have just crossed the East Fork of the Bitterroot. You must enter the water from the bridge. I suggest wading downstream for some fun fishing in what is actually creek-sized wa-

The East Fork of the Bitterroot River above the Sula bridge on Highway 93

ter later in the summer. Wait until the summer has arrived so that you can stay in the water and easily move downstream. The East Fork braids in this area and becomes quite shallow, but some heavy 12 inchers make their home here, as well as a few lunkers.

## MM 26: Hannon Memorial

Five camping sites, picnicking, toilet facilities, and a raft launch on the other side of the bridge.

MM 26: Junction with Highway 473 – West Fork of the Bitterroot River.

## Side Trip – Highway 473:
## The West Fork of the Bitterroot River

About four miles south of Darby, Highway 93 crosses the Bitterroot River. Just after the bridge make a left turn on the West Fork Road. The West Fork meanders and plummets down through the canyon from Painted Rock Reservoir. Above the reservoir the West Fork is a small brushy creek. The road mostly parallels the West Fork, although most of the property is private. Nonetheless, sufficient access will keep an angler busy.

Although progressively smaller as you head towards Idaho, the West Fork is over 40 miles long, and it is followed by a paved road to the dam and then a dirt road most of its length. Beautiful scenery and a clear running stream, combined with good catches of rainbows and cutthroats, make this a must-visit if you are in the area. Surprisingly, the West Fork is lightly fished after the June Salmon Fly hatch.

**MM 0:** Junction with Highway 93.

**MM 3: Connor Cut-off to Highway 93** Connor has a country store.

**MM 3.2: Access to the West Fork** On private property. A popular take-out for canoes and rafts, this private property was posted a number of years ago. As of 1998 people were still using this site to exit the river with their rafts.

**MM 6: Baker Lake access road**
Road 363; trailhead 10 miles. Baker Lake is a popular local fishing spot less than two miles from the trailhead on an easy trail. Under 10 acres, it is good fishing for small 7- to 12-inch cutthroats.

**MM 10.9:** Easy to miss, this access has one tent campsite on the river.

**MM 11.9:** A primitive campsite only with access to the river for rafters and canoeists.

**MM 13:** State access point for launching rafts or canoes.

**MM 13.1: Boulder Creek, Sam Billings Campground** Road 5631; one mile. Boulder Creek is a brushy little creek with lots of small pocket water for small cuts. The campground has 11 camping units, toilet facilities and no water.

**MM 13.9:** Ranger Station.

**MM 17.9: Rombo Campground**
15 camp units. Water, garbage, toilet facilities. Fee area. Excellent access to the river as well as beautiful campsites right along the river.

**MM 21.5: Dam, Access to Bluejoint Creek**
Bluejoint Creek is accessed by crossing the dam road and traveling to the north side of the lake. Bluejoint Creek has easy access. Fishing is good for 7- to 12-inch cuts.

**MM 21.6: Little Boulder Bay Boating Site**
Toilet facility and swimming area.

**MM 23.5: Slate Creek Campground** Four campsites, toilet facilities, boat launch and beach area. Take the Nez Perce Road just above Boulder Creek Campground.

**MM 25.2 Painted Rocks State Campground**
Camping, picnicking, toilet facilities, boat launch and

beach. Pack-in-pack-out policy with voluntary donations for maintenance.

##  MM 29.5: Alta Campground

15 camping units. Water, garbage, toilet facilities. Fee area. Alta is a beautiful campground above the lake. At this point consider the West Fork a creek, and a beautiful one at that!

## MM 29.8: Hughs Creek

Hughs Creek is a small, tumbling creek with easy access for small 6- to 9-inch cuts.

## Return to Highway 93 –
## Mile Marker 27 North to Darby

**Bitterroot River Access:** Hannon Memorial and the West Fork of the Bitterroot River

As you cross the bridge, you will see a boat launch to the right and a small campground to the left. Here is an excellent area for foot fishing. Just upstream from the campground, some children of out-of-state property owners screamed at me about private property.

After I portaged around a log, I educated them on the rights of fishermen and nature's obstacles. Stay in the riverbed and below the high water mark, and the law is on your side. Montana floaters are vigilant regarding stream access rights.

## MM 29: Darby, Montana; Tin Cup Creek

Look for J&D Body Shop on the left. From Highway 93 the road to the second trailhead is 4.5 miles. At 3.5 miles a sign will direct you left across a bridge where there is a trailhead. Continue straight one mile to the second trailhead which is through a piece of private property, a generous act of kindness these days.

The lower section of the creek that parallels the road is poor fishing for small trout. From the second trailhead to the first creek crossing is a 20-minute hike and another 20 minutes to the Wilderness Boundary. Tin Cup Creek looks better than it fishes.

I found the best fishing, naturally, in the wilderness area above and below the second creek crossing for 7- to 9-inch cutthroats. The trail is one of

Brandon and Darin taking a break from fishing on the Selway River in Idaho

the easiest trails to hike of all the canyon creeks. The scenery is stunning, and the pools above the second creek crossing are beautiful and large, although the size of the fish varied little. Looking at the high water mark tells the story of a harsh environment during spring run-off.

## Darby Bridge

Darby bridge has a small access on the south side of the bridge for floaters. Please do not block this access, and don't cross the bridge, as it is private and posted. If you are going to wade fish, keep in mind that all of the surrounding banks are private property so stay in the streambed. From Highway 93 in downtown Darby, turn east on Tanner for two blocks. Turn right on Water Street for a half-mile. Turn left on Darby Bridge Road.

## United States Forest Service

Bitterroot National Forest Information Center, Darby, Montana. Warning – 25 mph!

## MM 34.9: Como Lake Turn-Off

Como Lake, Rock Creek, Little Rock Creek and Little Rock Creek Lake access.

From Highway 93 to the boat launch is approximately four miles. Como Lake is a large lake, almost three miles long. Although it is popular with water skiers and jet skiers, it provides only fair fishing for smaller trout. The lake is subject to extreme drawdowns during low-water years.

**South Side:** Boating area, large parking area, floating dock, boat ramp and dispersed picnic area with drinking water, toilet facilities and garbage service. Rock Creek Horse Camp: nine camping units; two accessible camping units; toilet facilities; no garbage service.

**North Side:** Lake Como Campground Area: 11 camping sites; one accessible site; one group camping site; electricity, drinking water, accessible toilet facilities and garbage services. Campground hosts. Fee area.

**Upper Como Campground Area:** 11 camping sites; drinking water, toilet facilities and garbage services. No electricity. Campground hosts. Fee area.

During the past couple of years campground facilities have been upgraded, along with a new boat launch. The outlet is Rock Creek, which is diverted into an irrigation ditch. The creek is almost completely de-watered as it enters the Bitterroot River. From the north side campground an eight-mile trail loops around the lake. The trailhead to Rock Creek is 3.5 miles. Just above the lake are falls. The creek is excellent fishing for 7- to 10-inch cutthroats above the lake.

## Little Rock Creek

Follow the signs past the Como Lake boat launch up a dirt road for another three miles. The dirt road traverses the mountain in a series of switchbacks overlooking the lake for a breathtaking view. The road crosses over the ridge with an equally stunning view of El Capitan Peak. The road is bumpy and rough, but it is suitable for passenger vehicles with sufficient clearance. From the trailhead you will walk a short distance to an overlook of Como Lake, Rock Creek and its falls and Little Rock Creek canyon with El Capitan looming at the head of the canyon.

# Saga: Little Rock Creek Lake Fishing Trip

The trail goes straight down to the bottom of the canyon to the beginning of the designated wilderness. I remember my first visit a few summers ago when I was lured up the trail. It was August and late-afternoon thunderheads were swirling around the peaks, but I judged that they were breaking up. I had told my family I would be hiking up Tin Cup Creek, but I wanted to just check out the trailhead in the next drainage. Parked at the top of a mountain was one other vehicle from Minnesota. I thought to myself that I would just hike down to the creek, sample the fishing and head home before it rained.

I stepped down the trail at 1:45 PM knowing I would have to retrace my steps uphill on the way back, which seemed unusual. Shadow, my black Labrador, was eager. When I was a Boy Scout, I remember a father complaining about how difficult it was for him to walk down a steep trail. At 10 years of age, I thought it was the most ridiculous notion I had ever heard. I reached the bottom at 2:18, and my knees were already swollen. The narrow, glaciated canyon walls bring early shade to the creek. Shadow and I stood over a small pool and watched a number of six-inch cutthroats cruise and feed right in front of us.

With my Polaroid sunglasses I searched the dark crevices and spotted a larger fish. I hurriedly tied on an Elk-hair Caddis and caught three 9-inch trout in two little pools. I walked up the trail five minutes and repeated my catch. I looked at my watch and made the decision to head up to the lake, knowing I would have only an hour or so to fish before I would have to head back down the mountain and then up the mountain to my parked truck.

## Little Rock Creek Lake

The lake is 4.5 miles from the trailhead. The trail is both steep and rough. In many places water spills down the trail, leaving muddy bogs. Shadow eagerly ran up the trail. A few minutes later we met a Minnesota family heading out. No one in the party was a fisher, but they were detailed in their descriptions about all the leaping trout around the shoreline. What was their guess as to my hiking time? About two hours, they replied. From the trailhead to the lake, the hike took me three hours, and the return trip was only slightly shorter in duration. The trail gets thin in places, but I found the blaze marks on the trees and the piled rock cairns.

Although I had only an hour to fish, I was delighted with the numerous 9- to 10-inch cutthroats I caught in an hour's time. I caught all of these trout on the same caddis fly. I was letting it sink and twitch-ing it. They would hit it on the slow retrieve or when I paused. They would follow the fly right into my shadow. Reluctantly, I headed down the trail. I had asked the Minnesota couple to leave a phone message on our phone recorder for our bed and breakfast so that Pauline would know where I was and that I would be getting back after dark. The next time that I return to Little Rock Creek Lake I will get an early start so that I can fish both the lake and the creek and still have time for a nap!

## MM 35.3: Wally Crawford Fishing Access

Often referred to as the Como Bridge access, this is without a doubt the most popular stretch of water above and below the bridge for floaters. Although the fishery has withstood the increased pressure, as the summer flows decrease the larger fish head for cover. Plan on seeing up to 10 other floaters on a hot summer weekend. Floaters from Wally Crawford to Angler's Roost must portage around Sleeping Child Dam, which is easily done. Launching upriver, the floaters have a choice of floating down from the town of Darby for a short run or putting in above Darby at Hannon Memorial Access where the highway crosses the river again south of Darby. All of these access points are good fishing areas for foot fishermen.

## MM 37.9: One Horse Creek and Twin Lakes

From the highway to the creek is approximately four miles. From the highway to the first lake is 20.5 miles. One Horse Creek offers great picnic sites for the first five miles, but the fishing is poor, as the creek is very small. If you plan on driving to Twin Lakes, be sure you have a truck, preferably a 4X4. The road is rough for 16 miles, and you will average 10 miles an hour. The first lake is drawn down in the fall and is very shallow, which would account for the poor fishing.

The upper lake is said to be fair fishing for small cutthroats. Plan your trip so that you return in the evening as moose, elk and deer are frequently seen along the road.

**Schumaker Campground (Twin Lakes):** Five camping units, toilet facilities, no charge.

 **MM 38.2:** River access

The author launching his 10-foot Little Dipper at Angler's Roost

**MM 43.2: Roaring Lion Creek, Sawtooth Creek**
South of Hamilton on Highway 93, the highway crosses the Bitterroot River by Angler's Roost Campground. Look for Roaring Creek Road about eight-tenths of a mile from the bridge. The trailhead, a popular trail with horse people and hikers, is approximately 3.5 miles on a bumpy road. The trailhead has no campground or picnic site. The creek is fished heavily, and the majority of fish caught are in the 5- to 7-inch range. Roaring Lion Creek and Sawtooth Creek are located in two canyons side by side. However, access to Sawtooth Creek is from the Roaring Lion trailhead. "The dis-

tance from the trailhead to the first Sawtooth Creek crossing is approximately three miles. The first two miles of this section are in excellent shape. Between mile two and three, the trail generally is in good shape with several steep pitches. After the first creek crossing, the trail varies from fair to poor...." –USFS

**MM 43.4: Angler's Roost Campground**
A few miles south of Hamilton, the highway crosses the Bitterroot River. This is also a popular section for foot fishers. Angler's Roost owners have generously allowed floaters to launch their rafts from their campground. Be sure to sign their guest book and park in their designated parking spots. Show your appreciation by doing some business with them in their store.

**MM 43.9: Sleeping Child Creek, Skalkaho Creek**
Look for the Skalkaho Highway south of Hamilton on Highway 93. The highway actually turns south. Water diversion for irrigation and increasing development has impacted the fishing for the first 12 miles along Skalkaho Creek. Public fishing begins around mile 13 at Black Bear Campground. The best fishing is found in the upper reaches for 7- to 9-inchers between mile markers 15 and 19. After mile marker 19, the road climbs high above the creek. Look for pocket water, as this is a very small crick. Look for

Sleeping Child Road, which continues south off of Skalkaho Road. Sleeping Child Creek is not worth fishing as it runs through so much private property. Hiking into the headwaters is also not worth the effort, in my estimation, given the proximity of other great fishing creeks in the area.

**MM 46:** Hamilton, Montana

###  Bitterroot River Access: Hamilton

To the south of Hamilton the Bitterroot River is crossed at the Silver Bridge. In spite of heavy fishing pressure as well as swimmers, fishing is good downstream from the bridge to Blodgett Park, a short distance downstream. The river braids through this section, and it provides excellent cover from downed cottonwoods.

### Bitterroot River Access: Hamilton Sewage Treatment Plant

Don't let the facilities dissuade you. Some of the best fishing on the Bitterroot River runs behind the town of Hamilton. Turn west at the light at Adirondack Street from Highway 93. Two blocks up, turn right on Seventh and then immediately bear left. You can also reach the river by turning west on Main Street and driving a short distance to the Main Street Bridge.

### MM 47: Main Street, Canyon Creek, Blodgett Creek

Follow the directions to Blodgett Canyon as Canyon Creek is the first canyon south of Blodgett. Look for the Forest Service sign (road #735). Canyon Creek is a small, brushy creek that supports 6- to 8-inch cutthroats, but the creek is tough to access and even tougher to fish. The trail is steep. I would not recommend the trail for small children. However, from the Canyon Creek Trailhead, take the Blodgett Overlook Trail for a spectacular view.

"The Blodgett Overlook trail is open to hiking and mountain biking, but no motorized use is allowed. The trail winds around Romney Ridge and

Darin's hefty rainbow taken from a secret spot in the Bitterroot Valley

provides hikers with a scenic view of Hamilton, Blodgett Canyon, Canyon Creek and Canyon Creek Falls. This gradual 1.5-mile trail winds along the southeast-facing hillside of ponderosa pine, arrowhead balsamroot and exposed bedrock covered with ground moss and lichen. There are numerous benches along the way to rest on and enjoy the view. The trail ends at the steep cliffs of Blodgett Canyon Overlook." –USFS

Brandon at age 5 with his first big fish caught all by himself. "No! I am not going to release him." (Silver Bridge, Hamilton, Montana)

### Blodgett Canyon (Creek)

Traveling on Highway 93 through Hamilton, turn west on Main Street. After you cross the Bitterroot River, Main Street changes to West Bridge Road and then to Canyon Creek Road. From the intersection of Main Street and Highway 93, the distance to the campground and creek is 5.7 miles. The road out of town meanders until it intersects Blodgett Camp Road. Turn left on Blodgett Camp Road, which is designated as road 736. The last two miles to the campground are on a dirt road.

### Blodgett Canyon Campground

Six camping or picnic units, toilet facilities, no charge. The campground has an excellent shaded picnic site for those hot days in August. Blodgett Canyon is noted for spectacular rock formations. The creek is excellent fishing for small 6- to 10-inch trout.

**MM 48:** Headquarters for Bitterroot National Forest.

**MM 50.2:** Silver Bridge fishing access.

**MM 50.4: Blodgett Park** Fishing access, day use only.

**MM 52:** Turn right. Woodside Road to Corvallis Bridge fishing access.

### MM 52: Dutch Hill Road, Mill Creek

Turn west (left) on Dutch Hill Road and drive 2.5 miles until you arrive at Bowman Road. Turn left on Bowman Road. Drive three-tenths of a mile and turn right at the Mill Creek Trailhead. The trailhead is one mile. Mill Creek is a small creek tumbling down a steep canyon. For the first mile the creek is right along the trail and offers lots of pocket water for small trout.

Mill Creek fishes almost the same as its neighboring creeks, although I believe it gets a little more pressure. During the first half-mile the creek parallels the trail through a steep section of the canyon. Boulders ranging from the size of bean bags to bunk beds slow the water as it tumbles down the canyon into little pockets and pools. All along the trail are scuffmarks and slides left behind by eager fishermen. Looking down the 15- to 20-foot slides, I decided to wait. When the trail was only four or five feet above the creek, I scrambled down the trail and caught my first 9-inch cutthroat on a small hopper.

After I had released the fish, I thought of the question posed to me by a guest staying in my bed and breakfast. An accomplished fisher from back East, he asked me in all seriousness what I considered a pan fryer. I glibly mumbled, "I don't know. Anything that fits in a frying pan." No response was forthcoming. It was, after all, not a question to be expounded upon. Later I discovered I did indeed have an exact definition of a pan fryer. A pan fryer is an 8- to 9-inch trout with its head and tail cut off, and it fits perfectly at the bottom of a 5½-inch, official Boy Scout mess kit.

## MM 56: Tucker Crossing Fishing Access

Turn right. Look for Blackbird's Fly Shop and Lodge just in front of the access road on the east side of the highway. You will see an old, rusting teepee burner. In typical years I would not recommend floating downstream as the channel often splits and braids. The shallow water can make for some tough floating. This is also a popular site for walk-in fishing in both directions. On the other side of the highway, if you turn to the left, you will be on Bear Creek Road, which will take you to both the Bear Creek trailhead and the Fred Burr Creek trailhead.

## MM 56: Bear Creek, Fred Burr Reservoir

Turn west. Bear Creek is recorded in my endless favorite creek list. The first quarter-mile of the trail winds above the creek through a talus slide. Looking across the canyon and listening to the beckon-

ing call of the creek softly extolling its piscatorial praise of native cutthroats, I broke a vow I made to myself sometime around my 50th birthday – stay on the trail!

For years I have held the belief that 80 percent of fishers are too impatient to walk up the trail more than a half-mile. I also harbor the belief that 90 percent of serious fishers under the age of 50 look for areas that they are convinced no one else would bother hacking their way through the brush to reach. My third belief is that 75 percent of proficient fly fishers will pass up fishing a hole within the first half mile convinced that the local bait bugaboo has decimated the pool. A hodge-podge of contradictory beliefs? Of course! Acted on? Absolutely!

So there I was, poised high on the canyon trail overlooking a canopy of treetops and gnarly brush. "Don't do it," the 53-year-old in me warned. "Don't listen to that old curmudgeon," the kid in me responded. "You are only as old as you DO. Think of all those untouched pools. No one is going to bail off this trail after just leaving the parking lot. Even the impatient ones are going to go further on. And the serious guys are going to pass it up figuring the campers will have hit it pretty hard." Good point, I thought to myself. This could be worth the effort.

Off the trail I plunged into the Heart of Darkness. Bruised and scratched, only 30 yards off the trail, I was down on my knees thrusting my rod through any patch of light I could find. The horror! Even Shadow, my faithful Lab companion, was disgusted with me. When I finally broke out onto the creek, it was no more than a series of thin braids with little holding water. I finally worked my way up to the point where the creek was one, and after catching a number of fat 8- to 10-inch cutthroats, I was one with the creek, the canyon and the cascading brook. At one juncture I caught a small bull trout and a nice 10-inch cut in a pool right below the trail. A familiar worn path led from the trail to the pool. Unlike my youth during the '50s and early '60s, I am glad we live in a time of catch and release. I have no idea as to the fishing further up the trail. I only covered the first mile!

**Fred Burr Reservoir (Victor)**

Follow Bear Creek Road west towards the mountains until the road intersects with Red Crow Road. Turn west on Red Crow Road. The road will veer to the left (south), but keep straight ahead on Fred Burr Road for 1.5 miles to the trailhead.

Private landowners restricted access to the National Forest in Fred Burr canyon until 1995. Fred Burr Creek is heavily traveled by hikers, bikers and riders. Most of the trail is actually a jeep trail that leads to Fred Burr Reservoir, which is approximately five miles from the trailhead. Fishing along the creek is excellent for small 6- to 9-inch cutthroats. I spoke to a number of horseback riders coming down the trail, and all of them seemed pleased with the fishing in the reservoir. Huckleberry hounds, watch for those tiny purple treats along the trail late in July for an extra bonus.

I fished the creek in July with Tony Swallow, a long-time volunteer and board member for the local public television station. We only covered the first mile. Tony was one of those rare anomalies who had reached middle age without ever fly-fishing. I assured him he could be successful on his very first outing with me as his instructor. Over-confidence on my part? A touch of braggadocio after 15 years of being a fly fishing guide? None of the above. Summer fishing on any of the Bitterroot's canyon creeks should be considered one of those basic laws of nature – you will catch fish.

Keep in mind, however, that you must adhere to four principals: (1) Keep your fly high and dry. (2) Be sure your fly floats naturally without any line drag. (3) Allow your fly to land gently. (4) Get in the middle of the creek and cast upstream. Tony, hoping to catch at least a couple of fish, followed all of the above rules and lost count after catching 10 feisty trout.

### MM 59: Victor Crossing

The bridge at Victor Crossing washed out in 1997, but it was replaced in the summer of 1999.

### MM 59: Victor, Montana

Victor has a great steakhouse and a great Mexican restaurant and the Hamilton House Bar serves a great fish dinner! Sweathouse Creek is a small creek right above the town of Victor. A narrow canyon with fast, tumbling water, fishing is good for 6- to 9-inchers. From the town of Victor, turn onto Main Street and then right on Chief Victor's Camp Road and then left on Sweathouse Creek Road to the trailhead.

### MM 61: Bell Crossing Fishing Access

Turn east. Opposite the turnoff to Big Creek Lake, Bell Crossing is a state access point to the river for floaters floating down to Stevensville. Wade fishers will have to hike both upstream and downstream for selective fishing.

### MM 61: Big Creek

Turn west. The turn-off for Big Creek is between Victor and Stevensville on Highway 93. Look for the dirt road directly across from Bell Crossing Road. You will see an electric company's fenced substation across from the access road to the east. The headwater trailhead is approximately four to five miles from the highway. The road makes a few turns, but it is clearly marked with Forest Service signs and arrows. Big Creek is probably the most popular creek in the area, as it carries the most water and offers a more graduated drainage. It was not uncommon 10 years ago to land rainbows and a few browns in the 12-inch range. Now the creek is over-populated with 3- to 5-inch cutthroats in the canyon below the trailhead.

A short walk up the trail, however, will keep a fisher busy with 6- to 10-inch cutthroats. The trail to the lakes is approximately 12 miles and offers wonderful fishing all the way. Having once decided I would cut and hack my way through the brush to reach seldom if ever fished sections of the creek away from the trail, I will assure you that the fishing isn't much better than what is easily available to you from the trail.

## 🐟 🚶 Big Creek Lakes

Big Creek Lakes is really a misnomer as it is really just one large 240-acre lake that splits into two lakes on low-water years and during the fall. My son and I fished this lake in late August 1996, and it lived up to its reputation. The lake is loaded with 12-inch rainbows, and although I had heard that it was not uncommon to catch trout in the 16-inch range, we couldn't find them as the 12-inchers were harassing us on every cast. What fun we had. We caught fish on drys, nymphs and streamers. The scenery is breathtaking as the shore is edged with conifers in a large glacial canyon. For those individuals who are somewhat reluctant to meet the challenge of a 12-mile backpacking hike, I would recommend backpacking seven to eight miles and camping on the creek; then hike up to the lake the next day with just a lunch and fishing gear. This is the best of both wilderness experiences, and it is just a few miles above the populated Bitterroot Valley!

## 🐟 🛶 MM 66.8: Stevensville, Junction to Highway 269

**Bitterroot River Access:** Stevensville Bridge and Burnt Fork Creek

The Stevensville Bridge is a popular put-in and take-out point for float fishers either floating downstream to Florence or floating from Bell Crossing Bridge. This is a good access point for foot fishermen upstream or downstream. The entire area is a managed trophy trout section and, as such, is catch and release. During the last few years, the stretch from Stevensville to Florence has seen an increase in the number of boats plying the river on any given day of the season.

This section of the river can be fickle and torment floaters all day, or it can reward you with a most memorable day of fishing. I will confess to fishing a number of seasons without catching a trophy trout on the Bitterroot River (20+ inches). September 1997, I slipped my Little Dipper drift boat into the water at the Stevensville Bridge and within the first two miles I had caught a 23-inch brown, an 18-inch rainbow and a 17-inch rainbow.

I celebrated all day long as I floated down the river. The moon and planets and stars were surely all aligned.

## 🐟 🚶 🏕 Burnt Fork Creek, Gold Creek Campground

Four camping units, toilet facilities, no water, no charge. Not advised for RV or large camp trailers. I recently returned to Burnt Fork Creek after at least a 10-year hiatus. When my two sons were young, we would travel up the Burnt Fork for our first spring outing of catching little cutthroats and roasting hot dogs to celebrate the coming of summer. For solitude and fun fishing for small fry, the Burnt Fork is unsurpassed. From Stevensville's Main Street, drive one mile south to the Burnt Fork Road. Turn east and travel 10.1 miles to where the paved road curves to the right. At this point the road changes to Burnt Fork School Road. Exit from the paved road straight ahead on Mid Burnt Fork Road. Follow this dirt road approximately six miles to the Gold Creek Campground. From the Gold Creek Campground, you can continue on the same road for 2.4 miles until you come to the end of the road at the trailhead. The road is bumpy and narrow at this point, but it is still suitable for passenger vehicles with sufficient clearance.

Covered with a canopy of alder and mountain mahogany, the creek is shrouded in shade, which produces brilliantly colored cutthroats. Unlike their cousins in the Bitterroot River, who are drenched with sun all summer, the Burnt Fork cutthroats have a swath of bright orange from their jaw all along their underbelly. Their dark back and shaded penciled sides provide distinct markings, and best of all every pocket of water holds two or three 7- to 9-inch fish.

Like the creek I grew up on, this is not a place for purists and dry fly fishermen. The creek demands stealth and swing casts. A short, stout 3X leader provides all the necessary tensile strength when you miss a strike and find your fly snagged on a branch overhead. I recommend the bow shot for those hard-to-reach pockets where you can't even swing your fly. Get down on your knees, grab your fly between your fingers with the hook facing up, bow your rod, aim and let fire!

I recommend using a size 10 Girdle bug or Yuk Bug. Fish them just like a dry fly. Naturally they will sink, but their white rubber legs in the dark, moss-lined pools provide a lure which is easy to follow. When you see a trout flash, set the hook just as you would a dry fly. Here is a very small creek for the entire family to have fun.

### MM 67.8: Kootenai Creek Trailhead

The trailhead is two miles from the highway. Kootenai Creek is a fast, tumbling creek heavily used by rock climbers, backpackers and local fishermen. It is a great place to wet a line during the heat of the summer. Shaded most of the day, the creek offers an abundance of 6- to 8-inch cutthroats. This is pocket-water fishing, and as such it requires scrambling up and over boulders and staying right in the water. Don't come too early, however, as the creek rages down the mountainside long after the Bitterroot has settled into its summer flows.

### MM 70: River access.

### MM 70.2: Bass Creek, Charles Water Campground

20 camping units, four picnic spots, water, garbage and toilet facilities. Fee area. The trailhead is 2.5 miles from Highway 93. The campground is designed for trailers and RVs and is very nice. The creek is a brushy tumbling creek with difficult access. Nonetheless, there is fair fishing for small trout wherever you can climb down off the trail to a pocket. It is a moderate hike to the picnic spot. The area just above the shallow ponds is good fishing for small cutthroats.

## Saga: Bass Creek

When two four-legged animals come face-to-face on a precipitous trail at a blind spot, you have the makings of a high-country rodeo. Shadow, my black Lab, let out an alarmed woof. The mounted rider in the rear yelled, "Bear!" The horse reared, the rider grabbed the pommel with both hands, and I flashed forward to a courtroom where the first question asked of me was, "Did you have your dog on a leash and under control?"

"But your honor, not all the blame should rest solely on my shoulders. Shouldn't there be some shared responsibility with the wife who mistook my Labrador retriever who weighs 80 pounds for a premature grizzly release? And what about the husband? What's a pampered, citified horse doing on Bass Creek Trail? And what about Shadow? Doesn't she have the right to let out a choked snort when she is confronted by an alien sighting? Why, the man had on a huge white Stetson, a scarf and a John Wayne shirt with a string of buttons in a figure seven configuration!"

I wish I could say I made it all up, but it happened. I was horrified as I watched the horse spin on the up side of the trail with the rider holding on for dear life. I walked to higher ground where the horse could see us and talked to the two riders, but the horses were in a panic and would not come up the trail. I quickly leashed Shadow and walked down the trail, and all was well. The husband was apologetic for his horse, saying the horse had been trained around dogs and shouldn't have reacted. I was feeling much relieved when he openly confessed to his share of the responsibility. It seems that he had just looked down the cliff and thought to himself, "Oh, please, God, don't let me run into anyone on this spot." Suddenly Shadow appeared, his wife yelled, "Bear!" and he spooked an already panicked horse that was suffering from altitude sickness.

Bass Creek Lake trail winds up the canyon for eight miles to the lake at an altitude rise of over 3,000 feet, according to another middle-aged hiker I met. I planned a one night stay-over, and in retrospect I made the right decision. The lake was not at all as accommodating as Big Creek Lakes, my previous summer trek. I was too exhausted to hike to the back of the lake in search of a relatively flat 6X6 spot to pitch camp, so I joined the other two hikers and set up my camp on the level top of the earthen dam.

On the way back down I fished the creek in a beautiful park setting, but between the flies and the mosquitoes, we were punished severely for my off-trail fishing adventure. Sitting on a log in the middle of the tiny creek, I caught five small cutthroats, about the same size and the same number I had caught on the lake the previous evening. What Bass Creek lacks in fishing prospects, compared to the other creeks in the area like Kootenai Creek, it makes up for in scenery. One hour up the trail is a great picnic spot where the creek flattens out above an old timbered dam. The water is shallow, and it makes for a great day's outing for children. If you have never taken an evening stroll along one of these creeks, do so and discover the Bitterroot wilderness.

## MM 71.6: Poker Joe River Access

During the heat of the summer, fish a nymph on the bottom, or fish a hopper with a dropper down past the rip-rap car bodies above the railway bridge. This area is good foot fishing in the fall. Prior to the run-off in 1998, I floated through this section during an incredible drake hatch. I couldn't believe the number of 12- to 14-inch rainbows. Regardless of how poorly this section fishes during the heat of the summer, I can assure you that you are dragging your lure over more trout than I could imagine until I saw them all boiling on the surface. Yes, I caught a lot of fat fish, but I must confess that it wasn't easy. On every cast a regatta of brown drakes surrounded my fly. One other shore fisherman was on the stretch above me. After a while I walked up to him eager to share my experience. "Can you believe it?" I said. He replied, "Unbelievable, but you should have been here yesterday!"

## MM 74: Florence, Montana

Florence offers gas, food, bars and Rhino's sporting goods store, where you can buy a fishing license. After 18 years of being a resident of Florence, Montana, I packed into **Peterson Lake** with my donkey, Buddy, and two of my students, September 25, 1999. Peterson is only five miles into the wilderness, right above Florence. The trail is difficult in places, but the view is spectacular. A popular hiking spot for the locals, the fishing is, nonetheless, good for small 7- to 9-inch rainbows. Peterson is one of the few lakes in the Bitterroot Wilderness that can be reached in three hours, less if you are under 55 and in good shape! The lake is beautiful and fishes well at both the inlet and outlet, which is typical of most mountain lakes. A number of nice campsites ring the lake.

Duffy Lake, less than an hour's hike away, has a reputation for being the better fishing lake. We didn't make it to Duffy. Saturday morning the mountains were clouding up with telltale signs of snow. When my two senior students arrived at the house, I attempted to let them off the hook, but they just derided me for being a sissy. Besides, they pointed out, the paper said the clouds would break up in the afternoon and Sunday was supposed to be sunny with mild temperatures. Off we headed to a mountain lake just a few miles from my house. The trailhead is up Sweeney Creek. Take the Sweeney Creek Road, which is 1.5 miles south of Florence's only traffic light. From Highway 93 to the trailhead is approximately seven miles.

By the time we had Buddy unloaded from the back of my pickup truck and headed up the trail, the wind was blowing corn snow. When we reached the ridge, to drop down to the lake, the slightly warmer winds plastered us with wet snow. By the time we had our tents set up, it was cold and miserable. We spent the next three hours curled up in our sleeping bags. By 5 PM the snow stopped and the boys crawled out to fish. I started a huge "white man's" fire, and watched as the two young men pulled in fish after fish on a nymph setup I had devised for them. My wet feet never thawed. The next morning we woke to four inches of snow. After breakfast we took a vote to head home, even though the blue sky was breaking across the jagged cliffs and peaks above us. Packing out we stopped in awe at the beauty of the lake and the canyon. By the time we reached the truck, the Bitterroot Valley was bathed with the prospect of a return to Indian Summer. Thirty minutes later a Montana "Gotcha" clobbered us with cold winds and snow on the valley floor. I can't wait to return in the spring. If you are in the Missoula area, and you are not troubled by other hikers, Peterson Lake would be a great day hike or an overnight camping trip if you were pressed for time and wanted a wilderness experience.

## MM 74: Bitterroot River Access: Florence Bridge

As you enter Florence, watch for the Conoco Gas Station on the left and move into the right lane. Turn onto the East-Side Highway and drive one-mile to the bridge. The Florence Bridge is a popular exit point for floaters entering the river at Stevensville. This section of the river can be very productive fishing or VERY slow fishing. It is especially good fishing during the Skwala hatch during the spring and later when the autumn nights cool the river.

## MM 76.8: Chief Looking Glass Campground

Chief Looking Glass is a beautiful campground and local swimming hole. Watch for the sign between Lolo and Florence. This section of the river is poor fishing during the summer as the water is slow and warm. Comparatively speaking, this section has a low fish count, but I would recommend fishing this area in mid-September during the Ephemerella Hecuba mayfly hatch. The pattern is a size 10 rusty, green.

## Side Trip – Lolo Creek

**MM 83.3: Lolo Creek** Exit Highway 93 to Highway 12 West. Just a few miles south of Missoula, the community of Lolo rests at the junction of Highway 12, which leads to Idaho and the Lochsa River. A resting place for the Lewis and Clark Expedition, Lolo Creek parallels the highway for over 30 miles. Hosting a variety of species of trout, the creek proffers smaller 7- to 9-inch trout with the occasional spawning laggard. Years of logging and drought cycles have taken their toll on this pristine little crick. This creek gets pounded late spring and early summer. Some of the ranchers are becoming quite irritated over liberal interpretations of the high water mark. For a little seclusion, look for National Forest land where the creek falls away from the highway. Spring runoff turns this gentle canyon creek into an angry avalanche of water.

**Lewis and Clark Campground:** 15 miles west of Lolo. 17 campsites. Drinking water. U.S. Fee Area.

**Lee Creek Campground:** 26 miles west of Lolo. 22 campsites. Drinking water.

**MM 83.5:** Lolo, Montana.

### South Fork Lolo Creek

For years I had disdained fishing Lolo Creek, knowing it was heavily fished and heavily de-watered. But then I learned of the South Fork of Lolo Creek. It is a beautiful creek and loaded with 7- to 12-inch trout after you hike up the trail a few miles. If you would like to visit the South Fork of Lolo Creek, turn west on Highway 12 in Lolo and travel 10.2 miles until you see the sign for Elk Meadow Road on the left. Follow Elk Meadow Road 2.4 miles until it forks.

Follow the signs to the South Fork Lolo Creek Trailhead, which is two miles to the left. When you cross the bridge, you are at the trailhead. Just below the bridge is a parking and unloading zone. This spot is a picnicker's dream. Walk down the closed road a hundred yards to a field of daisies and bluebells. I fell in love with this spot on the creek. When I was there, July 19, the yarrow was in bloom as well as a number of other wild flowers. This beautiful creek is only 14.5 miles from Lolo, and it is perfect for children.

## Saga: South Fork Fishing

After huffing and puffing up through a series of switchbacks and then hacking my way down a steep canyon with downfall (an apt description), I was poised for my first cast at what looked like my only opportunity after such an arduous descent. The creek was raging, and I could see that it was still too early to wade up the creek and avoid the brush and downed lodge pole. Stepping into the creek, I made my first cast, and my faithful Labrador mistook the move for a crossing. Later I recalled reading about Jack London's dog Buck in *Call of the Wild*. In a demonstration of obedience, Buck almost plunges over a cliff.

Shadow is not nearly so dutiful; she is more on the impetuous side. In she plunged at the worst place. Shocked, I stood powerless to help as she tumbled and glided through a series of falls and chutes. Swinging to the far side about 20 yards down the creek, she reminded me of an Olympian kayaker. She didn't whine, but her forlorn look and those droopy wet ears clearly communicated that we were separated, and she wanted me on her side of the "Creek of No Return".

The far side provided three or four separate pockets to fish. In a space of 40 yards I caught six fish, the largest a 12-inch German brown. I also landed a 10-inch rainbow and four very small cutthroats. Satisfied, I looked for a crossing, knowing I would be back later in the month when I could stay in the creek and have more freedom of movement. Shadow refused to cross at the spot I selected and we subsequently lost considerable ground. Although it was less harrowing than her first crossing, I was still concerned for her. She appeared to shake both the water and the experience off as she lunged up the mountain with her faithful master huffing and puffing behind her. Up the mountain she would run and then back down to stop in front of me with tilted head. I couldn't tell if she was giving me a look of kindness or pity as I groped for every lodgepole in my reach.

### Return to Highway 93

**MM 83.9: Lolo Sewage Treatment Plant** River access. Turn east on Glacier Road. A few blocks down Glacier Road, you will come to a T-intersection in a residential neighborhood. Turn left and follow the road to the sewage plant where there is a day-use area on the river. This is the logical exit point if you are floating down from the Florence Bridge or Chief Looking Glass Campground, but you have to drag or carry your raft or canoe up to the parking lot.

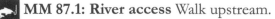 **MM 87.1: River access** Walk upstream.

Author fishing with his two sons – always on the oars!

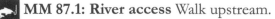 **MM 88.9: Blue Mountain Road**

Blue Mountain Road follows the Bitterroot River until it intersects with the Clark Fork. The first fishing access is Maclay Flat. Blue Mountain Road turns to the Southside Road that goes all the way to Petty Creek, which is an exit on Interstate 90. The road winds around the hillsides for miles. Sometimes it follows the Clark Fork River; at other times it follows the ridges far above the river. If you plan on wade fishing the lower Clark Fork, this is the road for you. It may also be accessed from Interstate 90 onto Reserve Street. Follow Reserve Street until you come to Mullan Road (Perkin's Restaurant). Turn right on Mullan Road. Follow Mullan Road until you come to Kona Bridge Road. Turn left on Kona Bridge Road until it intersects with Southside Road. Follow the signs to Deep Creek Shooting Range, and you will know you are on the right road. Past the turnoff for Deep Creek is the Old Harper's Bridge, which is a takeout point for floaters launching from Spurgin Road.

This area of the lower Clark Fork is a challenge for beginning fly fishermen, as it has long stretches of flat, unproductive water. The Clark Fork does not have high trout counts, but when you find one trout, you usually find a pod. I do not recommend this stretch for wade fishers during the heat of August unless you are on the search for sippers. If it is an overcast day in August or September with the promise of some light showers, do not pass up the opportunity to fish the Clark Fork.

**Highway 93 (Reserve Street)**

Traveling north on Reserve Street, cross South Avenue to Spurgin Road. Spurgin Road Fishing Access is tucked behind a very affluent neighborhood. In fact, you drive right between two fenced homes to get to the day-use fishing access. When you reach a T-intersection, just turn right and then left as Spurgin Road takes a jog. The access has a boat launch, but during dry years you will have to drag your boat down to the Bitterroot River where it joins the Clark Fork River.

Highway 93 from Missoula to Kalispell continues on page 57.

## Popular Float Trips on the Bitterroot River

**•Float Trip 1: West Fork of the Bitterroot**
During spring and early summer, this section can be dangerous. Check with one of the shops for the latest information.

**•Float Trip 2: Hannon Access (the bridge just south of the West Fork Road) to Wally Crawford (Como Bridge)**
By far this is the most heavily floated section, yet the fishing is excellent. Plan a full-day float or a short float to Darby Bridge.

**•Float Trip 3: Wally Crawford to Angler's Roost Campground**
Be sure to register at Angler's Roost. Plan for a full-day float, and be prepared to portage at Sleeping Child Dam.

**•Float Trip 4: Angler's Roost to Woodside (Corvallis Bridge)**
Be prepared for a sharp turn and a huge rock just above Hamilton's Main Street Bridge. Below the bridge you will have to portage around a diversion dam. If you go over it, unload your passengers on the right bank above the dam. After you float under the silver bridge south of town, the river forks to the left past Blodgett Park (an exit site) or to the right. The right channel gets very low late in the summer, and the left channel can be snaggy and dangerous during high water.

**•Float Trip 5: Corvallis Bridge to Tucker West**
Stay in the left (west) channel. This mid-section of the river from Tucker West to Bell Crossing loses a great deal of water from late July on, which makes for slow floating and, on low water years, some boat dragging.

**•Float Trip 6: Bell Crossing to Stevensville**
A full-day float.

**•Float Trip 7: Stevensville to Florence**
This is a very full day float if you fish hard. Plan on taking out after the cocktail hour.

**•Float Trip 8: Florence Bridge to Lolo Sewage Treatment Plant**
This too is a very long float both in mileage and slow water. You may shave off a couple miles by launching at Chief Looking Glass Campground. Keep in mind that you will have to portage your boat about 40 yards up a bank to the parking lot. Due to the warm summer water conditions, the fishing is generally poor until fall.

## Bitterroot River Mileage Chart

The following mileage between access points is approximate calculations starting from Missoula and moving to Hannon Memorial south of Darby.

• Maclay Bridge (Missoula–North Avenue) to Buckhouse Bridge (Missoula–Highway 93): 5.8 miles
• Buckhouse Bridge to Lolo Treatment plant: 10.5 miles
• Lolo treatment plant to Chief Looking Glass: 12.7 miles
• Chief Looking Glass to Florence Bridge: 2.2 miles
• Florence Bridge to Stevensville Bridge: 10.1 miles
• Stevensville Bridge to Bell Crossing Bridge: 9.5 miles
• Bell Crossing to Victor Crossing: 2.7 miles
• Victor Crossing to Tucker Crossing: 4.2 miles
• Tucker Crossing to Woodside (Corvallis bridge): 4.8 miles
• Woodside to Silver Bridge (Hamilton city limits): 3.1 miles
• Silver bridge to Main Street Bridge: 2.0 miles
• Main Street Bridge to Angler's Roost: 4.5 miles (Ask for permission at Angler's Roost campground.)

- Angler's Roost to Como Bridge: 9.8 miles
- Como Bridge to Old Darby Bridge (private): 6.3 miles
- Old Darby Bridge to Hannon Memorial: 3.8 miles

## Saga: Biking for Beatitudes and Beauties

Matched beauty. Photo courtesy of Stu Williams at www.montanaboat.com

On August 13, 1997, I replaced a flat tire on my mountain bike and cleaned out the saddlebags of old candy wrappers from a previous trek taken a number of years ago when I bought the bike as a way to keep in shape. I waited all morning, gauging the rain clouds over the Bitterroot Range. Finally, after pumping up the tire and my confidence, I decided it was now or never. I started up the Fred Burr Reservoir Trail at 11:40. At 11:42 I was walking. The entire trip, with intermittent riding, took an hour and 40 minutes.

I had only gone a short distance when my seat dropped, my knees pushed up to my chin, and I was soaked. My raincoat was tucked in my saddlebags, and I was hot and panting. Shadow's tongue was still concealed as she kept turning back waiting for me. Reluctantly, I put on the raincoat that I have been trying to wear out for 17 years so I can buy a Gore-Tex model. The coat was bought at a ranch supply store in Bozeman; made from rubberized canvas, it is destined to be a real Montana heirloom.

Huffing and puffing, my resolve weakened, and I thought of locking the bike to a tree with my combination lock, but I could not recall the numbers. Did I use my birthday numbers, my Social Security numbers or part of my telephone number? I gave up trying to remember. All I could think about was the ride down the mountain trail. Finally I arrived. It was pouring, and I huddled under a tree that a group of men and boys vacated just as I arrived. They, too, were soaked. They informed me that the fishing was lousy and headed on down the trail. Shadow and I shared a ham sandwich, and I hiked to the back of the lake up the trail to fish the upper portion of the creek. In spite of the rain and fogged-up glasses, I caught a number of colorful cutthroats from 8 to 10-inches. I made a few sloppy casts on the lake on my way back, and then I headed back down the trail, pleased with the beauty of the lake and the fun fishing I experienced.

Grasping the handlebars of my mountain bike, I prepared myself for the ride down the trail. My thoughts turned to Kiddo, a childhood friend who I had thought of for the first time in probably 35 years, on my way up the trail. As I pushed my bike up the trail earlier, my sweating brow and the long haul reminded me of Turnbow Canyon Road and a summer day in 1957. After visiting a half-dozen second-hand stores, I found my treasure, a 20-year-old beat-up baby buggy. I had promised Kiddo the adventure of his life, a soap-box ride from the top of Three Palms down to the valley floor.

Dismantling the buggy, I had the best ball bearing wheels and axles that money could buy, short of buying the official Soap Box Derby wheels, which only rich families could afford. We built the racer with the axle cut and mounted on a wide two-by-four with a large bolt in the center. The back axle was only about two feet wide. Our steering was a hemp rope nailed to the front two-by-four with a couple of old rusty nails. We pulled the racer up through the canyon for over six hours, stopping only to eat our lunches.

Reaching the top of the canyon divide, we could see the three palms above us gently swaying from the afternoon Santa Anna breeze. Off into the distance, we could see miles of carefully laid-out orange groves. Kiddo was a new friend. After his father died and his older brother was jailed, his mother packed up her family and moved to the country. Kiddo looked tough for a fifth grader. He wore a ducktail haircut that I admired greatly. He wore peggers, all of which my mother disapproved. But my mother encouraged the friendship, as she saw a very gentle and kind young man hidden behind the gang look of the fifties. Kiddo rarely laughed, but when we shoved off and began to pick up speed down the canyon, he laughed with gusto. We both began shrieking and whooping with reckless abandon, and reckless it was. Our makeshift brake broke on one of the first turns. We had passed the point of stopping, reaching speeds that I would have to guess was in excess of 40 miles per hour. Our laughter quickly subsided, replaced by white knuckles and quick maneuvering on hairpin turns. Suddenly, coming around a bend, we were faced with a sedan right in front of us traveling down hill. I had a quick decision to make – shoot off the cliff like a Stinger missile, be decapitated by a 1948 Packer or pass on a blind curve.

I attribute that reckless moment as part of my rite of passage. In the split second that I jammed my right leg forward to turn the axle, I knew the fear that all parents harbor for their sons. After I shot through the blind corner, Kiddo and I laughed hysterically. Kiddo's laughter was from turning to look at the old lady's expression; mine was initiated from a vision of death as the tears streaked from the corner of my eyes. Three miles down Turnbow Canyon Road, we lost a wheel. Kiddo shifted and two blocks later we crashed into a curb and were thrown into an orange grove. Bruised and dirty, we looked at each other and began laughing again. It was cool under the shade of that orange tree, and we lay on our backs for a long time just laughing.

Kiddo's mother, after losing her next eldest son to insanity, packed up her fragile family and moved to her rural hometown in Kansas. Two years later I received a report of Kiddo's death when he was thrown from the back of a pick-up truck on a Kansas farm road.

I pushed off on my mountain bike and thought, I still remember you, Kiddo. The return trip took less than an hour.

## Missoula-Area Fishing

Highway 93 runs south to north and intersects in Missoula with Interstate 90, which runs east to west. Before I continue with the fishing and camping prospects on Highway 93 north of Missoula, let me guide you through the Missoula area and all of its wonderful fishing opportunities on the Clark Fork, Rock Creek, and the Blackfoot drainage. The Seeley-Swan area is covered in the Northwest section. Highway 93 north of Missoula continues on page 57.

# Interstate 90 – St. Regis to Butte

## The Clark Fork River
## above and below Missoula

Like the famous Muhammad Ali match with George Foreman, the Clark Fork of the Columbia has been up against the ropes, pummeled and battered by powerful forces for over 100 years. Designated as one of the largest Superfund clean-up sites in the nation, the Clark Fork vies for the title of the comeback kid with the likes of Ali and Rocky Balboa. After a hundred years of mine waste discharge and heavy metal accumulation at the Milltown Dam, the river has yet to be declared champ, but the restoration and rejuvenation of the Upper Clark Fork has been stupendous. With fish counts at zero in the late '60s in the Warm Springs area and reaching over a 1,000 per mile 10 years later and almost doubling again, the brown trout population has attracted a great deal of angling pressure. From Warm Springs to Rock Creek the river varies considerably in the number of trout per mile due in part to thermal seepage, irrigation, years of drought, algae blooms and the insidious presence of whirling disease.

But the good news is that the river from Missoula's Kelly Island to the confluence of the Flathead River continually improves. Fish, Wildlife and Parks Biologist Rod Berg estimates on average about 600 rainbows per mile with the larger 18- to 20-inch fish in the Superior and St.Regis area. Beware of the Alberton Gorge just below the town of Alberton and extending for approximately 18 miles to Forest Grove.

Lewis and Clark were warned, and if you haven't already heard of this section, consider it the playground of experienced whitewater rafters and kayakers. During my first year of guiding in 1981 for Grove Hull, he came back jubilant from a fishing adventure in the gorge with an experienced whitewater oarsman. Constantly trying to balance himself and cast without being thrown out, he had one of those great bragging days on the river. When he suggested I join him, I quickly responded, "Your boat!" No deal, he said. To this day I have never wanted to risk my raft or my life fishing the canyon. Those big rainbows would just be too distracting.

## Popular Clark Fork River Float Trips
### •Float Trips 1 and 2: Beavertail State Park to Clinton and Clinton to Turah

Fishing the Clark Fork from Beavertail State Park past Rock Creek and finishing to Schwartz Creek Bridge has declined in the last number of years; however, given the right conditions, this section can be outstanding during the Salmon Fly hatch, as the hatch moves up Rock Creek. It is a long float trip, but it offers great scenery, albeit fair fishing. The section from Clinton to Turah is similar. The Turah takeout is a state campground, and right across the street from this campground is the Turah store and campground. Do not float past Turah, as there is no take-out from that point down to the Milltown Dam. Wade fishermen will find the Schwartz Creek access a better access point for hiking up and down the river.

### •Float Trip 3: Spurgin Road to Old Harper's Bridge

Missoula's first launching place is at the access on Spurgin Road. Don't be surprised when you drive through a very wealthy neighborhood and drive right between two houses. Fortunately, the access was in place before the developers plotted out the neighborhood. Take Reserve Street and turn west on South Avenue. Turn right on Clements Lane, and then turn immediately left again on Spurgin Road. Late summer during drought years, the small side channel drops really low, and quite often you must drag your raft through the shallows a short distance to the Bitterroot River. A hundred yards downstream the Clark Fork meets the Bitterroot. The takeout point for smaller craft such as canoes can be the Kona Bridge. Typically, however, floaters take out on the left side of the old Harper's Bridge.

**• Float Trip 4: Harper's Bridge to Huson (Interstate 90)**

Exit 85 is approximately 16 miles from the Reserve Street on-ramp.

**• Float Trip 5: Huson (Interstate 90 exit) to Petty Creek**

Leave Interstate 90 at Exit 85. Take the service road that runs west alongside the interstate. This is an excellent walk-in area, especially in the fall. It is also a rough take-out for floaters floating downstream from the old Harper's Bridge. Floaters may also launch from this spot and float down to Petty Creek.

## Petty Creek

Exit 77, 24 miles from the Reserve Street on-ramp. Petty Creek is a very small creek with very small fish. However, wade fishing is excellent on the Clark Fork above Petty Creek.

# Interstate 90 – Idaho Border to Rock Creek

**MM 0:** Idaho border

### Exit 22: Cabin City Campground

Exit 22 at Henderson. Travel east 2.5 miles on Camel's Hump Road #22148. Turn left (west) at the Cabin City Campground sign on Twelve Mile Creek Road #353 for two-tenths of a mile.

### Exit 26: Ward Creek Road

Follow Ward Creek Road (Road #889). The road is a single-lane road with very few turnouts. The creek is very small and almost impenetrable, although it does hold small brookies. From the I-90 exit to the

**Hazel Lake** trailhead is 6.6 miles, and the trail to Hazel Lake is 3.2 miles for small cutthroats.

### Exit 30: Two Mile Road Fishing Access

### Exit 33: St. Regis, Montana; the Lower Clark Fork River

During my tenure as a guide in western Montana, the furthest I had ever floated and fished the Clark Fork was from Forest Grove down to Superior, and those trips were few and far between. The lower Clark Fork has excellent pre-season fishing in March and April, but in typical years the fishing doesn't get good again until mid-July.

I recommend using Woolly Buggers and Bitch Creeks in the spring along the lower St. Regis River, as the browns follow the spring spawners to feed on the egg deposits. The opening day for the St. Regis River is the third Saturday in May. When I asked about the St. Regis River in general, one of the local guides said that the river gets scoured every year. The best fishing is in the first two miles, and he wouldn't fish any further up than four miles, except during spring and fall spawning runs. Pre-season flies include Skwala stonefly from March 15–May 15; Gray Drakes (Amoletus), April 1–June 15; Blue-Wing Olives, April 1–June 1; Nemoura stonefly, March 1–April 30; and March Brown, March 25–April 30.

Most of the locals are spin fishermen and favor black Panther Martins and black Mepps. During mid-summer local guide Brooks and his wife Jackie prefer floating from St. Regis as far down as the 14-Mile Bridge. Brooks recommends a caddis pattern in the evening until mid-August as well as a Parachute Hopper right into September. September through October they recommend a Blue-Wing Olive and the October Caddis. Brooks said his favorites are the Royal Wulff and the Madam X. As the water drops later in the summer to around 9,000 cfs, the fish in the Superior to St. Regis area tend to pod together as the water drops, providing an opportunity for some great fishing. In the late summer and fall, Brooks and Jackie also recommend hoppers, Slate-Wing Olives and Mahogany Duns. When I pressed Jackie for her favorite local lakes that could be reached by driving or a short hike, she said that there were a lot to choose from, but her favorites were Moore Lake, Diamond Lake and Cliff Lake.

## Moore Lake, Little Joe Creek

Follow the main street in St. Regis a half-mile west. Turn left when you see the sign South Fork Little Joe Creek and Moore Lake. The mileage to Moore Lake is 14 miles, and this is the only sign to Moore Lake you will see again until you are zig-zagging up Road #221. (If you miss Road #221 you will wander like I did to the top of the pass and the Idaho State Line.) Turning at the sign just outside of St. Regis, the road will cross over the Interstate and St. Regis River. The road turns to gravel, but it is well-maintained. At 3.3 miles there is a camping spot and an access to Road #221. Turn left on Road #221. The road follows the creek and is one lane and bumpy at times, although you don't need a 4X4. Follow this road 6.9 miles until the road makes a turn to the right, at the second Moore Lake sign. The lake is 3.4 miles from the sign. Moore Lake has a turn-around and an outhouse. The lake is 200 yards from the parking area and does not have any campsites. Nestled in a tight bowl, this 13-acre sub-alpine lake offers good fishing for 8- to 12-inch brook trout.

## Little Joe Creek

Little Joe Creek is a very small creek, but up in the canyon on the way to Moore Lake the creek is backed up by many downfalls, providing little pools for small brook trout and cutthroats.

## Exit 43: Diamond Lake, Cliff Lake

Heading eastbound, take Exit 43 off Interstate 90. Turn right at the stop sign and proceed over the railroad tracks. Continue seven-tenths of a mile and turn right on Road #342. The lake is 13 miles. Four miles from the lake, you will make a left turn at a T-intersection. Diamond Lake Campground is suitable only for tent camping. The road is a one-lane, steep climb suitable for cars. Diamond Lake is a popular spot, as it is one of only a few lakes reached by road in the area. It is a 17-acre, deep lake in heavily timbered country, and it is full of small brookies. To define small, I fished the lake with a father and son from Maine. We dragged and carried three of my one-man boats about 200 yards before we could launch them. (The campsite end of the lake is jammed with logs so if you plan on launching a canoe, plan on a portage.) In the space of two hours, Tom, Lincoln and I managed to catch only 15 fish between us. Not one measured over 9 inches.

Much larger than Diamond Lake, Cliff Lake is reached 1.5 miles up the trail from Diamond Lake. The lake reportedly has 14-inch cutthroats. I spoke to two fishermen coming down the trail, and they said they couldn't even cast from the shore because of the cliffs and the debris and half-sunken logs surrounding the lake. Eager to float the Clark Fork that same day, we passed up the hike.

## Exit 43: Dry Creek Road

Camping and fishing access. After you exit the Interstate, you will come to a T-intersection. Turn right for the boat launch and turn left 3.2 miles for **Slowey Campground**. The campground is right on the water with numerous campsites adjacent to the river. This would make a nice destination for a short evening fishing trip from Superior. Slowey offers 16 campsites plus 10 trailer pull-through sites as well as horse camp facilities, cold drinking water, and a canoe or raft launch.

## Exit 47: Superior, Montana, Fishing Access
Cross the bridge and make a right turn. Head east one mile to the Big Eddy Fishing Access.

## Trout Creek Campground
Seven miles southwest of Superior on Trout Creek Road #257. 12 campsites. Drinking water. No garbage facilities.

**Exit 55:** Floaters wishing to float down to Superior will find access points along the access road, but most of them require sliding your raft down an embankment.

## Exit 58: Quartz Creek Campground
(USFS) Quartz Creek Campground is divided by the Interstate although there is a tunnel joining the two loops. Popular with travelers and white water rafters, loop C has access to the river. 52 campsites. Cold drinking water. Flush toilets. Waste disposal site. U.S. fee area.

## Exit 61: Tarkio Fishing Access
The fishing access is a popular whitewater boat launch one mile from the Interstate 90 exit. The access provides toilet facilities and long stretches above and below the access for wade fishermen.

## Exit 66: Fish Creek
Fish Creek empties into the Clark Fork. From the Reserve Street on-ramp, Fish Creek is 35 miles due west. Take Exit 66 off Interstate 90. Take a right turn to Rivulet if you want to fish the creek from the confluence upstream. Spin fishers and fly fishers heavily fish this section. Deep pools and heavy pressure keep the trout very wary and shy. Nonetheless, what it lacks in numbers, it can make up for in the size of the fish. In the first half-mile of the creek, I caught only three fish on a hot August day, but one of the fish measured 16 inches and jumped eye-level to me three times.

Further up the creek the water is flat and shallow and heavily fished as the road parallels the creek. Years ago I used to take my sons to Fish Creek early in the summer for good catches of 8- to 10-inch trout. Having talked to three high school students from Huson, not much has changed, with the exception of some crafty bull trout which makes Fish Creek very fishy!

If you fish the lower section, you might as well make a day of it and fish the Clark Fork as well. Continue the four miles to Rivulet, which is a railroad spur with two houses. Just above the two houses the river offers a half-mile of riffles with large side pools. You will have to slide on your butt down to the river through a lot of brush. Take a lunch and keep an eye on the pools.

## Exit 70: Cyr Boat Launch and Fishing
Whitewater section.

## Exit 72: Fishing access
East-bound only.

## Exit 75: Alberton, Montana
Fishing access.

 ## Exit 77: Petty Creek
Petty Creek is really not worth fishing, although there is some great fishing access to the Clark Fork River above the creek.

## Exit 82: Nine Mile Road
The upper stretches of Nine Mile Creek offer some

nice camping sites, but the creek is not worth fishing, and the lower stretches of the creek pass through private property.

 **Exit 85: Huson, Montana**

The 32" trout was caught and released two miles downstream from Missoula in April 2000. Photo courtesy of Stu Williams at www.montanaboat.com

Fishing access. Primitive boat launch that is impractical to use during low water years.

**Exit 89:** Frenchtown, Montana.

**Exit 96:** Highway 93 North to Flathead Lake.

**Exit 99:** Missoula airport.

**Exit 102:** Reserve Street Exit – Missoula, Montana .

**Exit 104:** Orange Street Exit – Missoula, Montana.

**Exit 105: Van Buren Street, Rattlesnake Creek**
Here is a great creek right outside the city limits, but you need to be prepared to walk about six miles before you can wet a line in the catch-and-release section. The creek is closed to fishing from the city water supply dam of Mountain Water Company up the creek to the mouth of Beeskove Creek, which is a distance of about six miles from the parking lot to Beeskove Creek. But what a spectacular hike! The trail is a popular trail for both hikers and mountain bikers entering the Rattlesnake Wilderness. Wait until at least mid-July if you plan on fishing for pure strain Western cutthroat. From Beeskove Creek all the way up to the headwaters is catch-and-release fishing. If you have a bike, go all the way to the footbridge and fish above and below the bridge for 7- to 12-inch beauties. Van Buren changes to Rattlesnake Drive. Follow the Rattlesnake Wilderness signs. (The lower section of Rattlesnake Creek below the city water supply site to the mouth is open to fishing. Be sure to check the regulations.)

**Exit 107:** East Missoula, Montana.

**Exit 110: Junction Highway 200, Blackfoot River**
Read about the Blackfoot River drainage from Highway 200 in the Northwest section of this book.

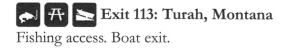 **Exit 113: Turah, Montana**
Fishing access. Boat exit.

**Exit 121: Clinton, Montana**
Fishing access. Boat launch.

## Exit 126: Rock Creek

Rock Creek is probably the most famous creek in western Montana. It is a 20-minute drive from Missoula traveling east on Interstate 90.

**Norton Campground:** Follow Rock Creek Road 11 miles south of I-90 on Rock Creek Road. 10 campsites. Drinking water from hand pump. Toilet facilities.

**Dalles Campground:** 14.5 miles from I-90. 10 campsites. Drinking water from hand pump.

**Harry's Flat Campground:** 17 miles south from I-90. 18 campsites. Drinking water from hand pump.

**Bitterroot Flat Campground:** 23 miles from I-90. 15 campsites. Drinking water from hand pump.

**Sira Campground:** 28 miles from I-90. Four campsites. No drinking water.

# Nymphing on Rock Creek for Bigger and Better Returns

By Doug Persico

Western Montana fly fishers overwhelmingly rate Rock Creek as their favorite dry fly stream. Generating legendary hatches, this quintessential stream offers riffles, pools, long runs and deep holes. Best of all, it is the perfect size to wade and cast, especially to rising fish. Except for a fairly brief period in the spring during the spring runoff, the stream can be waded almost anywhere along its 50 odd miles, and it is almost never crowded compared to the more fabled waters of the Yellowstone Park area.

However, if a fisherman were to consider Rock Creek as only a dry fly stream, he or she would be missing the best fishing opportunity Rock Creek has to offer. Rock Creek nymph fishing exceeds its reputation as a classic dry fly fishery. Nymphing produces consistently bigger fish and greater numbers of fish. Best of all, nymph-fishing produces during those times when there is no dry fly fishing.

### Techniques

Dead drifting a nymph on the bottom and fishing a nymph on or near the surface, either by itself or in tandem with another fly, are the two most productive methods of nymph fishing. Dead drifting simply means figuring out where the fish are holding on the bottom, weighting either the fly or the leader enough to get the fly down to where the fish are, and drifting the fly through the holding water until a fish takes it. Recognizing the take and setting the hook follow. Sounds simple, right? It is, until you consider such questions as, how do you know if you are deep enough, and how do you recognize the take.

The answer to the first question is easy. If you are getting hung up on the bottom and losing an occasional fly, you're deep enough. To answer the second question opens up one of the big debates currently in fly fishing – are strike indicators nothing more than bobbers and an open acknowledgment that the fly fisher hasn't mastered his craft?

Most of my customers use strike indicators to recognize takes when dead drifting a nymph. Strike indicators are simply something the angler can see under any condition. They are attached to the leader far enough away from the fly so that they can be seen on the surface as the fly drifts on or near the bottom. The strike indicator telegraphs to the fisherman the fact that the nymph is no longer drifting. The angler must then quickly set the hook before the fish spits the fly out. Strike indicators are a valuable aid to increase productivity. As a fly shop owner, I make and sell indicators, and I consider them a valuable source of revenue for the shop.

The other method of nymphing used most often on Rock Creek is fishing a nymph unweighted either as a wet fly on the swing or as a trailer to a dry fly. To fish a nymph on the swing, simply cast across the current and start stripping line slowly in as the fly starts swinging below you. In most cases the fish will hook itself.

A technique that is becoming increasingly popular is to fish an emerger imitation in tandem with a dry fly during the hatches. A section of tippet is attached to the bend of a dry fly hook. The tippet section is from 16 to 18 inches long, and an emerger nymph is attached. The dry is drifted and catches fish in its own right as well as acts as a strike indicator for the trailing nymph. This method is proving itself deadly and increases in

Landing a Rock Creek rainbow

popularity every year.

**Fly Patterns**

Just as there are a number of techniques that work on Rock Creek, there are a number of patterns that seem to work well. Some patterns work well all the time, and some work best during a particular time of year. If I were limited to just one pattern and size of nymph to use on Rock Creek all year long, that pattern would be a size 10 Prince, with or without a bead head. For some reason known only to the trout, this pattern works any time of year. Other patterns will work better than a Prince at various times, but day in and day out during the entire year, a size 10 Prince will always produce fish.

During the winter the fish are not very active, but when the weather is warm and sunny enough, and there is no slush ice floating down the creek, a dark stonefly dead drifted through the deep holes can produce some big browns. I sell more Kauffman and Brookes' stoneflies in sizes 4 and 6 than all other patterns combined.

During the latter part of March, Skwala stoneflies and Western March Browns start to hatch. This is the time to dead drift smaller stone fly patterns for the Skwala and size 14 Pheasant Tails for the March Browns. It is also the time to trail a crippled March Brown emerger behind a dry fly. We have particularly good results sinking a Quigley Cripple in the surface film behind a size 14 Parachute Adams or even a size 10 Skwala Stimulator. For a lot of locals, this time of the year is their favorite. I know that this is my favorite time of year to fish dries on Rock Creek, as long as I can trail the emerging nymph behind them.

Once the Skwala and March Brown hatches are over, we begin the countdown to the Salmon Fly. This hatch is easily the best-known in the state, since it occurs in a lot of our major streams. I consider Rock Creek's hatch to be at least as good as any in the state. However, to a dedicated nympher, the hatch itself is less important than the weeks preceding it. During this time there are caddis emerging. Dry attractor patterns are fooling some good trout, but the nymph fisherman knows that the major story is being told on the stream bottom where both the Salmon Fly and Golden Stone nymphs are preparing for their destiny.

Both of these stonefly species hatch on land. When the time is right, the nymphs wiggle out of the water, split their cases, and emerge as adults from the cases and climb onto bushes near the stream banks, which is where they will spend the major part of their adult lives. Prior to this momentous event, the stonefly larva have been moving around the stream bottom. The trout, of course, are not indifferent to this movement since the larva of the various stoneflies is a major part of their diet. As the date for their hatching gets closer, the larva migrate closer to the stream bank. Finally, on the appointed day, out they come.

Not all stoneflies hatch on the same day. The hatch is progressive. It starts near the mouth of the creek and progresses several miles upstream from where the insects are actually hatching. I dead drift a big black nymph as close to the bank as I can get it. Anyway, I used to fish like that. Since opening a fly shop, my outings during the stonefly season have been few and far between. I have sold a lot of large black nymphs, however.

Rock Creek, 20 miles up, and the Salmon Flies are on the water.

After the stoneflies are done, Rock Creek settles into its summer pattern. The primary hatches are caddis and Pale Morning Duns. This is the premier time to fish emerging nymphs just under the surface, trailing behind a high floating dry. Sparkle Duns and Quigleys work extremely well for PMDs and Sparkle Pupas are devastating in the evenings as caddis imitations. For those anglers who like the bottom, Gold Ribbed Hares Ears, Pheasant Tails and the ever-popular Prince, either with or without bead heads, will almost always take fish.

As the season starts to wind down, the hatches change. Late August brings the Blue-Wing Olive and the beginning of the Giant Orange Caddis.

Fishing the olives is pretty much like fishing the PMDs. Small Pheasant Tails do a good job on the bottom, and olive Sparkle Duns in the surface film can be killers.

But the real star of the fall on Rock Creek is the big orange caddis. This guy is big with a body almost two inches long. If you want to see the adult, they will be on the water in the evening although not in large numbers. My personal experience with this insect, at least as a dry, has been frustrating. I can count on one hand the number of fish I have taken on dry imitations of this caddis.

A couple of years ago I began experimenting with different nymph patterns to try and imitate the insect. After a lot of false starts, I came up with a size 8 Serendipity. This is perhaps the simplest caddis nymph there is, but it has proved to be absolute dynamite on Rock Creek in the fall. It can be dead drifted on the bottom for big browns or fished as a wet fly to imitate an ovipositing caddis. In either case, we've had a lot of success with the pattern.

The orange caddis stays with us until the snow starts to fly. As soon as the ice and snow start to build up on the banks, both the trout and the an glers seem to go into hibernation. The cycle has been completed, and we are back into the stone fly larva on the bottom we started with. If you're planning to fish Rock Creek at any time during the year, the techniques and patterns discussed here should help to make your experience more enjoyable. Even if you're a dryfly bigot, remember that there will be times when there is no dry fly fishing. And if you're going to fish and want to catch something other than a cold, you're going to have to go under the surface. And when you do, you will be surprised both by how challenging it is and by how rewarding it is.

**About the author:** Doug Persico is the owner of Rock Creek Fisherman's Mercantile, located at:

15995 Rock Creek Road
Clinton, MT 59825 (Exit Interstate 90 at Exit 126)
(406) 825-6440

The Blackfoot River (See Highway 200 – Northwest Montana, page 67.).

# 4
# ROCKY MOUNTAIN FRONT

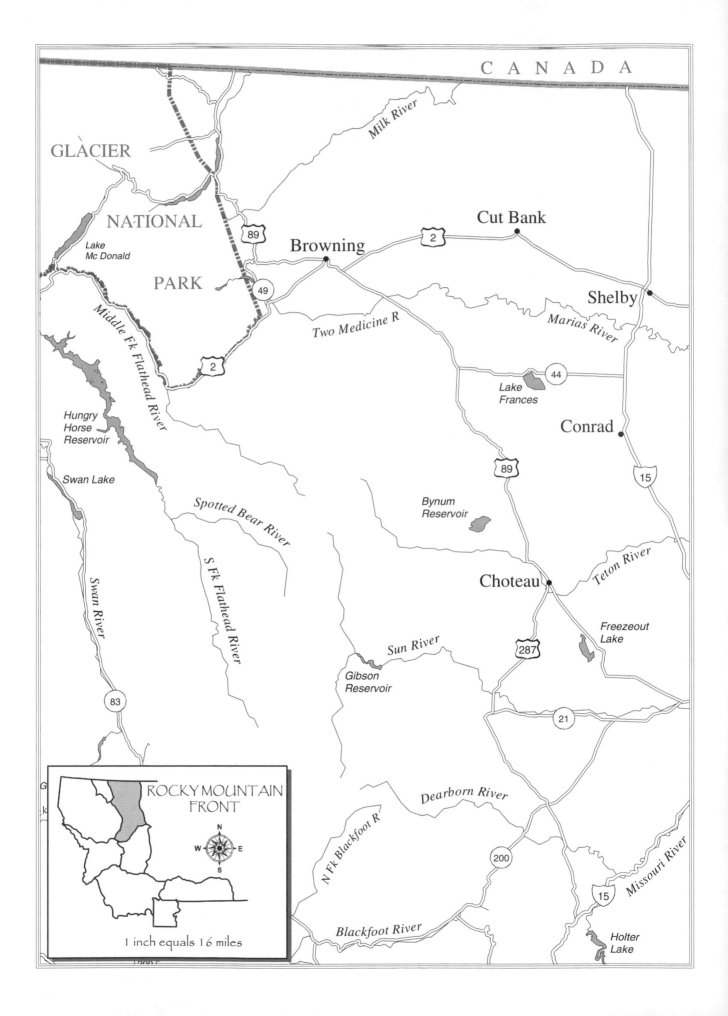

The Rocky Mountain Front has always stood as a fortress or battlement to challenge travelers plying their way across the vast and sweeping prairies. Extending from the eastern flanks of Glacier National Park to the Missouri River in the Helena area, this towering mountain range encompasses one of the most awesome wilderness areas in Montana. With more than 1.5 million acres of towering peaks, nestled lakes and pristine streams, travelers by foot or horseback may weave their way across the Continental Divide in Glacier National Park, the Great Bear Wilderness, the Bob Marshall Wilderness and the Scapegoat Wilderness.

It is easy to imagine native Americans following the bison across this vast grassland at the entrance to the Rocky Mountain Front. With a sparse population of 2.8 people per square mile, and cattle outnumbering people 10 to one, the area still retains its heritage as both cattle country and farm country, most notably in barley and wheat. Three rivers flow out of the Front. The first of these is the Dearborn River, which is closest to Highway 200 (the main artery which connects Missoula and Great Falls). The Upper Dearborn River is restricted to trail access only. The trailhead is just that – a trailhead. The small parking area restricts camping. The Lower Dearborn River meanders through private ranchland and may only be floated in good water years. The next drainage is the South Fork and North Fork of the Sun River, both of which are accessed from the town of Augusta. The final river to drain this wilderness extravaganza is the Teton River, accessed from the

town of Choteau. Finally, the visiting angler has the opportunity of fishing the Blackfoot Indian Reservation, which is the gateway to the East Entrance of the Park and offers excellent rainbow trout fishing in the reservoirs.

**Upper Dearborn River – Devils Glen**
**General location:** Highway 200 north of Lincoln and south of Augusta on the Rocky Mountain Front.

The Bob Marshall Wilderness

**Directions:** From Missoula take Highway 200 north past the town of Lincoln and over Rogers Pass. After crossing the Middle Fork of the Dearborn, watch for a highway crossing. To the right (south) will be a paved road 19 miles to Wolf Creek and the Missouri River. Turn left (north) on county road #434, a graded dirt road, 11.4 miles to the intersection to **Bean Lake**. At 11.4 miles turn left and go seven-tenths of a mile to Bean Lake. Continue on Dearborn River Road #577 past Bean Lake to the canyon trailhead, a distance of 5.1 miles. Bean Lake is a small, popular pothole lake and good fishing for stocked rainbows in the early summer.

**Trailhead:** Located on BLM land, the trailhead prohibits overnight camping and offers only an outhouse and a hitching rail. The trail to the canyon and National Forest land passes through private property, so please stay off the private road and on the designated trail. At the trailhead the USFS sign states that it is 1.8 miles to National Forest land. However, at three-quarters of a mile from the

Pauline and Shadow soak up the beauty of the upper Dearborn River.

trailhead, the trail crosses the Dearborn River on a newly constructed bridge. The property owner's sign next to the bridge claims three miles of private property after the bridge crossing. Regardless of which sign is accurate, the first campsite is approximately four miles from the trailhead.

**Backcountry Camping:** One of the gateways to the Scapegoat Wilderness, the Dearborn River plunges over granite rock out of the Rocky Mountain Front. The mountains command your attention. Steep and rugged, the river-carved granite presents a stark contrast to the rolling prairie grasslands and pocket lakes just a few miles away. Cross-

ing the bridge by the last summer cabin a little less than a mile from the trailhead, the trail winds its way up the northern side of the river to the first spectacular view of the canyon. The timeless art of water-carved rock inspires a moment of reflection before pushing up the trail. From the trailhead to the bridge is a 25-minute hike. From the bridge to the first campsite is about a 45-minute hike. About five minutes up the trail from the first campsite, the trail forks down to the river past a second nice campsite. Just past this campsite on this spur trail, the trail crosses the river to a large flat area, which can accommodate a number of campers. Another mile or two above this fork, the trail climbs up a steep-walled canyon past Devils Glen, a carved canyon of granite at the base of Steamboat Mountain. After you cross a steep slide of shale, the trail follows close to the river again and offers a number of shaded campsites in a narrow part of the canyon. The trail offers an easy to moderate hike for all ages.

Although this creek-sized river appears to be a sterile environment of rock pools and slides in gin-clear water, the fish are fairly abundant. However, do not come looking for the more common riffle-pool run. Instead, plan on fishing pools and pockets with very short riffles in between. The pools, with vertical rock cliffs on both sides can be quite restrictive. Scrambling around the ledges, hide behind rock outcroppings and make your first cast be your best shot. If your cast is delicate, you may raise a small 10- to 12-inch rainbow fanning just under the surface in the shadows of sheer rock ledges. If you are lucky, you may bring up one of the big boys hugging the bottom of the pool, 10 to 15 feet below your fly. The best time to fish this giant rock garden is late August through September, when detours up and around these mini canyons are minimized and the hoppers are crackling everywhere. I found the fishing to be both challenging and novel. After fishing for about three hours, I never succeeded in bringing up one of the big rainbows from the bottom, but I did talk to a fly fisherman who had landed an 18-inch rainbow on a hopper towards evening.

## South Fork of the Sun River • Nilan Reservoir

**General location:** West of the town of Augusta

Nilan Reservoir

**Directions:** From Highway 200 take the Four Corners Junction north on Highway 287. (The opposite direction would take you to the Missouri River at Wolf Creek.) From the junction the town of Augusta is 20 miles and Glacier National Park is 135 miles. When you enter the small cow town of Augusta, follow the road to Nilan Reservoir, seven miles from town.

### South Fork of the Sun River, Benchmark Campground and airfield

The Benchmark access to the South Fork of the Sun River is actually the headwaters of the South Fork. From the town of Augusta, Nilan Reservoir is

seven miles, and Benchmark's trailhead is 32 miles. **Nilan Reservoir** is considered by many to be the premiere reservoir in the Rocky Mountain Front; however, it is best fished in the early spring and fall, as the heat of summer drives the fish to the deeper water and they become quite unresponsive. The two most popular hatches are damselflies and the Callibaetis hatch in June and mid-July. The reservoir is heavily stocked with fingerlings and by the following spring they have grown to between 10 and 12 inches. Each year fly fishers ply the water in kick-boats and belly-boats to catch 6- to 7-pound rainbows and browns right off the shoreline with nymphs. Be cautious, however, because Nilan is renowned for high winds.

### Wood Lake

Wood Lake is nine miles above Nilan Reservoir and offers camping and fair fishing in a small lake. **Benchmark Campground** is 15 miles above Nilan Reservoir. Although Wood Creek holds fish, they are tiny and not really worth fishing, unless you have children. A number of primitive campsites can be found along this road. In addition, Double Falls

Campground offers an outhouse and a few picnic tables in a beautifully secluded spot on Wood Creek. **Benchmark Runway:** Built in 1966 as a joint-funding effort between the Forest Service, the Federal Aviation Agency and the Montana Aeronautics Commission, this 6,000-foot runway was constructed for

An enchanting creek in the Bob Marshall Wilderness

both public recreation and administration of the national forests in the area. At an elevation of 5,309 feet, the runway is often empty due to the wind shear factor in the area. Benchmark Campground provides 25 campsites with trailer restrictions above 22 feet. It is a fee area and provides toilets and water.

### Benchmark Trailhead
The trailhead offers trailer parking, loading ramps

and feeding areas for live stock. The trail follows the South Fork down to Gibson Reservoir. About seven miles down the trail, the trail crosses the West Fork of the South Fork of the Sun River.

### West Fork of the South Fork of the Sun River
Sadly, I never made it to the West Fork of the Sun. I did, however, speak to a ranger who told me the West Fork was good fishing for smaller cutthroats.

## South Fork and North Fork of the Sun River • Gibson Reservoir

**General location:** The trailhead is west of Augusta, Montana, which is north of Highway 200, the connecting highway for Missoula and Great Falls.

**Directions:** From Augusta to Gibson Reservoir is 26 miles. Take Highway 287 north. Just outside of Augusta, take the turn-off to the left, which leads to Willow Creek Reservoir. The reservoir is 5.3 miles from the highway turnoff. The road is a dirt road for 19 miles. Drive past Willow Creek Reservoir to the campground at the base of Gibson Reservoir, or turn right, cross the bridge and follow the road up and over the mountain to Mortimer Gulch Campground, which establishes the trailhead for the Sun River.

### Willow Creek Reservoir
A treeless, barren lake just off the road to Gibson Reservoir, the reservoir does hold stocked trout, but it is more popular as a recreation lake for water-skiers and jet-boat enthusiasts.

### Sun River
Much of the prairie lands in the Augusta and Choteau area did not attract a large number of homesteaders after it was opened in 1862. Once the prime river-bottom land was claimed, the re-

maining lands were dry and wind-swept. Adding to this was the area's bleak and chilling winters. Typical government homestead offerings of 160 or 320 acres could not sustain a small rancher or farmer without irrigation water. The first irrigation project, completed in 1918, brought renewed interest to the area. The Bureau of Reclamation concluded that, in order to bring prosperity to the area, the Sun River would need to be dammed. With the completion of the Gibson Reservoir in 1929, the area enticed new settlers to the region. Today Gibson Reservoir provides boating and fishing recreation to residents and visitors. More importantly, it is the trailhead for the North Fork of the Sun River and the South Fork of the Sun River, as well as the majestic Bob Marshall Wilderness. Although some fair to poor fishing may be experienced across the grasslands that the Sun River

Gibson Dam

traverses, for the most part the river is restricted by private property.

## ⬛⬛⬛⬛ Gibson Reservoir

Gibson Reservoir offers a boat launch, Mortimer Gulch Campground, and a horse facility. Just above the boat launch, Trail 201 leads seven miles to the head of the lake. For day hikers wishing to fish the North Fork of the Sun River, plan on a three-hour hike. Although the trail is not arduous and mostly level, horse people need to be forewarned that the trail follows along the contours of the lake, and for about 30 minutes of travel time the trail is chiseled out of solid rock, high above the lake's waters, often with little room to pass or maneuver.

One of the first scenic areas to camp on the lake may be reached in just a little more than an hour, and it offers both shoreline and shade. At the head of the lake, the trail forks to the right up over a saddle and down into the North Fork drainage. Trail 201 continues to the confluence of the North Fork and the South Fork, approximately two miles.

Trail 201 ascends the north side of the valley mountainside cresting at a saddle, which offers a splendid view of the South Fork drainage. Hikers pass through two gates as they descend down through aspen groves and the early summer abundance of wildflowers. From mid-June through early July, plan on seeing a host of wildflowers representing the color palate. On my trip on June 11, 2000, I noted wild roses, sunflowers, orchids, iris, Indian Paint Brush, lupine, and my favorite, the shooting star. I wish I could take photographs of all the beautiful flowers that I am sure I had never seen before, but my lead donkey, Buddy, becomes impatient and pushes me when I pause, and Banjo also usually resorts to some impatient mischief when I stop.

Although I did not travel very far inside the Bob Marshall Wilderness designation, the river beckons with promise. I would estimate that I walked nine miles before I viewed the **North Fork of the Sun River**. Camped on a bluff overlooking the river, I fished for only 30 minutes before I was drenched

The road to Gibson Reservoir overlooking the Sun River

with a chilling rainstorm. Although I caught one small cutthroat, it was difficult fishing during the silted runoff. Nonetheless, the North Fork is considered good fishing for nice-sized cutthroats. The next morning I broke camp and headed back to meet Trail 201 to the South Fork of the Sun.

### South Fork of the Sun River

Trail 201 continues following the lake shore past the narrow cliffs that back up the North Fork and the South Fork. At the head of the lake the North Fork tumbles past the K-Bar-L Guest Ranch. Relocated in 1927 with the construction of the Gibson Dam, the ranch was originally patented in the 1880s under Soldier's Script. The ranch, supplied with natural energy systems, offers a traditional guest ranch in the heart of a wilderness. Owned and managed by third- and fourth-generation members of the Klick family, the ranch is only reached by boat or by trail. Passing through the Klick Ranch, hikers will enter the Bob Marshall Wilderness about a mile above the bridge over the North Fork and just above a series of rapids. From this juncture the trail splits. The lower trail is the low-water trail and it fords the river within the first mile and winds its way up the South Fork to Benchmark. I camped where the two trails split. The upper trail circumvents the canyon on its way 14 miles to Benchmark. At this same junction a third trail leads eight miles to Bear Lake, which offers excellent fishing for 10-inch cutthroats.

The best fishing in this area is just up from the Klick Ranch, where the South Fork of the Sun backs up to the cascading rapids. During the spring when the water is high, boaters motor the seven miles right up to the confluence and drop anchor. Fishing mostly with bait and roe, they catch a lot of small cutthroats that mingle around just below the rapids. Later when the water drops, the boaters have to hike up the trail a little ways. Having been "skunked" due to the high and roiled water above the falls, that evening I couldn't resist moving down to the slower water, where all the boats had been anchored. (I dare say many of you, too, would succumb to this fish-pond mentality if you had hiked upwards of 15 miles in two days and found yourself cheerless having caught only one dink.)

I attached an "Oscar-the-Grouch" look-alike. It was bright green, two inches long, had big bulbous eyes, as well as yellow rubber legs. Well, I thought, that should be heavy enough to pull down my San

Juan worm to the bottom. To my surprise, on the very first cast, I caught my first 10-inch cutthroat on this frightful Woolly Bugger. On the third cast I caught another 10-incher on the San Juan. In 30 minutes I had caught six cutthroats and one grayling.

Off in the distance I heard the supper bell on the Klink Ranch. I knew that it did not toll for me, and that the guests were going to sit down to a delicious ranch meal, but one mile away in a small meadow next to the river, I was content. I look forward to returning.

Before I left, my camp was inspected by a game warden. I queried him about the fishing reports that the South Fork was only fair fishing above the Klick Ranch. He had no insights, although he conceded that he would only describe the South Fork as fair, unlike the North Fork, which he rated good to excellent. He did acknowledge that the West Fork of the South Fork of the Sun offered good fishing up in the meadow section.

I must say that my donkeys were fairly well-behaved the first two days, but on our return Banjo started

acting up long before I got to the granite cliff section. This was the first trip handling both donkeys by myself. I tied Banjo's lead rope to Buddy's pack with a slipknot. Each time we came to a rivulet trickling across the trail, Buddy would flair his nos-

North Fork of the Sun River

The author and his two donkeys, Buddy and Banjo

trils and leap forward. Right behind him Banjo would react by jumping back. What a mess this created. A number of times the rope did not slip, and I had a tug-of-war between the two asses. Finally, I gave up and completely unhooked Banjo and let him walk as a free agent. When I got to the cliff section, I fretted about what to do with two critters. The trail is literally blasted out of sheer rock high above the lake, not to mention the fact that it is very narrow in places. Would Banjo behave better and create less

Trailhead to Bear Lake

tension if we passed someone on the trail and he was free to freak-out or hug close to Buddy and myself? Or would I be able to keep control of him if I tied him to Buddy with a serious knot? Every time I came to a blind corner, I nervously called out and listened for a reply. Gradually, my confidence grew as I gingerly led these two donkeys closer to the end of the cliff section.

The trail in one spot descended straight down to the water's edge and another blind corner. We rounded the corner and headed straight up the cliff again. Nearing the crest about 80 yards away, I could see the trail was vacant for another 100 yards. I breathed a sight of relief. Suddenly the pressure of

the climb proved too much for Buddy, and he cut wind so loud he shattered Banjo's poking complacency. Head to butt, naturally Banjo jumped backwards. On hearing loose rock dropping down to the water below, Buddy panicked and lunged forward. Banjo, overwhelmed with fear, naturally followed his flight instinct, spun around and galloped back down the trail hell-bent for leather. I yelled, but it was no use. I prayed that no one would be on the trail behind us, as Banjo bucked and kicked around the blind corner. By the time I found a root on the side of the cliff to tie up Buddy, Banjo came charging around the trail again. I was quite amazed that all of his packs were still securely tied. He ran up to me and buried his head in my chest as if to say, I'm sorry. I wasn't polite in sharing with him the frustration and anxiety he had caused me. The cute donkey routine just didn't cut it. Ah, dear reader, I know by now you must by thinking to yourself, is this guy reckless, irresponsible, crazy, foolhardy, or just experiencing beginner's luck? I, too, am beginning to raise those questions.

### Teton River
**General location:** Like the Sun River, the Teton River winds its way out of a canyon to meet the rolling prairie west of the town of Choteau.

### West Fork of the Teton River
Take Highway 89 north of Choteau towards Browning. At mile marker 46.5 turn left (west) to

wards Eureka Reservoir. The turn-off for the reservoir is 2.7 miles from the highway. At 17.5 miles the paved road splits to the South Fork or continues ahead for the West Fork of the Teton River. Follow this road until the bridge crossing above a campground. Follow the trailhead into the wilderness section for fair to good fishing for 6- to 12-inch cutthroats. The main stem of the Teton River was scoured in the flood of 1964, and subsequent flood years wiped out the river's holding water and insect populations.

Mission Lake on the Blackfeet Indian Reservation

### Eureka Reservoir

A treeless, barren lake just off the road to the West Fork of the Teton River, the reservoir holds stocked trout, but it is more popular as a recreation lake for water skiers and jet-boat enthusiasts. The lake has eight to 10 campsites and some outhouses.

### Blackfeet Indian Reservation

Out of the way for most Montana visitors, the Blackfeet Indian Reservation east of Glacier National Park offers some of the finest still-water fishing in the state. Consider yourself lucky if you arrive on a day without bone-chilling winds. If you are willing to brace yourself against the elements, the reservation offers a bounty of rainbows and browns in the trophy class. The Blackfeet pride themselves on their fishing resources. In 1999 they planted 470,462 fish on the reservation's waters. Duck Lake received over 50,000 rainbow trout in the spring, and Mission Lake received 107,448 kokanee salmon, not to mention close to 60,000 rainbow trout. Planted trout grow big and fast in these pothole lakes on the prairie. It is not uncommon for 7-inch fingerlings to reach 18 inches in two years and up to 10 pounds at maturity in five to six years. The most popular lakes and reservoirs are Duck Lake, Kipp Lake and Mission Lake. A tribal fishing permit is required. Contact the Blackfeet Fish and Game Department for Blackfeet Tribal Licensed Outfitters:

Blackfeet Fish and Game Department
P.O. Box 850
Browning, Montana 59417
(406) 338-7207

Camping is permitted only on tribally-owned campgrounds or on private property with the owner's permission. Motels are located in Browning, Cut Bank, East Glacier and St. Mary.

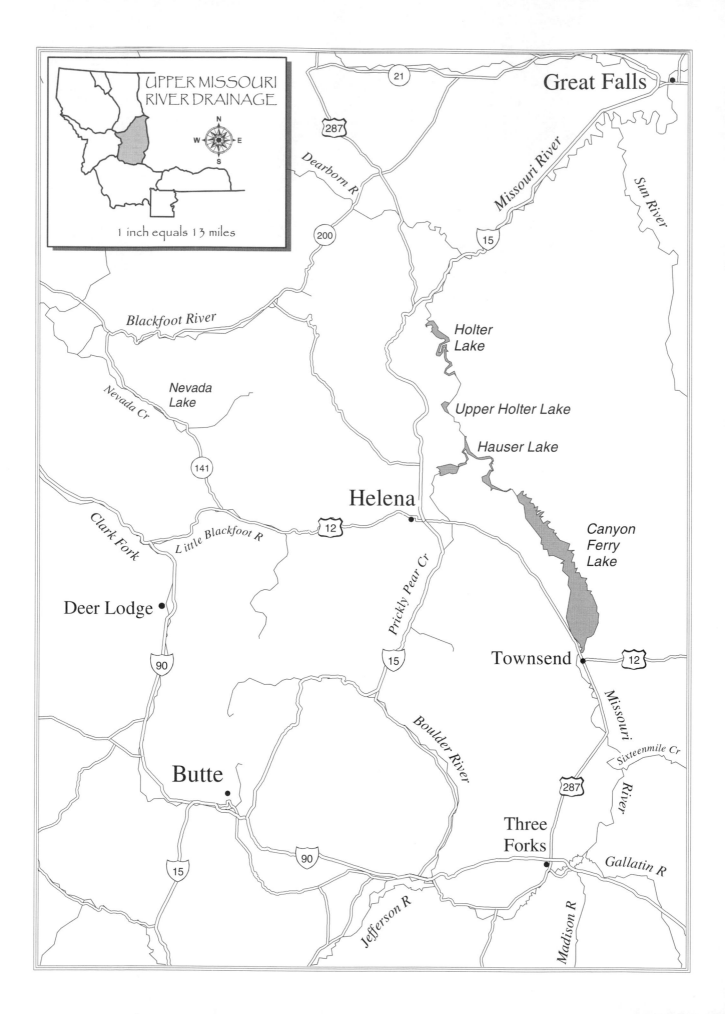

# UPPER MISSOURI RIVER DRAINAGE

To reach the upper Missouri River from Three Forks to Great Falls, take Exit 278 from Interstate 90 to Highway 287. The mileage from Three Forks to Townsend is 31 miles, and it is 65 miles to Helena. The information covering the Upper Missouri River Basin follows Highway 287 north to Helena and then Interstate 15 from Helena to Great Falls.

The Missouri River provided a corridor of trade amongst the indigenous tribes along its 2,466-mile

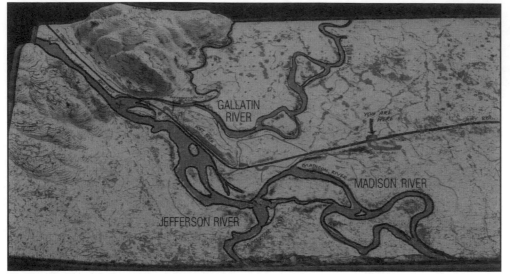

Three forks of the Missouri River

journey to the Mississippi River. Later, trappers, traders, gold seekers and settlers would follow this river thoroughfare to the gates of the Rocky Mountains and to the present-day town of Three Forks, where the Missouri is formed. From the days of the Lewis and Clark Expedition to the mid 1900s, the mighty Missouri River shifted and changed channels. Many of the original campsites of the Lewis and Clark Expedition are miles from the present riverbed. The Missouri River claimed many steamships as they plied their way up the river as far as Fort Benton. During the Depression, taming nearly 2,500 miles of the Missouri challenged the Corp of Engineers to safeguard against flooding and provide safer passage for boats plying the lower river.

The Fort Peck Dam and Reservoir, the second-largest earth-filled dam in the world, commenced construction in 1933 and was completed in 1941.

The 250-foot earthen dam, with a mile-long spillway, generates 185,000 kilowatts of electricity per year. At peak performance the generating plant discharges up to 250,000 cubic feet of water per second. Just a few years after its completion, the next ambitious project for the Army Corps of Engineers was the Canyon Ferry Project.

The Bureau of Reclamation's Canyon Ferry Project, authorized by Congress under the Flood Control Act of 1944, was completed in 1954. The snowpack drainage area covers 15,760 square miles. Canyon Ferry catches the annual spring runoff to prevent flooding downstream, generating 425 million kilowatts hours annually, as well as providing irrigation water and recreational opportunities. The concrete dam is 225 feet high and 1,000 feet long at its crest. The U.S. Army Corp of Engineers estimates that the project has prevented $93 million in flood damages from 1950 to 1996. The first and smallest of the dams is Toston Dam, which is a large diversion dam 20 miles north of Three Forks. The next downstream dam is the Canyon Ferry Dam, followed by Hauser Dam and then Holter Dam.

For opponents of the damn Corps of Engineers, one only has to look to the Big Horn River and the Missouri to be reminded that cooler water in the summer and controlled flows in the spring provide great trout fishing opportunities. The added benefits of the upper Missouri system of reservoirs is the spring migratory spawning runs of rainbows in the 6- to 10-pound class, along with the fall browns, which exceed this weight. From each impoundment, huge trout head upriver looking for spawning beds between dams. Few places in Montana offer the fly fisher such opportunities for trophy-sized trout as the upper Missouri River.

## Missouri Headwaters State Park

Three miles east of Three Forks, the park is open year-round and offers 20 campsites for both tents and trailers. Water, toilets, hiking trails and a rough boat launch are also available. Three Forks KOA Kampground is a few miles south of Three Forks on the road to Ennis. Drouillard Campground and boat ramp on the Jefferson River provides a primitive campground or resting spot just off Interstate 90. Take Highway 287 south for one mile and make a left turn heading east to Three Forks, which is three miles. The campground is less than a half-mile and is to the left as you cross the Jefferson River.

Missouri Headwaters State Park

## Canyon Ferry Lake Recreation Area

Canyon Ferry Lake offers 13 campgrounds and nine day-use-only sites. Half of the campgrounds are fee areas, which provide water, toilets, tables, grills and boat ramps. All of the campgrounds are on a first-come basis. Three of the campgrounds offer group-use sites. Most of the campgrounds are accessible from Highway 12 / 287, the main route to Helena.

If you are a tent camper, head towards the dam and turn south on West Shore Drive, one mile past Yacht Basin Marina, to Fish Hawk Campground, which is restricted to tents only and offers six sites, and more importantly, shade and toilets, although it lacks water. The eastern shoreline has four campgrounds evenly distributed (Jo Bonner, Hellgate, Goose Bay and Confederate). Follow the East Shoreline Drive, which may be reached off Highway 12 just outside of Townsend or the Highway 284 cut-off towards Helena, or cross the dam and pick up the East Shore Drive by Chinamen's Gulch. Shade is scarce along the lake, but campers may find both shade and a little more tranquility at Jo Bonner Campground, which is just a few miles south of the dam on the East Shore Drive. The Bureau of Land Management has published an excellent map of the Canyon Ferry Lake Recreation Area. Write:

BLM
7661 Canyon Ferry Road
Helena, Montana 59602

For fishing licenses and up-to-date fishing information contact::

Yacht Basin Marina
3555 West Shore Drive
Helena, MT 59602
(406) 475-3440

Kim's Marina
8015 Canyon Ferry Road
Helena, MT 59602
(406) 475-3723

Goose Bay Marina
300 Goose Bay Road
Townsend, MT 59644
(406) 266-3645

### Trident (Headwaters State Park) to Toston

One would only have to look down from a helicopter during spring and early summer to understand the powerful forces of spring run-off, which shapes the meandering channels each year. Once the Missouri is formed from the Jefferson, Madison and the Gallatin, the newly-formed river is big, flat and turbid. The riverbed, up to 100 yards wide in some places, is scoured each spring leaving behind bleached banks with few trees. Bank fishers at the headwaters are synonymous with bait fishers, and in truth, these leisurely, arm-chair fishermen pull in an occasionally large trout with their patience. For the summer fly fisher, however, thermal heating on the lower Madison coupled with the heat of summer in an arid area drives water temperatures to the critical low 70s. The area features dry hillsides with sparse junipers, eroded riverbanks and low vegetation. This seemingly barren stretch, however, does contain a healthy population of large rainbows and browns, as well as impressive numbers of whitefish, carp and rough fish. The problem, however, is that in proportion to its size, the trout get scattered over a large volume of water. In my mind, this is not a viable stretch of water for the one-time fisher wanting to fish Montana's mighty Missouri.

Missouri Headwaters State Park is reached from Exit 278 on Interstate 90 at Three Forks. The only public river access between the park and Toston Dam is the Fairweather fishing access in the Clarkston Valley, which is nestled between the Belt Mountains and the Elkhorn Mountains. The boat launch has been washed out at Fairweather. The water slams into a five-foot bank, making it next to impossible to stop and unload your craft. To reach this fishing access, drive by the Trident Plant at the end of the park, cross the railroad tracks and follow the county road 1.9 miles to where it forks to the left. From the Trident Plant to Fairweather Fishing Access is a distance of 11.3 miles. Norman Strung in his book, *Fishing the Headwaters of the Missouri*, recommends big streamers for the pools and deep holes. He also suggests trolling the streamers by casting upstream as you float downstream. At the same time twitch or jig the streamer with an upward motion of the rod tip. Launching from the boat ramp in the state park, the float time to Toston Dam is a long day with an early start, if you don't have an outboard to push you along. Toston Dam backs up water for almost five miles!

Most fishers fish deep with heavy spoons or Rapalas, streamers, night crawlers or sucker meat.

### MM 90: Toston Dam

From Highway 287 look for the dirt access road on the eastern side of the highway. Follow the road five miles to Lower Toston Dam Recreation Site, which offers a boat ramp to the river, outhouses, and picnic tables. Above the dam is another boat ramp with a picnic facility. I feel it is only fair to say that this site is generally unattractive, but I am reminded that beauty is in the eyes of the beholder. Just above the dam the Lewis and Clark Expedition camped on July 25, 1805. According to the historical marker, Lewis and Clark had been looking for this spot from the description given to them by the Mandans in North Dakota. The Indians had described significant landmarks and cliffs for the Little Gates of the Mountains, the second chain of Rocky Mountains that approach the river. The more notable Gates of the Rocky Mountains are located approximately 60 miles downstream.

## Toston Dam to Townsend

Located about halfway between Three Forks and Canyon Ferry, the dam stops the fall spawning run of brown trout. This section is popular with anglers during the fall, but it is closed from March 1 to June 15 to protect the spring spawners. Some of the local sportsmen motor upriver from Toston Dam for a day of fishing and duck hunting (Blast and Cast). What the area lacks in numbers of fish is made up for in the solitude above the dam. Fishing from the Toston Dam to the bridge at Toston is popular with bank fishers and floaters. From Toston to the Deepdale Access, however, is restricted to float fishers, as the river flows through the scenic Toston Valley and heavily posted lands. This entire section of river offers broken water, riffles, runs and pools. Below the dam from Canyon Ferry to the Deepdale fishing access, large numbers of migrant browns make their runs and provide fall fishing for anglers seeking trophy sized trout.

## MM 89: Crow Creek

The road leading to the fishable sections of Crow Creek is just across from the exit to the small community of Toston. Public fishing begins in the Helena National Forest above the town of Radersburg. Unlike western Montana, the upper Missouri River does not offer an abundance of good fishing creeks. For this reason, Crow Creek, Beaver Creek and Little Prickly Pear Creek get fished fairly heavily during the summer. In spite of this pressure, Crow Creek offers good fishing for 7- to 10-inch rainbows and brookies, with the occasional fat rainbow.

## MM 81.5: Deepdale Fishing Access

Deepdale provides a lovely campground under a canopy of cottonwoods. In addition to the campground, a cement boat launch is provided.

To access the Missouri River as it enters Canyon Ferry Reservoir in Townsend, look for the bridge crossing on Highway 287 after the intersection with Highway 12. This section may also be accessed at the Indian Road Campground or the Cottonwood Campground west of town. This section is popular for both the spring and fall spawning runs, but be sure to check the fishing regulations. During the heat of summer some of the trout at the southern end of Canyon Ferry move upriver to escape the thermal heating on this shallow section of the reservoir.

## Deep Creek

From Townsend take Highway 12 east until the highway meets the creek as it drops down a steep canyon. The lower section flows through private property. The canyon section offers small pocket water for small rainbows and brook trout, but the highway is right next to the creek.

## Canyon Ferry Reservoir

Although fly fishers have good fishing during the spring for rainbows around the marinas and campgrounds at the upper end of the lake, the lake is best fished from a boat for rainbow trout, brown trout, perch, ling and walleye. Late April through the month of May is generally considered the best fishing from shore and boat. Plentifully stocked each year and drawing anglers year-round, Canyon Ferry is one of the most heavily fished reservoirs in the region. During the summer months, when surface action slows, boating enthusiasts enjoy this 25-mile-long stretch of water, which includes an island offering overnight camping.

## Beaver Creek

The easiest route to Beaver Creek is to cross Canyon Ferry and turn left to the base of the dam, which provides a campground and boat launch. Follow the York-Nelson dirt road north until it intersects with the Beaver Creek Road. Turning left will lead to the mouth of Beaver Creek at the Missouri, which is a popular spot during the spring. Turning right will take you to the headwaters in Refrigerator Canyon. Beaver Creek, along with Little Prickly Pear Creek, is one of the more popular creeks in the area and offers 10 miles of good fishing for 8- to 12-inch rainbows, a few good browns and a host of smaller brookies in the upper stretches.

## Canyon Ferry to Hauser Lake

From the base of the dam to Hauser Lake, a little more than a mile in length, boat fishers seek out good-sized rainbow trout from the comfort of their boats. This is big water. Holding large numbers of both resident and migratory trout, the area is heavily fished. Those fishers willing to face the blustery winds of fall may be rewarded with trophy-sized browns moving up from Hauser Lake. Hauser, like Canyon Ferry, offers year-round fishing with 3,700 acres of water

## MM 70: Silos Campground

One mile off the highway, look for pronghorn antelope grazing in the fields. In addition to the BLM public campground, campers may also camp and shop at the Silos Campground and Grocery, which also provides boat rentals.

## White Earth Campground

Just a few miles north on Highway 287 is the White Earth Campground. Exit at Winston and take the Beaver Creek Road 5.5 miles to the lakeshore campground, which also offers a nice boat ramp.

## MM 51.6: McClellan Creek

Folks, unless you have small children and you are visiting or live in the Helena area, pass this one up. It is a tiny creek that flows out of the mountains west of Helena to join Prickly Pear Creek just south of East Helena. Drive eight miles back into the mountains to reach public lands. The creek is small and produces very small brook trout and rainbows.

## Helena, Prickly Pear Creek

Here is a little brushy creek outside of Helena, which offers both small trout and a few good-sized migratory trout. More aptly described as a "crick", this small body of water wanders out of the mountains sandwiched between Interstate 15 and old Highway 15 through mostly residential developments. Nonetheless, access is available in isolated spots from the old Highway 15 south of Montana City.

Eight inches deep and eight feet across during late summer, Prickly Pear Creek's best lower access is at Ash Grove Corridor. From Montana City, follow the road that crosses over Interstate 15. The road swings away from Interstate 15 following a narrow ravine east of the Interstate. Ash Grove corridor is a trashy, willow-lined section of the creek above the ARCO Plant property. The best fishing is from the mouth of McClellan to Ash Grove.

The road and creek continues down through the rolling hills to meet East Helena. This loop road exits right across from the Conoco gas station in East Helena. One of the state fish biologists that I spoke to told me that the creek has been losing ground on the numbers of migratory fish moving up the creek from Lake Helena, but the opportunity still exists for landing something much larger than a resident dink.

## Helena-Area Mountain Lakes and Smaller Reservoirs

### Spring Meadow Lake State Park

This park is located on the western edge of Helena and provides fun fishing for children, as well as offering swimming and wildlife viewing. The lake is encircled by a nature trail. The 30-acre spring-fed lake provides good fishing opportunities for perch, bass and rainbows. The lake is open to non-motorized boats only. Take Highway 12 west and turn north on Joslyn towards the Country Club.

### Northern Pacific Reservoir (Quarry Pond)

From East Helena take McClellan Creek Road, which is the loop road to Montana City that joins Interstate 15. Look for the gravel road turn-off and procede another half-mile to this 15-acre reservoir, which lies close to Interstate 15. The reservoir offers good fishing for 7- to 10-inch rainbows.

### Park Lake

A small three- to four-acre alpine lake, Park Lake is nestled in an alpine setting less than 15 miles from Helena. The lake fishes well for stocked rainbow trout in the 7- to 12-inch range, along with some fair-sized grayling. The lake is restricted to non-motorized watercraft and offers 22 camp sites. Travel south on Interstate 15 to the Clancy exit. Follow Lump Gulch Road (Forest Service Road #4009) to the lake.

## Interstate 15 – Helena to Great Falls

### Hauser Lake

From Interstate 15, 13 miles east of Helena, turn off on Exit 200 to Hauser Dam on Lincoln Road. Hauser Lake is a popular summer recreation lake. Just six miles down from Canyon Ferry Reservoir, this 3,700-acre lake offers good fishing for trout, kokanee, walleye and perch. The only campground on the lake is Black Sandy Beach Campground, and it should be considered a boater's campground. The campground offers 30 campsites, toilets and a boat launch. On the route to the dam, you will drive by Lake Helena. Lake Helena is a 2,100-acre Bureau of Reclamation reservoir. It is carp-infested, as well as holding tons of rough fish. It does have some numbers of rainbows, but local fishers generally shun this algae-infested impoundment. From the Interstate to Hauser Dam is 9.5 miles.

### Trout Creek

Reached from Hauser Lake from the York Bridge crossing onto the York-Trout Creek Road, the creek passes by many new residential houses until the visiting angler reaches the canyon section. The creek offers fairly good fishing for both rainbows and brookies. The creek may also be reached by taking the York Road at the base of the Canyon Ferry Dam.

### Hauser Dam to Upper Holter Lake

Although never really a secret, this section enjoyed relatively little pressure through the years. During the past 10 years, however, increasing numbers of fly fishers have congregated on this four- to five-mile section both for the spring run of rainbows from March to mid-April and the fall brown runs, which generally run from mid-October through the end of November. Fish with a nymph and a strike indicator during the spring. During the summer dry-fly enthusiasts will find excellent evening hatches, and standard attractor patterns work as well. The road dead-ends at the dam with limited parking, but an outhouse is provided.

The Montana Power Company provides access to trails on both sides of the river downstream from the dam. Fishing is excellent until June when large volumes of water are released from the dam due to spring run-off. Large migratory rainbows from Holter Lake move through this stretch. On an exploratory trip in late March, I walked down the eastside trail about a half-mile and watched a lone nymph fisherman land a hefty rainbow on a very cold, blustery day. Perched on the trail high above him, I could see three other large rainbows in the shallows within 20 feet of where he was standing. They all ignored his offerings until he nailed a big hen. The trail leads down the east side about three miles to Beaver Creek, which is the next access point that may be reached by road. (See directions from the Canyon Ferry Dam.)

## Holter Lake

Leave Interstate 15 at Exit 226 at Wolf Creek, which is about 28 miles north of Helena. Holter Lake, covering over 4,800 surface acres of water, winds its way a number of miles to the Gates of the Mountains and then beyond to Upper Holter Lake. The lake is best fished deep with trolling methods. Access to the lake for shore fishing is provided by the Beartooth Road on the east side of the lake, which also provides campgrounds and boat launches. The section known as the Gates of the Mountains provides spectacular scenery of towering cliffs that rise above the water to merge with Montana's Big Sky. Upper Holter Lake may be reached from Exit 209. Holter Lake, considered the most scenic of the man-made lakes, is surrounded by the Beartooth Wildlife Management Area on the eastern side of the lake and the Sleeping Giant Wilderness Study Area on the western side of the lake.

Holter Lake provides three campgrounds on the Beartooth Road on the eastern side of the lake. The first of these campgrounds is **Log Gulch Campground**. The campground offers 80 camping sites, the majority of which are most suited for tents. Many of the sites have shade and a swimming area.

## Exit 226: Holter Dam (Wolf Creek) to Craig to Cascade

State fish biologists sadly noted the presence of whirling disease in 1999 on this most famous stretch of the Missouri River. Since other areas of the state have not been decimated like the Madison River debacle, devotees have taken a wait-and-see attitude. Typical catches range from 10 to 16-inches, although 16- to 18-inch trout are not uncommon. During the spring when the dam spills over the top, still-water fish drop over to visit their river cousins, and local anglers congregate in large numbers to greet both of them. From Holter Dam the river freely courses its way 90 miles to Great Falls. The best blue-ribbon trout fishing is found between the dam and the town of Cascade. Punctuated by few riffles, the river is wide and flat and holds an abundance of rainbows and smaller numbers of browns. The water slows as it nears the Smith River, and the river loses both clarity and riffles. Trout populations plummet from this point downstream.

From personal experience, I would have to say the Missouri River challenges first-time visitors a great deal more than other famous rivers in Montana. Float fisherman will have the greatest advantage due to the sheer size of the river. Fish the scum-lines in backwater eddies, weed beds and the tail-end of islands. Pods of trout will follow these shifting scum lines, which channel the bugs in a large rotation. Sometimes a raft or a drift boat will actually depress or break up these slow patches of foam and disperse the feeding trout. Look ahead and see if it is possible to drop anchor or beach your boat. Start with the tail end of the foam and work your way forward. Look carefully for noses and the tops of dorsal fins. Lunkers like these Lazy-Susan luncheons. During early summer don't hesitate to try smaller attractor patterns such as a Royal Wulff, a yellow Humpy or a Renegade during the evening hours.

Known for its prolific hatches, the early season is best fished with Wooly Buggers until the arrival of the Baetis hatch in April and May. Baetis like the slower water in the weed beds along the banks and will typically emerge during midday with an evening spinner fall. Stick to a size 18. When I have to scale down to a size 20 Blue-Wing Olive, I instead switch to a size 20 Parachute Adams. Following on the heels of the Baetis hatch, as is typical of most Montana rivers, is the arrival of caddis followed by PMDs. These two hatches are the most important summer hatches followed by the appearance of Tricos in the latter stages of summer, which emerge in the morning with the spinner fall typically an hour or two later between 8 and 10 AM.

As is typical in most flat-water rivers, long leaders and small tippets prevail, along with sighs of disappointment when a fat rainbow pops off in the deceptively strong current. During the dog days of summer, hoppers and droppers work best, although I must confess that I personally search out other waters during those blistering hot days. With the arrival of fall, the Baetis re-emerge along with the tactic of tossing wooly buggers and streamers.

In his excellent book, *Flyfisher's Guide to Montana*, Greg Thomas reminds visitors that the vagaries of fishing the Missouri are most often attributed to water releases. A rapid raising of water level alters the feeding response of trout, which leaves them sulky for a day or two. The same is true on free-flowing rivers and streams. When the water crests and then drops gradually for a day or two, the fish go into a feeding frenzy. Thomas reports that the best flows for float fishing range from 5,500 cubic feet per second to 8,000 cfs, which is about four to five miles an hour. To optimize your fishing chances, he recommends calling one of the local fly shops for up-to-date information.

### Interstate 15 – Exit 226 (Wolf Creek): Little Prickly Pear Creek

In all of my forays to the Missouri River, I had never once stopped to fish the Little Prickly Pear Creek or read about it in the numerous fishing guide books that I have acquired through the years. Perhaps a few of my disappointing days on the Missouri could have been redeemed on this fine little creek. The creek is host to both migratory spawning rainbows and browns, along with a serious population of rattlesnakes. Sadly, the creek turned up its first reporting of whirling disease in 1999. The creek opens on the third Saturday in May and is good fishing for large rainbows returning to the river in the lower section from the town of Wolf Creek down to the river. Popular patterns for these spring spawners include Woolly Buggers, leech patterns and large Yuk Bugs. The creek is closed after Labor Day to protect brown trout spawning beds. Above the town of Wolf Creek, Little Prickly Pear Creek has fewer public access points as it moves through private land, except where it parallels Interstate 15. Fishing is generally considered good from the mouth of Canyon Creek to Sieben. Keep in mind, however, that permission is needed to fish private lands, and landowners no longer have to post their lands to warn against trespassing.

### Canyon Creek

A tributary of Little Prickly Pear Creek, the creek may be accessed along Highway 200, the Lincoln Highway. Although small and running mostly through private property, the creek is good fishing for 7- to 9-inch rainbows hiding under the brushy overhangs. The creek enters Little Prickly Pear Creek five miles north of Marysville.

# True Confessions of a Fly-Fishing Guide: Natural Selection

A while back I marveled to a colleague on the complexities of matching up 20 fishing clients with 10 guides in less than 30 minutes. Typically the clients are guests of a CEO, ducking out of a convention or involved in a seminar where the "bottom line" is a code word for dropping a Wooly Bugger into a deep pool with a sink-tip line. Rolling up to the hotel parking lot and joining the ranks of the other guides and their rigs, I was always amazed at the process that matched 30 men for a day's outing. Social Darwinists would have a field day watching this natural selection.

On a personal level, I had already discovered a form of this "natural selection" between men and women by way of the "Invisible Velcro Patch Natural Law of Selection". I believe that dysfunctional adults wear an invisible Velcro patch attached to their shoulders. Healthy males and females have tiny patches enabling them to thread their way through a crowded dance floor. Confident of finding their soul mates, they hum the refrain, "Some enchanted evening, you will find a stranger across a crowded room." Their search for a soul mate and their ultimate success is principally the result of a small patch that doesn't reach out and grab weirdoes, losers, neurotics and other dysfunctional individuals. Dysfunctional individuals like myself, on the other hand, have invisible flaps the size of a mud flap on a 16-wheeler. Thwack! We have a match. We have lift-off! Mission soon to be aborted.

I have suffered through this matrimonial, mating phenomenon more times than I care to admit, but it is even more interesting to watch the natural selection take place in a parking lot where 20 powerful titans of capitalism match up with 10 self-assured Montana river guides. The consummate guides arrive early and position their rigs after first reconnoitering the layout. When the men file out after breakfast, these professionals efficiently scan the group, weeding out the unworthy neophytes. The tailgates of their trucks are down to display hundreds of fly boxes holding a myriad of traditional patterns, as well as their own secret killer flies. They shake hands with the first group of men and casually dismiss the gawkers and gushers. They know their man when an individual picks up a pattern, inspects it carefully and comments, "Have you ever tied the thorax with rabbit fur and used partridge feathers for the tail rather than mallard fibers?"

The joke tellers and football fanatics match up quickly. These extroverts bond instantly. On any given day on the river with a large group, you can hear laughing and joking all day. I was always envious of these men. Regardless of how poor the fishing was, both clients and guide enjoyed each other's company, as if they were long-lost fraternity brothers. Another quick match-up is made between the high-performance salesmen and the hyperactive college guides. These guides attend college one semester a year with a lot of cutting classes during the Skwala hatch. They are passionate and intense about the sport. Witty and self-assured, they work the parking lot like evangelists. Pro-active and assertive, these young men resemble a more sophisticated version of Mike Fink, the famous river boatman. "I can catch more fish than anyone in Montana. I can thread the eyelet of a size 22 Adams at sunset. I can out drink, out fish and whup any man who says the contrary." Well, exaggeration aside, they exude charisma.

The quiet, confident guides in the Henry Fonda tradition patiently wait for their men. Before anyone notices, these stoical men part from the group and quietly go fishing. My tactic was to wait patiently for the newcomers to the sport who were seeking a teacher and instructor. I never could seem to play any other role so comfortably. It was usually thrust on me. "Go talk to Dave Archer over there. He's a schoolteacher. He'll get you all set up…. You don't know how to cast! Well, hell, you're in luck. There's a schoolteacher right over their leaning up against that Avon. He's fixing someone's old fly fishing outfit that the guy inherited from his grandfather when he was 10 years old. As soon as he is finished, ask him to teach you to cast over there on the lawn. He's your man!" I was always the last one to roll out.

Sadly disappearing from the guide ranks are the old timers who seem to be guides transported from a Faulkner novel. They don't mix well, and their rig and boat usually display signs of use and abuse. The antithesis of a yuppie fly fisher, they wear worn, old denim shirts or threadbare western shirts with a circular, worn spot in the shirt pocket that holds their chew. Rarely do they adorn themselves with the accoutrements of fly fishing. They stand by idly working a pinch of Copenhagen waiting for their guys to show. The wad of chew keeps their jawbone and cheek constantly in motion. Almost as predictable as Old Faithful, their left shoulder dips slightly, they pull down their head in a slight, downward dip and launch a brown luggie. Puuut! Launched from the side of their mouth, the brown spittle bursts from the side of their mouth, stalls in mid-flight and plops unceremoniously on its unintended target.

When they talk to a client, their jaw rotates in a circular fashion as they squint their eyes a bit. If they are interested in what you say, there is a slight nodding of the head, which precipitates a premature release. Puuut! Quietly intense, they capture the persona of a frontiersman. Many clients find these guides' demeanor appealing, especially after spending years confined in a high-rise office building. "Puuut! You pilgrims ready to catch some fish?" Once on the river the clients succumb to their piscatorial prowess. "Shhh, over there. See him? Not the little guys flashing at the tail end of the log. The big guy next to the rock below the log. See 'em. Yeah, Old Brown Bart. You son-of-a-bitch. You outsmarted that New Yorker last week, but I got me a Bostonian who's gonna stick you!"

"Yeah, I see him," says the client, hands trembling.

"OK. You're only going to get one cast with no margin of error for slop. You've got to make a reach cast up against that log, but not so close to the edge that your fly gets sucked under. Puuut! Yeah, easy does it. Mend that line just a little. YEAH! Fish on! Puuut! Hey, you in the back, you ready to catch a fish?"

## Gender Equity and Fly Fishing

Few co-ed sports or activities exist free of sexual tension. If social scientists are correct in their assertion that humans dwell on sex, in some form, six to 10 times an hour, few co-educational activities escape this human tendency for mischief, miscommunication and wanton reveries of the mind. Fly fishing, on the other hand, is as pure and tension-free as one can imagine. An increasing number of women are joining the ranks of fishermen, creating such gender free words as fly fishers and just plain fishers.

Any fly fisherman worth his salt will confirm the intense concentration one must possess with a well-presented fly on or under the water. This rapt attention precludes any possibility of conjuring a sexual image or a dalliance of the mind. If you have reached your 50s and wear trifocals like I do, you will confirm my assertion that a day on the water casting precludes any chance for the mind to wander, even if you are surrounded by a bevy of beauties from a famous modeling agency in New York.

A number of years ago I was hired to join about five other guides to guide a number of models from a famous New York agency who were guests on a rather exclusive ranch in western Montana. We were told that only a couple of them had ever fished, but all of them wanted a float fishing trip rather than a scenic float trip. We chuckled and joked about the daunting challenge of instructing the nuances of fly fishing to pampered models, models who most likely had not had an outdoor adventure in years. After checking over miscellaneous equipment, we waited for our cover-girl clients. Leaning against the rafts and drift boats, the guides started reminiscing about celebrities and movie stars they had guided. I remember being quite surprised with the list. Finally, the models arrived. We were shocked. In moments each of the guides had regained his composure. We promptly went to work preparing our assigned beauty with both equipment and advice.

Proclaimed as some of the most beautiful women

in the world, they presented themselves. They were strikingly plain-looking. Perhaps it was a joke, I thought to myself. Uncombed hair, no mascara, and zinc oxide in place of lipstick, these cover-page women further disguised themselves in old shirts and pants that I wouldn't have bothered to save for a fiberglass boat project. They joined us for a day of float fishing on Montana's famous Rock Creek. Gender issues slipped into the curling foam on the backwater eddy, as we slipped our crafts into the current and began our search for sipping rainbows. Floppy hats, bulky vests, ballooning waders and polarized sunglasses keep men and women focused on life's second-greatest pleasure.

# 6

# SOUTHWESTERN
# MONTANA

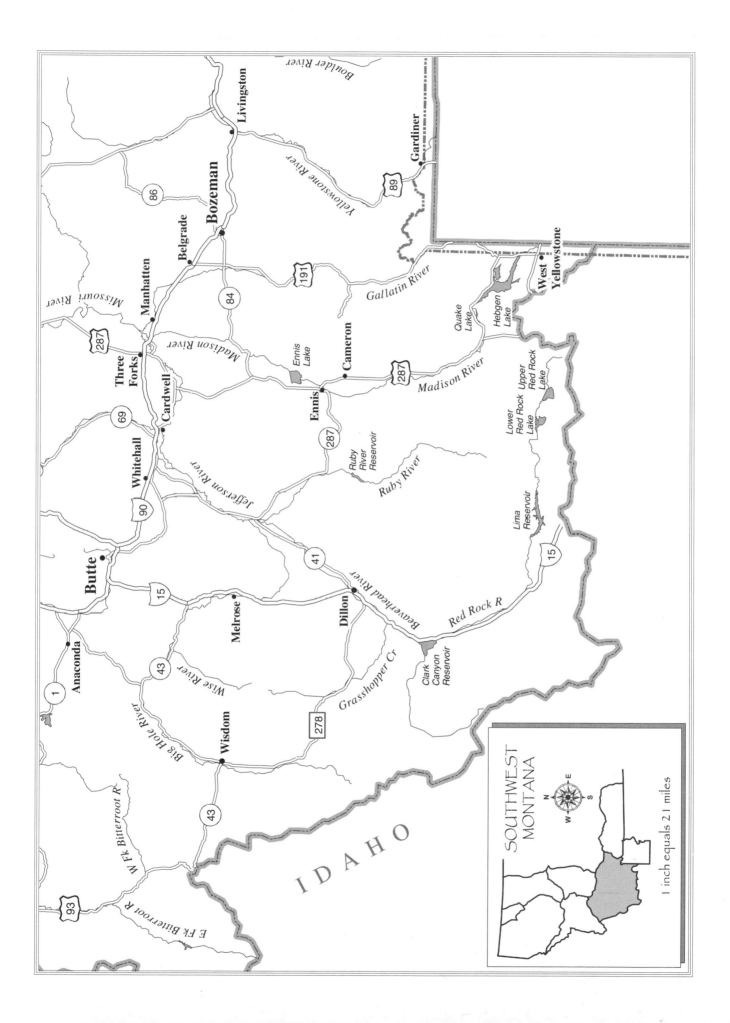

# Interstate 90 East – Rock Creek to Livingston

 **Exit 126: Rock Creek** See Western Montana.

**Exit 130: Beavertail State Campground**
Twenty-six miles east of Missoula, Beavertail State Campground includes a half-mile of river frontage on the upper Clark Fork River under a canopy of tall cottonwoods. The campground has 26 camping sites with toilets, water and a hand-launch boat site.

**MM 143:** Rest area

## Side Trip – Georgetown Lake
**Exit 153: Drummond, Montana** (Anaconda, Georgetown Lake, Phillipsburg)
If you are not in an "interstate hurry", the scenic route to Anaconda via Georgetown Lake provides spectacular scenery as well as great fishing opportunities. Exiting Interstate 90 at Drummond, the mileage markers begin with mileage marker 64 and work backwards six miles north of Anaconda, where Highway 1 meets Interstate 90 again at mileage marker 0. From the interstate at Drummond, Phillipsburg is 27 miles. If you arrive in early June or in the fall, you may want to wet a line on **Flint Creek**. At mile marker 63, turn left. Drive one mile and enter Drummond City Park and Rodeo Grounds.

The park offers a nice shaded picnic site right along the upper Clark Fork River. Camping is allowed for a daily fee of $10. At the back of the park, you will see a train trestle. Walk under the trestle and follow the Clark Fork River for a 10-minute walk to where Flint Creek enters the river. This section fishes poorly during the heat of summer, but fair-sized browns enter the creek during the fall.

Flint Creek fishing improves further towards Phillipsburg. Look for county roads off Highway 1 that cross Flint Creek. Two such access points are located at mileage marker 54.9 (Douglas Creek Road) and at mileage marker 51.7 (Henderson Creek Road). A few miles from Phillipsburg, Flint Creek travels through a narrow valley. The creek lazily cuts and winds through willow-lined banks and produces good catches of 10- to 12-inch browns. This section is mostly unposted and located between mileage markers 42 and 47.

A few miles past the old mining town of Phillipsburg, Highway 1 intersects with Highway 38. Highway 38 will take you over Skalkaho Pass and then on down to Hamilton, Montana, to the Bitterroot River, or you may want to follow Highway 38 a few miles to the upper end of Rock Creek. This loop will take you around to Interstate 90 again at Exit 126, a few miles from Missoula.

From Phillipsburg, continuing on Highway 1, the highway passes by Flint Creek Campground at mileage marker 30.3. The campground offers 16 camping sites, some of which are just large parking areas for trailers. Some of the camping sites lack tables. Although the campground is old and somewhat run-down, it is a good place for older children who want to play in the creek, as Flint Creek at this point is very small. From the campground, Highway 1 climbs up the mountain to meet the reservoir dam for Georgetown Lake.

**Georgetown Lake**
Georgetown Lake is a shallow, weed-infested meadow lake. A little over four square miles, the lake sits at an elevation of 6,350 feet. Bordered by meadow grassland and alpine hillsides, Georgetown Lake is picturesque by any standards. A popular recreation lake during the summer, Georgetown Lake is renowned as a prolific aquatic lake in both insect production and fish growth. Although whirling disease has impacted the native runs of rainbows, stocking programs have minimized losses. Arlee rainbows and Eagle Lake rainbows average 14 inches with impressive numbers of 16- to 18-

inchers. Although less in numbers, brook trout grow to impressive size, and, yes, trophy trout abound.

Late spring and early summer bring about heavy hatches of Callibaetis. By mid-summer, look for emerging damselflies followed by prolific hatches of caddis fly. Because of the gradual gradient along the shore, most fishermen prefer to fish from boats or float tubes. Smaller tippets, heavy fish, and thick weed beds create a fun and challenging fishing experience in a beautiful setting. The lake is easily accessed around its entire length, and the immediate area offers numerous campgrounds, boat launches, picnic sites and swimming.

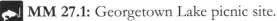

### Phillipsburg Bay Campground
USFS. The campground has 69 campsites which accommodate trailers up to 32 feet. The boat launch is suitable for trailers and two-wheel-drive vehicles.

 **Piney Creek Campground**
USFS. The campground has 49 campsites and can accommodate trailers up to 48 feet. The boat launch is suitable for trailers and two-wheel-drive vehicles.

**MM 27.1:** Georgetown Lake picnic site.

**MM 24.8:** Grassy Point boat launch.

**MM 19.5: Spring Hill Campground**
Spring Hill Campground offers 15 campsites with 22-foot trailer space. The campground is 11 miles northwest of Anaconda on Highway 1.

**MM 8:** Anaconda, Montana.

**MM 5: Lost Creek State Park**
Take Route 273 north from Highway 1 and then follow the signs six miles to the campground. Lost Creek tumbles over a 50-foot ledge, which makes this one of the more scenic campgrounds in the area. The campsite provides 25 campsites with water and toilets. Lost Creek is a small creek offering fair catches of smaller brook trout and cutthroats.

**MM 4.4:** Road to Wisdom, Montana (Big Hole River).

**MM 0:** I-90. End of the scenic route from Drummond to Anaconda.

## Return to Interstate 90 at Drummond
**MM 169:** Rest area.

 **Exit 171:** Fishing access to the upper Clark Fork River.

### Exit 174: Garrison Junction and the Little Blackfoot River
The Little Blackfoot River is really no more than a creek, but it is well worth fishing. Although no public access points are available, numerous pullout spots may be seen from the highway on the way to Helena, a distance of 44 miles. Most of the land is not posted, but permission to trespass is the law of the land now. The creek runs parallel to railroad tracks for a number of miles north of Garrison. Although some sections hold larger browns, a typical brown runs 8 to 12-inches.

 **Exit 179:** Beck Hill Fishing Access.

**Exit 184:** Deerlodge, Montana.

**Exit 187:** Deerlodge Information Center.

**Exit 197:** Galen Fishing Access.

**Exit 201: Warm Springs Wildlife Management Area**

Warm Spring Ponds, one of the largest Superfund clean-up sites in the country, has been transformed into a wetlands management area for wildlife and trophy trout management. After a century of copper mining and milling contamination, the area became barren. ARCO and the Anaconda Company have spent millions of dollars to prevent metal seepage from Silver Bow Creek. Today fly fishers stalk trophy browns and rainbows in these ponds. The most popular method, however, is fishing from a float tube. Brochures and fishing regulations are placed at the entrance. Camping is non-designated camping, and you will need to bring your own water (pack it in – pack it out). The trout average two pounds, and there are still some monsters that cruise along the bottom. The problem, however, is that they are satiated from an abundance of aquatic insects and great populations of scuds and leeches.

Upper Big Hole River

I have fished it only once back in 1983 with Charlie Miller, who at the time owned a fly shop in Hamilton. I have bittersweet memories of that day. I broke a Sage rod on the first cast. Earlier in the morning I had leaned my rod on the hood of the truck, and the wind had blown it down. Charlie inadvertently stepped on it, but the only damage we could detect was a tiny chip in the enamel. One cast and it exploded. I borrowed Charlie's spare rod, and we fished all day in one pond. Finally, I landed a 24-inch brown. Just before the end of the day, I landed one big fish. How hard are you willing to work for a trophy trout?

The best time to fish is in the spring and fall. Be sure to read the special regulations.

**Exit 201:** Anaconda, Montana.

## Side Trip – The Big Hole River and the Beaverhead River

**Exit 219:** Junction with Interstate 15 to the Big Hole River and the Beaverhead River.

## The Big Hole River

The natives first named the Big Hole Valley the Land of Big Snows and Ground Squirrel Valley. Captain Meriwether Lewis of the Lewis and Clark Expedition named the forks of the Jefferson River, Wisdom and Philanthropy, to honor President Jefferson's virtues. Later on the return trip, William Clark would name the present area of Jackson the

Hot Spring Valley when they camped for the night near the hot springs. Fur trappers seeking valleys (holes) which were bounteous with beaver gave it its lasting name. With the passing of time, ranchers sprinkled the valley with rich hay fields, producing some of the finest hay in the region. They nicknamed the valley 10,000 Stacks Valley with the invention in 1910 of the Beaverside Haystacker. By the late 1930s and '40s, the Big Hole achieved piscatorial pre-eminence from local fly fishers and then by fishermen from around the country, who came to pay homage to another one of Montana's fluvial wonders.

From its headwaters down to Jackson, the river, more aptly described as a small meadow stream, meanders northwards to Wisdom, Montana, and then to Sportsman Park. From there the river heads east and then south to Melrose and Glen. From Glen the river runs east for a short distance and then heads north again to meet the Beaverhead and form the Jefferson River. From the town of Wisdom to Twin Bridges, the river winds a little over 100 miles. The most famous section, particularly during the Salmon Fly hatch in mid-June, stretches from Divide to Glen. From the second week in June through the end of the month, this section of river rivals the Madison in its heydays for boat traffic. The runoff, typically beginning in May, makes the Big Hole most difficult and perhaps dangerous to wade fish with the arrival of the Salmon Fly hatch in early June.

The powerful current and half-submerged sweepers and rocks pose serious consequences for inexperienced rowers as well. Early July brings the arrival of the golden stoneflies, caddis and mayflies. With the arrival of mid-summer, irrigation drawdown and slow, heated water shuts the river down in some sections. In drought years the trout are barely able to survive in some sections of the river, and playing a fish to shore adds significant stress to their survival chances after release.

With the exception of the Salmon Fly hatch, the Big Hole River provides lots of elbowroom for an-glers seeking solitude. During early summer the Big Hole fishes well with attractor patterns, particularly in the upper stretches above and below the town of Wisdom, where anglers also have the opportunity to catch Arctic Grayling. The Big Hole River holds the last survivors of river-dwelling grayling in the lower 48 states, and their numbers are growing under the careful protection of the state after the severe drought years during the 1980s. In addition to the grayling, the upper section holds high concentrations of brook trout and to a lesser extent cutthroats and rainbows.

With the discovery in recent years of whirling disease, the verdict is still out on the rainbow population, but recent research holds promise for securing a place for rainbows in the drainage. The mid-section of the river below Wise River picks up both volume and gradient speed as the river flows through canyons, offering floaters a mixture of riffles, rocks and pockets. Larger rainbows and browns are found from the Divide Bridge down to Melrose, the most popular float on the river. Some sections of the Big Hole River have produced shock-counts of over 3,000 trout per mile.

From Glen to the confluence at Twin Bridges, the river returns to pasture land and cottonwood bottoms and braided channels. Check with one of the shops before you float this section, as it often contains many obstacles and impediments for safe floating. The river holds mostly browns hidden under downed trees and undercut banks. The lower stretch may be accessed from a county road from Glen to Twin Bridges, but there are no public access points except bridges. Access to the upper river, on the other hand, has improved greatly, thanks to the efforts of the Big Hole River Foundation.

Fishing the Salmon Fly hatch requires patience, luck and good oaring skills. The greatest challenge to fishing this river is to wait for your turn to launch your boat. The last time I floated from Divide to Melrose, almost 10 years ago, I was shocked at the number of people patiently waiting to take their launch turn. Fishermen were dropping drift boats in the water everywhere. As I drifted down the river, I was reminded of all those nature films I had seen through the years of crocodiles charging through the marsh grass and silently entering the water. I suppose the best attitude to embrace for this bevy of boats is to just enjoy the circus-like parade and be as generous as possible in sharing the river. Once the hatch is over, the crowds

Hefty Big Hole brown

disappear for another year.

The hatch moves typically four to five miles a day upstream from the confluence all the way up to Wisdom, although the heaviest concentrations are from Glen to Wise River. The Salmon Fly hatch on the Big Hole is generally earlier than the hatch on the Madison. As a result the Big Hole draws outfitters and guides from all over the region, including from the Missoula area, which offers a good Salmon Fly hatch on the forks of the Bitterroot, Rock Creek and the Blackfoot about the same time.

Nymph fishermen like to get ahead of the hatch, but the bulk of the fishermen enjoy fishing right in the middle of the hatch. Most of them enter the river between 9 AM and 10 AM hoping to catch the first ovipositing females as they warm up. Timing and good luck determines whether or not you will have a memorable hatch experience. Most camping

fishermen come to stay for a while, knowing that cold, rainy June days are a reality in southwestern Montana. About 20 years ago I fished the hatch for the first time with a former principal of mine from Jackson, Wyoming.

Nick Holmes, who at the time was the principal in Whitehall, Montana, almost always fished with a nymph. He is an excellent fisherman, and he would softly chuckle every time he watched me tie on a dry fly. Invariably he would out-fish me. Nick had no use for strike indicators or tapered leaders. He carried a few spools of monofilament in his vest and tied on short leaders. As I was his junior, coupled with the fact that he always out-fished me, I generally took Nick's advice, including switching over to a nymph after watching Nick land three or four fish.

The night before I had driven over from the Bitterroot Valley and camped at Divide Bridge, where I was to meet Nick in the morning. I spent that first evening talking to every fisherman who would answer my questions. The general consensus was that it was not worth getting out on the river early until the bugs were warmed up and landing on the water. Eager beavers, I was told, just pass up good water that would be productive water later in the morning. I had planned on meeting Nick at 6 the next morning!

When Nick arrived earlier than our scheduled time, I was groggy-eyed. I told him of my findings, and he let out that soft chuckle, which from past experience assured me he had some experience that I wasn't about to challenge. It was chilly, but the sun was coming up when we backed up to the launch and slipped into the river at 7 AM. I was on the oars first and ribbed Nick about using a nymph today. "No," he said, "I'll fish with drys today. Here, I tied up a couple for you as well."

Tied would be an overstatement. Nick was also a goose hunter, and he had carved magnum Salmon Fly bodies out of balsa wood and attached them to what I guessed to be shark hooks. Richly painted and finished off with bright feathers, they looked more like floating Rappalas. As I received the two gigantic flies in my hands, Nick good-naturally said, "Be sure to cut off about half of that tapered leader of yours." It was good advice. Our agreement was two fish caught and you are on the oars. Within 10 minutes, Nick landed his first 20-inch trout. Within the hour I was on the oars, and although my first two fish weren't quite as large as Nick's, I was jubilant. As the day progressed, we both lost our two hand-carved Salmon Flies and the fish became progressively smaller and tougher to catch. I never fished the Big Hole River again with Nick, and I have never carved balsa wood Salmon Fly patterns, but each spring I wonder if they would work on Rock Creek. The Big Hole Salmon Fly hatch is a great experience if you time it right, if the run-off is not severe, and if the sky is free from pounding rain.

**March and April:** During this pre-runoff period, the river is best fished with a variety of Woolly Bugger and streamer patterns along with stonefly nymphs.

**May:** The month of May begins the run-off season along with prolific hatches of caddis. Unlike many of Montana's other famous rivers, the Big Hole does not typically get blown out with mud. If the weather cooperates, the upper and mid sections are certainly worth fishing using Elk Hair Caddis patterns as well as emerging nymphs.

**June:** The Big Hole's famous Salmon Fly hatch is usually in progress by mid-June and essentially over by the end of the month with the exception of some late bloomers. Followed closely on the heels of the Salmon Fly hatch, Golden Stones and a few Green Drakes appear along with PMDs.

**July:** Early July offers opportunities for standard attractor patterns such as Humpies, Wulffs, Trudes, and Parachute Adams.

**Late summer:** Hoppers, ants and Tricos.

**Fall:** Hoppers, Tricos, Blue-Wing Olives, streamers and buggers.

# Highway 43 – The Big Hole River

The Big Hole River may be reached via Highway 93 from Salmon, Idaho, from Interstate 15 from Idaho Falls to Butte or at the junction with Interstate 90 and Interstate 15 west of Butte. The Big Hole River parallels Highway 43, which begins at the junction with Highway 93 at Chief Joseph Pass. From the junction to Wisdom is 27 miles. Dillon is 93 miles.

## MM 16.5: Big Hole National Battlefield, North Fork of the Big Hole River

The Nez Perce, refusing to accept a re-negotiated treaty in which their people would lose nine-tenths of their reservation, refused to move into the newly-restricted reservation. Tensions mounted, deadlines were mandated and a few young warriors precipitated military reprisals when they killed some settlers. Thus began a journey of flight and a series of skirmishes. The Nez Perce elected Chief Joseph as their leader. At the Big Hole the 7th US Infantry, under the command of Col. John Gibbon, mounted a surprise attack. The Nez Perce tribe suffered the loss of almost 98 members, only a third of whom were warriors. In military terms, the Indians had won the battle, but their loss of horses and provisions would soon exhaust them on their journey of escape. Thirteen hundred miles later, Chief Joseph would surrender to Col. Nelson A. Miles, just 40 miles south of the Canadian border: "Hear me, my chiefs, I am tired; my heart is sick and sad. From where the sun now stands I will fight no more forever."

## MM 23: Lower North Fork Road, Mussigbrod Lake: 18 miles, Pintler Lake: 18 miles

Mussigbrod Lake Campground (USFS) has 10 campsites. The lake fishes well for grayling and brook trout, but be prepared for ugly drawdown during the summer. Pintler Lake offers much more in scenery, good fishing from a boat and a small campground. The lake is a little over 30 acres and does not offer good fishing from the shoreline due to plant growth.

**MM 26:** Junction with Highway 278 to Dillon, Montana.

The North Fork of the Big Hole River runs through the Battlefield and holds an abundance of brook trout.

## Highway 278 to Dillon

 **Twin Lakes**

The route to Dillon leads to Jackson, Montana, which has a commercial hot springs resort. Seven miles south of Wisdom on Highway 278 is the turnoff to Twin Lakes, which is 16 miles from the highway. The lake, actually two lakes joined by a channel, is popular with locals and offers good fishing for rainbows and brook trout. Although large lake trout are present, their numbers seem to be in decline. Twin Lakes Campground has 21 camping sites and a boat launch.

**Lower Miner Lake, Upper Miner Lake**

From Wisdom to Jackson is 18 miles. Just out of Jackson a half-mile is the turnoff to Lower Miner Lake, which offers 18 campsites and a boat launch. The fishing, however, is only fair as the lake is shallow and suffers from oxygen depletion during the summer and periodic freeze-outs. Upper Miner Lake, along with Rock Island Lakes, offers good cutthroat and brook trout fishing for day-hike fishing in the backcountry. The hike is approximately four to five miles and well worth the hike for the scenery alone. My sons and I have fond memories of catching lots of 9-inch brookies in these lakes. **Note:** The last time I visited the area the access road from Lower Miner Lake to the Upper Miner Lake trailhead was rough and suitable only for high-clearance vehicles.

**Van Houten Lake**

A half-mile further from the Lower Miner Lake turnoff is the access road for Van Houten Lake, which is 10 miles from the highway. South Van Houten campground has three tent sites, while North Van Houten has four tent campsites. The lake is barely 10 acres.

**Bannack State Park and Campground**

Located four miles down a county dirt road off Highway 278 five miles south of Dillon, Bannack was Montana's first territorial state capital after a major gold discovery in 1862. A number of buildings remain on Main Street. The campground has 20 campsites for both tents and trailers. Grasshopper Creek runs through the campground and offers fishing for 14- to 16-inch brown trout. The creek runs through miles of ranchland. Be sure to ask for permission.

## Highway 43 – Wisdom to Divide
**MM 26:** Wisdom, Montana

 **MM 42: Squaw Creek**
Squaw Creek has a launch site and parking. This is also the junction with the Lower North Fork Road. Pintler Lake is 10 miles and Mussigbrod Lake is 22 (See MM 23.).

**MM 48.7: Fishtrap Fishing Access**
This access provides a boat launch, but there is no shade for a picnic.

**MM 52. 5:** Roadside tables.

**MM 54.4:** Junction with Highway 274 to Anaconda. Anaconda is 25 miles.

**MM 57.1: East Bank Campground**
Eight miles west of Wise River, the East Bank Campground offers five campsites with a boat launch.

**MM 58: Dickie Bridge Recreation Area Campground**
The campground has eight campsites. The first four have tables; the other four sites are primitive. The area also has a boat launch.

**Wise River, Montana**
Thirteen miles from Interstate 15, Wise River offers services and accommodations. The Wise River nearly drys up some years in its lower stretches. The upper reaches of the river offer fair fishing for smaller rainbows. Following Pioneer Mountains Scenic Byway along the Wise River will lead to many campgrounds.

 **MM 67.1:** Jerry Creek Bridge access and launch

 **MM 71:** Dewey fishing access and launch

**MM 74: Old Divide Bridge** If you are floating down to Old Divide Bridge, you must take out at this point, as below the bridge is a dam. The next put-in site is a mile away at the new Divide Bridge.

**MM 75: Divide Bridge Fishing Access and Boat Launch**
From this point to Melrose and Glen is the most famous stretch of water on the Big Hole. Divide Bridge is 2.8 miles from Interstate 15, Exit 102. The BLM site offers lots of parking as well as 25 campsites.

**Exit 102:** Divide, Montana; Junction with Interstate 15.

**Exit 93: Interstate 15 to Melrose, Montana**
Melrose is a very small community. The launch site or takeout is right in Melrose at the Salmon Fly Campground. The campground, if you can call it that, is a patch of grass, which is non-designated, close-quarter camping ("parking"). Six miles further is Maiden Rock Campground. Maiden Rock Campground (FWP) has 30 campsites, which can accommodate 32-foot trailers, and it offers a boat launch. From Melrose you may follow the frontage road south to Browne's Bridge.

## The Beaverhead River

Throughout the many years of my guiding and teaching in the Bitterroot Valley, I heard exciting tales of summer and fall trips to the Beaverhead from fellow guides. Regaled stories, combined with the "shocking" reports of Montana's fish biologists, heightened my desire to fish these fabled waters. But the culmination of each summer guide season, the arrival of a new school session and fall hunting kept

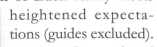

Beaverhead River

me from sampling the Beaverhead.

Like the endless stories of gamblers who return from Las Vegas, no mention is ever made of losses. When pressed, most recreational gamblers mutter that they broke even, or better yet, their winnings paid all of their expenses. In 20 years of listening to river guides talk about their Beaverhead trips, no mention was ever made about a slow day in paradise.

And for the record, this paradise is verifiably evident with biologists proclaiming record populations and record-size browns from their shocking studies even to this day. In the days when Blue Ribbon was bantered around so lightly, the Beaverhead studies reported astonishing numbers

of trout per mile with record-breaking browns waiting to enter the record books.

Today the numbers are only slightly down due to whirling disease, and anglers truly have the opportunity to catch "Five Pounders", which, in my mind, is another term lightly bantered about. No other river between Glacier and Yellowstone holds such promise for a catch-of-a-lifetime as this national treasure! But into this Garden of Eden reality meets heightened expectations (guides excluded).

The Beaverhead hosts abundant insect life, half-submerged willows and a tailwater rich in nutrients. By all standards this narrow river holds challenges for seasoned veterans, yet each passing season, innocents from abroad proudly photograph their "jackpot" reward. From the Clark Canyon Reservoir to Dillon is approximately 20 river miles of water, which races past a double-wall barrier of thick willow and undercut banks. Dangling willow arms greedily reach out to snatch a fisherman's offerings, and weighted nymph patterns and buggers stumble through underwater deadfalls. Shooting past a target, he who hesitates is lost, and lost flies mount up as the day progresses. Typical flows in mid-summer on a high water year reach in excess of 1,000 cfs, which makes it tough for both guides and clients. The upper section from the dam to Barrett's Dam is the most famous stretch of water. Here wade fishers are even more challenged during high water releases. Optimum flows for floating this upper section are from 600 to 800 cfs. Compounding the aforementioned physical conditions is the simple fact that heightened pressure has produced some very educated browns. Whereas in the past heavily weighted buggers with incredibly short and stout leaders was the preferred method, realistic nymph patterns properly presented prevail today.

Rather than be intimidated, however, relish the prospect of fishing over 300 trophy-sized browns per mile after first taking a teaspoon of lowered expectations. If you can afford it, by all means hire a guide. During my last visit to the Beaverhead, I sat in my truck outside a shop in Dillon arranging notes and brochures. I heard two out-of-state visitors debating the merits of hiring a guide. Money wasn't even a consideration. The men had pulled a drift boat behind them from another state and felt sheepish about hiring a guide on that basis alone. Sitting in my truck, I couldn't pretend to be oblivious to their dilemma so I hopped out and approached them. Within 60 seconds they returned to the shop to book a trip. Here is an almost word-for-word argument I gave them.

"Excuse me. I couldn't help but overhear your conversation. I am a former guide from out of the area, and I can tell you that I dearly wish I could afford to hire a guide. If money isn't the issue, consider this. Only one of you will be able to fish at a time while the other person is on the oars. That's half the day watching your buddy fish. You are going to be speeding down the river five to six miles per hour not knowing what lies around the next bend. Before you can even react, you're going to

blow through a good pocket that you could have got out of the boat and fished. Even if you are an experienced oarsman, you are going to miss a lot of prime water, and hopefully you will miss rapping the top of that boat of yours on a low bridge. Lastly, you will probably doggedly cling to a non-productive pattern in the absence of a voice of authority."

The opener begins May 17, and the preferred fly

Three generations of Beaverhead fly fishermen: Alex Day, age 7, with Grandfather Robbie Garrett and Uncle Jeremy Garrett on the oars.

patterns are small mayflies, small yellow stoneflies and caddis. Keep in mind that for the first stretch down to Grasshopper Creek, the water remains clear as it comes out of the dam. Grasshopper Creek muddies the water during runoff and during heavy rains, but this section above provides clear opportunities, albeit for a short distance of a little over 10 miles.

Early summer brings PMDs and then later Tricos, but these hatches tend to be early and late in the day. The upper section lacks green pastureland for hoppers who gradually work their way to the water's edge; however, crane flies fill this void, and late summer and early fall scattered hatches of Baetis emerge. Throughout the river drainage, the Beaverhead is primarily known for fishing down and ugly versus sitting high and pretty. Floaters fishing below Dillon to Anderson Road will find conditions much better for dry fly fishing along with far fewer boats, and from Barrett's Bridge to the town of Dillon, wade fishers delight in catching smaller trout but in greater numbers.

## Popular Sections and Access Points on the Beaverhead River

The Beaverhead is easily accessed from Interstate 15 at Exit 44 at the dam, Exit 52 at Grasshopper Creek, Exit 59 with the junction to Highway 278 to Wisdom, and Exits 62 and 63 in the town of Dillon. For a quick preview of the river, follow the secondary road just past Poindexter Slough south of Dillon near the junction with Highway 278. This secondary road winds its way all the way up to the dam, crossing the river and at times under the Interstate. At times it joins with old Highway 91. In some places it looks like a private ranch road. Wade fishers can travel this road to fish, and floaters new to the river should follow the road to check out each of the access points.

### Clark Canyon Dam or High Bridge to Grasshopper Creek Access or Barrett's Park

Built in 1965, the base of the dam provides a launch site and a picnic spot, along with a couple of camping sites. Less than a mile downstream, High Bridge offers an easier launch site. Wade fishers have a short stretch above and below the bridge to fish. This upper section is renowned for its swift current and river bends. Henneberry Bridge is about six miles from the dam, and it too offers a good exit point or boat launch along with a picnic area. Henneberry Bridge is most easily found by following the secondary road south from Exit 52. Grasshopper Creek Access is the next access downstream, about 10 miles from the dam. From Grasshopper Creek to Barrett's Park is the last floating stretch of the river. During

high water the park takeout can be tricky as it is right in front of a low bridge, and there is no room for error. When you see the bridge, slip over and hug the left bank.

### Tash to Cornell Park

Referred to as "Tash to Trash" by the local guides, the Tash access point is near the junction with Highway 278 by Poindexter Slough. A short float of about five miles, this popular evening float exits at the weir, a low irrigation diversion dam, in Cornell Park in the town of Dillon, not too far from the dump. To find Cornell Park, follow North Montana Street past the museum and depot until it comes to a T-intersection. Turn west and follow the KOA signs. The park is about a half-mile further and offers a hand-launch site.

### Cornell Park to Anderson Road

Be sure you take note of the low bridge and debris at the train trestle on Highway 91 at the north end of town. It could prove tricky during high water periods for a high bow drift boat. The exit point for this 12- to 14-mile float is Anderson Road, which may be reached at mile marker 7.4 north of Dillon on Highway 41. The road is unmarked, but across the street is a ranch complex with silos. Turn west 1.3 miles. The access is small and next to a county bridge. Anderson Road may also be reached at mile marker 5.6 on Highway 91 north of town on the way to Butte.

Fly fishers should also consider fishing Poindexter Slough for good catches of browns in a spring creek environment as well as Clark Canyon Reservoir, which produces exceptionally large rainbows. Stocked in the lake in the spring at four inches, these Eagle Lake-strain rainbows grow in excess of 12 inches the first year and easily reach 5-pounder status in three years. Although popular with boat fishers, the lake is likewise popular with float tubers prowling the shores for those lunkers.

## Public Campgrounds

Dillon has a number of private campgrounds, and Barrett's Park has a few campsites. The best public campground facilities, however, are up on Clark Canyon Reservoir, which offers eight non-fee campgrounds provided by the U.S. Bureau of Reclamation. Most of the campgrounds are on the west side of the lake, and for the most part they lack any shade.

# Interstate 90 – Butte to Livingston

### Exit 249: Whitehall, Montana, and the Jefferson River

Having spent a number of days fishing the Jefferson the one year I lived in Whitehall, I can with a clear conscience steer you away from this one. Even before the days of whirling disease, the Jefferson presented a challenge. Primarily a brown trout stream, the Jefferson River flows 80 miles through farmland, which adversely impacts late summer stream flows. Locals, like my former high school principal Nick Holmes, know how to reap the bounty of the Jefferson, as do most of the ranch kids. If you are traveling through the area and short on time, pass this one up, as you are close to the Madison, the Big Hole and the Beaverhead!

**Exit 256:** Cardwell, Montana, and the Boulder River.

### Lewis and Clark Caverns

"Located in the rugged Jefferson River Canyon, Lewis and Clark Caverns features one of the most highly decorated limestone caverns in the Northwest. Naturally air-conditioned, these spectacular caves are lined with stalagmites and columns. The Caverns – which are part of Montana's first and best known state park – are electrically lighted and safe to visit. To avoid peak use periods, call the park for suggested visitation and tour times at (406) 287-3541." –Montana State Parks brochure

**Exit 274:** Exit to Ennis, Montana (Madison River)

**Exit 278:** (Madison River) Three Forks, route to Yellowstone National Park via the Madison River to West Yellowstone Entrance (Hwy 287).

**Note:** Interstate 90 from west to east continues after the Madison River.

## Side Trip – Highway 287: The Madison River

The Yellowstone River, deemed one of the most abundant trout fisheries in the world, has a challenger less than four hours away. Montana's second crown jewel is still a showcase. Having been ravaged by whirling decease during the early part of this decade, Madison loyalists watched the number of rainbow trout plunge from 3,500 per mile to 600 per mile. Juvenile populations dropped 90% in a few short years. Clearly the Madison fishing frenzy has waned. No longer do wade fishermen curse the steady stream of drift boats. But newcomers will find no memorial markers with epitaphs lamenting the death of the Madison. The loss has been profound, but the Madison River is still one of the top fisheries in Montana. Brown trout average 1,500 to 1,800 per mile with a healthy population of trophy fish.

Research continues on solutions to mitigate the whirling disease impact on rainbows. One promising solution is looking at early spawning rainbow trout, which would have less exposure to the WD parasite. In temperatures below 50 degrees, the host worm actually produces very few spores. In an article published in the *Missoulian* August 6, 1998, Dick Vincent, FWP Region 3 Manager, suggests that finding strains of rainbows and cutthroats that are predisposed to spawn early holds promise for the future. "We may be able to actually spawn fish in the wild, imprint the colder temperature on them, then put them back out there in the hope that they would imprint their young to spawn earlier."

What is not missing from the Madison River to

day is the opportunity to fish a great brown stream that offers pristine settings and some of the most beautiful water in the world. Whether in the Park or in the Ennis area, the Madison River deserves respect.

P.S. Fat rainbows are still present!

The Madison River originates 15 miles from the West Yellowstone Entrance inside Yellowstone National Park. Just above the National Park Meadow,

The author taking a break on the Madison River

the Gibbon River joins the Firehole to begin the Madison's journey for over 130 miles to Three Forks, where it joins the Gallatin and the Jefferson to form the Missouri River. Although the Park section is fished throughout the summer, the best fishing occurs in June during the Salmon Fly hatch and the Green Drake hatch. Migratory trout spawn in this section during both the spring and fall. The fall receives heavy pressure as anglers anticipate the fall brown spawning runs out of Hebgen Lake. Large streamer patterns work best, but fishermen are also successful using nymphs and egg patterns.

Keep in mind that by mid-summer the Park section water begins to rise in temperature due to the summer heat and the thermal activity in the Firehole

River. An additional challenge is that Madison River trout are hammered all year long, and they become vary educated. Just inside the Park boundary, fishermen can take a left on a dirt road to the Baker's Hole area if they want some semblance of solitude. With the advent of fall and the anticipation of brown spawning runs, the area becomes quite a popular gathering spot. Regardless of the season, be cautious in disturbing wildlife.

Leaving the Park, the Madison takes a short run and enters Hebgen Lake. Hebgen Lake runs 16 miles long and the area provides a number of campgrounds. Most of the arms of the lake offer good fly fishing for float tubers. For camping information contact:

Hebgen Lake Ranger District
PO Box 520
West Yellowstone, MT 59758
(406) 646-7369

All Hebgen Lake Ranger District fee sites are available to reserve on the recreation reservation system by calling (800) 280-2267. Hebgen Lake offers seven campgrounds. Rainbow Point Campground and Baker's Hole campground exclude tent camping because of bear activity. Baker's Hole Campground is right on the Madison River just above where it joins the Madison Arm of Hebgen Lake. Anglers will find a white stake denoting the Park boundary.

At the outlet of Hebgen Lake, Quake Lake was formed during a 1959 earthquake. Below Quake Lake to the Junction with Highway 87, the scarred remnants of the quake make floating this section of the river extremely dangerous; even expert rafters shun this short section. The junction with Highway 87 begins the mileage markers. Ennis, Montana, is 41 miles downstream.

## MM 0: Highway 287 junction with Highway 87 to Henry's Lake, Idaho

The water from Quake Lake to the junction with Highway 87 is both sobering and challenging. The 1959 quake registered 7.8 on the Richter scale, and an entire mountainside slid down on one of the most productive stretches of the Madison River. A campground was buried, and many lives were lost. More than 40 years later, gray pine tree stalks lean at all angles in the river, and the boulder-strewn piles of gravel and rock testify to this horrific event. The water looks barren above the junction, but dedicated nymph fishermen take fish in the fast foam and surface film. From the junction to Ennis, a distance of approximately 50 miles, this famous section of the Madison has been described as a 50-mile riffle.

Hebgen Lake

The best time to fish this section of the Madison is early summer and fall. The first awaited hatch is the prolific caddis hatch of late May and June, but the Madison River's Salmon Fly hatch is justifiably famous and eagerly awaited. But like the Big Hole and Rock Creek, making flight and motel reservations six months in advance can lead to great disappointments when you are confronted with lingering storms, late run-offs, or heavy or late snow accumulations. Hitting it just right is a craps shoot, but if you have the time and the money, it is more than worth the gamble. Traditionally, the hatch starts during the last week of June through mid-July followed by the presence of golden stoneflies. With the announcement, "Gentlemen, start your engines," an interesting rush to the water takes place. Nymph fishermen head upstream above the hatch to chuck weighted Bitch Creeks and various other stonefly nymphs into the cold water. Dry fly enthusiasts rush around probing the river and chasing guide rigs. And the leisure set move behind the advancing hatch knowing that trout have orange memories and rise readily to smaller yellow and orange Stimulators.

The dog days of August calls for terrestrials, but those enticements are often ignored. One popular and effective technique is to add a bead-head Prince as a dropper. Realistically, during the heat of August, expect to catch smaller fish. By all means pound the water mid-day with hoppers, beetles and ants, but do not ignore early morning nymphing techniques and evening hatches of Blue-Wing Olives. September and October call for a change of tactics with heavy streamers.

### Wade Lake and Cliff Lake

Wade Lake and Cliff Lake turn-off is just downstream from the junction. Both lakes are fairly large and may also be reached from the West Fork Bridge access at mile marker 9.6. Both lakes have campgrounds, but fishing from shore is somewhat difficult due to the steep shoreline. Both lakes support healthy populations of 10- to 14-inch trout. Wade Lake Campground offers 30 camping sites, Hill Top Campground offers 20, and Cliff Point offers six sites and a trailer boat launch

### MM 9.6: West Fork Campground

The West Fork Campground offers seven shaded tent camping sites right along the West Fork of the Madison, which is a beautiful stream in its own right, offering fair catches of rainbows and browns. The West Fork may be accessed for almost 14 miles on a dirt road. The West Fork blows out early during spring run-off and after a heavy storm. Above the West Fork the river clears earlier due to both the nature of the Park and the addition of Hebgen Lake, which tends to settle the silt. Next to the West Fork Campground is the West Fork Cabin Camp and RV Campground.

### MM 15.7: Lyon Bridge Recreation Area
Boat launch and picnic area.

### MM 22.7: Palisades Campground

One mile off the highway, Palisades Campground offers seven camping sites along the river with a towering bluff on the other side.

### MM 30.8: McAttee Bridge
McAttee bridge offers a day-use site as well as a boat launch. Three miles down a well-maintained road is the Wall Creek Wildlife Management Area and **West Madison Campground**. If you like sagebrush and full exposure to the sun, then this campground, with 22 camping sites and a boat launch, is for you.

### MM 38: Cameron, Montana
Cameron has a post office and the Blue Moon Store and RV Park.

### MM 40: Varney Bridge
The road to Varney Bridge is over three miles on some rough road. Although the campground has a self-deposit fee requirement, it is somewhat old and run-down. Nonetheless, the five or six campsites are next to the river with mature cottonwoods providing welcome shade. Most locals take the secondary road out of Ennis on the westward side of the river to Varney Bridge.

Floaters may choose a half-day float and spend more time out of the boat fishing if they take out at the Eight-Mile Ford boat launch, or they may float down to Ennis Campground. The stretch from Varney Bridge to Ennis Campground, unlike the water upstream, separates into many braided channels and islands. Even with this separation of water, the Madison flows swiftly against undercut banks and tiny islands. This section has traditionally maintained the largest browns.

### Ennis Campground
Just across the bridge from Ennis, Ennis Campground is a shaded campground on the river. The campground is a Fish, Wildlife and Parks Campground with 25 camping sites with mowed grass. Before the bridge crossing, look for the turnoff to Valley Garden Campground, which is on the secondary road leading to Bear Trap Canyon. Float fishing from Ennis Campground to Ennis Lake is closed.

## The Madison River from Ennis to Three Forks

### Ennis Lake

The lake is shallow, no more than 20 feet in most places. Solar heating of the lake often raises the water temperature close to 80 degrees during the heat of summer, which threatens both the trout in the lake and the trout downstream. In spite of this, healthy populations of 3- to 5-pound Eagle Lake rainbows and browns entice boaters and float tubers.

### Ennis Lake Outlet to Three Forks

The outlet of Ennis Lake picks up speed as it drops down through the Lee Metcalf Wilderness in Bear Trap Canyon. Bear Trap Canyon is wicked white-water country and should be avoided unless you are knowledgeable about the vagaries of this rushing canyon water. For floating information contact:

Bureau of Land Management
Box 3388
Butte, MT 59702

Highway 287 splits at the town of Norris and heads to Cardwell and Interstate 90. The Madison River is reached again by taking Highway 84 to Warm Springs and then to the outlet of Beartrap Canyon. A secondary road, Madison Road, follows the river to Three Forks. The lower Madison is broad and much warmer as a result of the shallow water of Lake Ennis. Lower in elevation, the lower Madison's water temperatures slow

down the fishing by mid-summer. Released fish are highly stressed and frequently die. Spring and fall are most assuredly the best time to fish the lower Madison.

### Bear Trap Wilderness Canyon of the Madison River

**Directions:** Hikers reach the Bear Trap Canyon from the north, off State Highway 84, near the

Ennis, Montana

bridge, which crosses the Madison River eight miles northeast of Norris, Montana. The easiest route, however, is to take Highway 84 right out of Bozeman.

Managed by the Bureau of Land Management as part of the Lee Metcalf Wilderness, Bear Trap Canyon of the Madison River offers a day hike of wilderness fishing or a nine-mile Class IV whitewater adventure. Cutting its way through 1,500 feet of granite rock of the Madison Range, the canyon offers camping at Bear Creek, about three and a half miles from the trailhead. Above the campground the remainder of the canyon is closed to camping. The canyon is best fished from spring until the heat of summer. Due in part to the thermal warming of the shallow lake above the canyon, the Madison reaches critical levels of heat stress for trout. In extremely hot and dry years, such as 1988, trout mortality alarmed biologists and the general public.

Although concerns had been voiced as far back as the 1960s, the summer of 1988 brought a coalition of state biologists, Trout Unlimited and the general public decrying the loss of a once-great fishery. When Montana Power applied for re-licensing, the Federal Energy Regulatory Commission required consultation with local agencies and the public to establish a plan to mitigate the negative impacts of thermal heating. A consensus plan called for an infusion of pulse flows during the heat of summer. During these periods, pulsed flows of 12,000 to 21,000 cfs reduced maximum temperatures by five degrees, with an overall aftereffect of lowering the water temperature 3.2 degrees. Clearly, the canyon is making a comeback as larger trout draw fishermen into the wilderness section.

The best fishing is in early spring until mid- or late July. The canyon has healthy populations of 16- to 18-inch rainbows and browns with some genuine lunkers. Although being in the canyon mid-June during the Salmon Fly hatch can be a piece of heaven, timing your arrival to coincide with the hatch can be hell. Depending on the spring runoff and what the dam operators are doing, the hatch can be impacted greatly and last only five or six days. After the trout have gorged themselves, they sulk under the high, muddy water until the river clears. When this happens, watch for prodigious caddis fly hatches. Stripping in sculpin patterns provides the best chance for catching trophy trout from the canyon down stream to Greycliff Campground in late November through March. This wild canyon, which has taken the lives of a number of rafters and kayakers, poses some risk to the walk-in fisherman as well.

The canyon is home to hordes of rattlesnakes. I talked to a college student at Bozeman State who fishes this section of the river every chance that he can get. He loves the phenomenal fishing so close to his dorm room. He recommended snake guards. Ticks can also be a problem, and bring a water-purifying pump if you plan to camp, as giardia is present. Much to my surprise, the area is covered with poison ivy, and I fell victim to a very serious infection.

The campsites by the trailhead are primitive. Across the highway, however, a fee campground provides eight campsites with tables and lots of room. This campground also offers a water pump. Keep in mind that this is hot country with no shade to speak of in the campgrounds. The most popular float outside of the canyon begins at Warm Springs Access just above the trailhead. Float fishermen begin at Warm Springs and float down to Greycliff Campground, a distance of 8.5 miles. I recommend the campground at Greycliff, as it offers an abundance of shade.

Greycliff Campground may be reached between mileage markers 10 and 11. Highway 84 swings away from the river at Black's Ford. Black's Ford offers a boat launch at the junction with Highway 84 and Madison Road. From this junction Greycliff Campground is five miles. The road then continues to the next fishing access, Cobblestone, 12 miles from the highway junction. Continuing north on Madison Road will lead to Madison Buffalo Jump State Park and Missouri Headwaters State Park, where the Jefferson River, Madison River and Gallatin River form the Missouri River.

For further information and a map of the canyon write to:

Bear Trap Canyon
Bureau of Land Management
1005 Selway Drive
Dillon, MT 59725
(406) 683-2337

## Side Trip – Highway 191: The Ruby River

Follow Highway 287 out of Ennis to the restored mining towns of Virginia City and Nevada City, then to the town of Twin Bridges where the Ruby River and the Beaverhead join to form the Jefferson River. The Ruby River really looks more like a large creek than a river, especially late in the summer. While populations of grayling increase, rainbow populations seem to be decreasing. Even with stream access laws, the Ruby offers few public access points, with the exception of three or four bridges. Similar to the Beaverhead, the Ruby meanders down through a willow-lined valley. Unless you have access on private property or a lot of free time to seek out those few and far-between public penetrations, my advice would be to turn south on Highway 41 towards Dillon and fish the famous Beaverhead.

## Interstate 90 East to Bozeman

**Exit 283: Madison Buffalo Jump State Park**
"Prior to the introduction of the horse to the Indians of the Northern Great Plains, the Blackfeet, Flathead and Shoshone tribes stampeded herds of bison over this precipice in order to secure the necessities of food, shelter, and tools. The top of the jump affords impressive views of the Madison River Valley and surrounding mountain ranges." –Montana State Parks brochure

**Exit 288:** Manhattan, Montana.

**Exit 298:** Belgrade, Montana.

**Exit 305:** Bozeman, Montana; route to Yellowstone National Park via the Gallatin River along Highway 191 to the West Yellowstone Entrance.

## Side Trip – Highway 191: The Gallatin River

**Note:** For a camping and picnic guide to Gallatin National Forest along the Gallatin River, call (406) 587-6920 or write:

Bozeman Ranger District
3710 Fallon Street, Suite C
Bozeman, MT 59718

Years ago, float fishing was prohibited on the Gallatin from the park boundaries to the East Gallatin River to avoid conflict with bank fishermen. Today bank fishermen must share the canyon waters with an amazing number of commercial raft companies as well as kayakers. The only section open to float fishing is from the East Gallatin River down to Logan Bridge on Highway 205 or further down to Missouri Headwaters State Park. The West Fork of the Gallatin during spring run-off challenges floaters with Class III and IV whitewater. If you are going to float the river even during the summer, I would recommend buying the Gallatin River Montana Afloat map, which may be purchased in any fly shop throughout western and southwestern Montana. This is a no-nonsense river that I personally choose not to float.

Steep timbered mountains, towering crags, steep canyons and fluttering aspen leaves lend a transcendentalist aura to the 40-odd miles of the Gallatin Canyon. Unlike the Madison River, which is surrounded by benchland sagebrush, the Gallatin Canyon section inspires a sense of wonderment. The Gallatin River from the Park boundary to Taylor Creek primarily holds small rainbows and whitefish in abundance. Still resembling a creek, the water is easily waded and easily accessible with many pullouts along the highway. For the most part the river is shallow and easily fished with dry fly patterns. Taylor Creek is renowned for mudding up the river long after spring run-off subsides the last week of June. So if by chance you arrive after some heavy rains, fish above Taylor's Fork in the park.

From Taylor Creek to the West Fork of the Gallatin harbors an astounding number of 10- to 12-inch rainbows with estimates up to 3,000 per mile! This section can only be described as just fun fishing. Drive along the river and pick the type of water you enjoy fishing. Riffles, pockets, pools and boulder-strewn sections provide a diversity of habitat for dry fly fishermen, nymph fishermen and spin fishermen. The best part of this fun fishing is the fact that the fish readily rise to attractor patterns in the fast waters. Although weighted nymphs and streamers work best in this boulder-strewn section, dry fly purists catch trout behind the rocks in those hard-to-reach places. Be very cautious when wading, however, as this section is potentially dangerous, even late in the summer. For the most part rainbows average 8 to 12-inches with enough 14- and 15-inchers to offset complacency. Prepare yourself for company, however, as you will be confronted by a constant stream of rafts and kayaks.

Leaving the red sandstone cliffs and the canyon behind, the Gallatin enters agricultural bottomland. Heavy agriculture use leaves a scarcity of water in some parts of the braided bottomland. Access is difficult with the exception of public bridge crossings, which are numerous above and below Four Corners. Be sure to stay under the high water mark to be legal. During the heat of summer, this section is difficult to fish with the exception of pools and banks, which often hold good-sized browns. If you are a visitor with a limited time to fish, skip this section of water. From the Logan Bridge on Highway 205 at the junction with Logan-Trident Road to Missouri Headwaters State Park, the river is open to float fishing. This is an especially popular section during the fall for spawning runs from the Missouri River. Access to the East Fork of the Gallatin is restricted with the exception of bridge crossings from Logan upstream towards Bozeman.

## Side Trip – Highway 191: West Yellowstone to Bozeman along the Gallatin River

### MM 1: Access road to Baker's Flat Campground

Located three miles north of West Yellowstone, the campground has 72 camping sites and is restricted to hard-sided campers only.

### MM 2.8: Access to Rainbow Lake Campground

Located five miles north of West Yellowstone, take Road #610 west three miles and then turn north on Road 6954 two miles to the campground. The campground has 85 camping sites and is restricted to hard-sided campers only.

### MM 7: Cougar Creek

Meandering through the Madison Valley, Cougar Creek crosses Highway 191 to join Duck Creek a mile or so above Grayling Arm of Hebgen Lake. West of the highway the creek travels through mostly private property. Take the Cougar Creek Road one mile east to reach the Park boundary. Cougar Creek is swampy and host to small browns, rainbows and brook trout, the latter being quite small and quite populous. Richard Parks in his excellent book, *Fishing Yellowstone National Park*, points out that Cougar Creek is actually Maple Creek, as Cougar Creek seeps into the meadow prior to reaching Maple Creek. Parks speculates that the 1959 earthquake altered the course of these once-joined creeks. Names aside, the creek is swampy, willow-lined and sedimentary and offers poor fishing. Maple Creek can also be reached from the Gneiss Creek Trail about seven miles from the West Yellowstone Entrance on the road to Madison Junction.

## MM 8: Duck Creek, Richards Creek, Gneiss Creek and Campanula Creek

Duck Creek may be reached by turning east off Highway 191 onto an unmarked road next to the highway department's maintenance shop. Just beyond the shop the road turns to a dirt road. After three-tenths of a mile, veer right following the WNP Duck Creek sign. After six-tenths of a mile the Park boundary posts force you to turn left or right. Turn left for another two-tenths of a mile to the turnaround, which borders a private pond and the backed-up waters of Duck Creek. A few hundred yards from the parking area, the trail overlooks miles of meandering meadow water. At some point in this maze, Gneiss Creek joins Duck

Cougar Creek

Creek. Having accessed Gneiss Creek from the Gneiss Creek Trail further up Highway 191, I never did find the junction of the two creeks. You will appreciate this confession when you, too, stand gazing across this swampy, willow-lined valley. Although I brought up a very good-sized trout to inspect my presentation on Duck or Gneiss Creek (pronounced 'nice'), I never landed a fish over 10 inches. The best time to fish Duck Creek is early June when the spawners return to Hebgen Lake, unless, of course, you follow the belief that they should be undisturbed on their return journey to Hebgen Lake. Duck Creek outside the Park is closed to fishing until June 15. Bring your favorite terrestrial patterns for late summer.

While speaking to one of the landowners on the pond, I discovered that one of the record browns was taken on Duck Creek back in the 1930s. A few years later one of the landowners on Duck Creek decided he wanted a pond so he built a small dam, backing up the waters into the park. By the early 1990s the Park threatened to remove the dam through litigation, unless the surrounding landowners built a fish ladder for what was once a thriving spawning ground. After completion of this $22,000 fish ladder, the very next spring found large numbers of 16-inch trout heading up Duck Creek. The owner ruminated that he wished they had built it years earlier.

Standing at the overlook just beyond the turnaround, you will note a faint trail leading across the swampy grass in a southeasterly direction. The trail leads to Richards Creek and Richards Creek Pond. Of the creeks coursing through this swampy valley, Richards Creek is said to be the best fishing for dinks; however, the headwaters of Richards Creek produces good fishing for cutthroats and brook trout in the beaver ponds. The entire area is part of Yellowstone's Bear Management Program and regulations should be reviewed. In the last couple of years some very aggressive moose have been defending the ponds from angler intrusion.

## Saga: Yellowstone Park's Gneiss Creek, August 1999

The Yellowstone Backcountry Office holds open one-third of backcountry campsites for first-serve

Duck Creek

availability. It was clear that they discourage stock use. They only permit lakeside camping 12 to 15 miles into the backcountry, which is no problem if you are riding. If you are leading donkeys and only want to hike five to eight miles, good luck. They offer only sites far from lakes and streams. I also heard a man complain that the previous year his party could not find their backcountry campsite and had to return. The park official made no comment. Pauline and I continued watching the mandatory back-country travel tape, signed our backcountry permits and together with our two donkeys headed for the Gneiss Trail. We were told the campsite had no shade and was not on the creek. Since this is a bear-management area, fishing is restricted to areas

where the trail intersects a creek. We never found the campsite, nor were there any trailhead signs or information.

Banjo, my smaller donkey, demonstrated what happens when you don't properly train a donkey before you take him into the wilderness. Although he was four years old, up until four months previous to this trip, he had never been around humans. This little wild ass has come a long way. In fact after five days on the road and trail, he had become quite affectionate and bonded with both Pauline and myself. But this came about only after the two of us stumbled off the trail and fell down the side of a steep mountain.

The previous day we had taken the donkeys up the Nez Perce Creek Trail, which drains into the Firehole River. I wanted to fish further up than I had before. We didn't get very far, perhaps two miles, as both donkeys were acting up. We gave them a hard lesson in crossing a creek. Banjo was terrified, and we had to use the whip to get him to re-cross. Buddy displayed his worst case of stubbornness, refusing to cross back, even when we used the whip. I told Pauline we would just pack up and leave him like a little kid. As we packed up Banjo, Buddy nibbled the grass and snubbed us. Leading Banjo through the trees broke Buddy's nonchalance. As if he had been struck by lightning, he frantically plunged into the water and charged through the deadfall to meet us. A few minutes later Banjo acted up and tried to run over me when Pauline led Buddy ahead of us. That should have been sufficient warning for the next day's pack trip up the Gneiss Trail. Although the Nez Perce fishing was disappointing in both size and numbers, the training for the donkeys was invaluable.

The next day we picked up the Gneiss Trail about 8.5 miles north of West Yellowstone on Highway 191. The trailhead is right next to the cemetery as you come up a rise. The Gneiss Creek meets Campanula Creek to form Duck Creek, which crosses the highway a mile or so from the trailhead. Campanula Creek is crossed 1.5 miles from the trailhead in a beautiful canyon just before it enters the marshy Madison Valley. I fished a number of spots close to the trail and never caught a fish over seven inches; the same is true for Gneiss Creek, although I did raise a 16-incher. Later, I talked to a resident of Duck Creek. He laughed and said that

Buddy and Banjo

some of the books have generously attributed better fishing than what exists. For every large trout caught, plan on landing a dozen dinks.

Crossing Campanula Creek with the donkeys was an improvement from the previous day on the Nez Perce. The crossing is short, perhaps as little as 10 feet, but the crossing is at the tail of a pool up against a jagged fallen log. When we got to the other side, we had a choice in trail directions. I selected the fool's route, which led up the hill on an old path probably used prior to the 1988 firestorm. Pauline said she would lead Buddy up the trail as I re-adjusted Banjo's pack. Banjo immediately became alarmed that he was being separated. About 60 feet up this steep trail, Banjo tried to run me over to join

Buddy. As I fought to maintain control, I looked up the hillside to see Buddy acting up and breaking away from Pauline. I flashed a brief bit of irritation at Pauline for loosing control of Buddy, until I realized I, too, was in a struggle to hold on to Banjo. Banjo panicked when he saw Buddy lunging up the hill by himself. Banjo's bond with Buddy negated any fear of reprisal from me.

I literally fought with Banjo to keep him from running over me. Suddenly, both of us were off the trail falling to our knees, desperately struggling to keep from tumbling down a very vertical hillside to the creek below. Banjo is short, so he was very top-heavy with his pack. I held on to the lead rope trying to keep his head pointing uphill. If he were to roll, it could have lead to a life-threatening injury. At some point in the struggle, I found myself directly below Banjo, as he spun around trying to catch his momentum. I was sliding on all fours staring into the ass end of a floundering donkey. Finally, he was pointed directly uphill in front of me. His back legs dug into the loose rock and soil, pelting me with debris. His sawbuck and pannier bags askew, and slipping on every forward lunge, Banjo recovered and headed up the slope. I could no longer hold on and watched him struggle up the slope with his pack slipping off to one side.

By the time he met up with Buddy and Pauline, his pack and pannier bags were dragging beneath him. I was so out of breath and exhausted I couldn't even talk to Pauline. Pauline was sucking air as well. Finally she said, "What have I let you talk me into? And we are in grizzly country, no less!" Banjo had

Gneiss Creek

his head buried in Pauline's bosom and was shaking violently. My rush to the backcountry with an untrained donkey was impetuous and shortsighted.

Even though the fishing was relatively poor and we were pounded by two days of hard rain, we gained some hard-knock donkey experience! Arriving at the trailhead, we were pelted with rain. That night, tucked away in our hard-sided RV donkey trailer, Pauline lifted up her head from the pillow and asserted, "You're not going to make an outdoor woman of me. I am glad to be right here in this trailer rather than some flimsy tent in a Grizzly Management Area!"

## Campaunla Creek

Campanula Creek joins Duck Creek from the north. The creek can best be accessed from the Gneiss Creek Trail. The trailhead is located north on Highway 191 a mile past the junction with Highway 287. Look for the cemetery at the top of the hill, as the trailhead parking area is located just above the entrance to the cemetery. If you have younger fishers in your party and you want to take a short hike into a beautiful creek for a large population of small trout, than take the time to fish this little creek 1.5 miles from the parking area. Keep in mind, however, that the area is a Bear Management Area and may be subject to fishing restrictions that may change. The trail wanders across a ridge with pockets of aspen and wild flower fields down into a canyon where Campanula Creek winds its way a half of a mile to meet Duck Creek.

### MM 11.1: Grayling Creek

Grayling Creek is an overgrown, swampy creek holding fair numbers of trout, but bring along plenty of mosquito repellant and pepper spray for the bears if you fish the lower end of the creek. The lower section as it makes its way to Hebgen Lake is heavily posted. Highway 191 parallels the creek between mileage markers 11 and 17 and provides a more typical freestone creek in a timbered canyon setting. Spilling down from the Gallatin Range to the

Madison Basin, Grayling Creek offers good fishing for cutthroats and rainbows from 7 to 10-inches. The creek is slow to settle after spring run-off so the best fishing is mid-summer. In spite of the proximity of the highway, the creek offers long stretches of quiet solitude with small pocket water to ply. Fall spawning runs of browns out of Hebgen Lake add spice to this little creek, which hosts smaller trout the further you travel up the canyon.

**MM 20:** Gallatin River Drainage inside the Yellowstone Park Boundary

**MM 22: Fan Creek**
Fan Creek is within the Yellowstone Park boundary and holds 7- to 10-inch cutthroats and rainbows; some are quite plump. Fan Creek is easy to locate. Look for the big turnout overlooking the meadow section of the upper Gallatin. Looking across

Specimen Creek, Yellowstone National Park

the meadow, you can see the point where Fan Creek slips in to join the meandering Gallatin. The trail drops right off the side of the parking lot and crosses three little bridges. If you are just going to sample the first mile of Fan Creek, drop off the trail where it meets the bench. Be sure to come prepared for bears and bugs. The flies and mosquitoes can be overwhelming in June and July. After about 1.5 miles, Fawn Pass Trail meets the Fan Creek Trail. The trail drops down and fords Fan Creek.

**MM 26.5: Specimen Creek**
One would be hard-pressed to find a more beautiful mountain creek. Here is a perfect little creek for

a picnic or fun fishing. The creek hosts some nice fat cutthroats in the first two miles below the north fork and the east fork of the creek. Neither of the forks is really worth fishing due to the steep terrain, difficulty in casting and the smaller water. The trail begins at the Specimen Creek picnic area and trailhead. For the most part the trail gently climbs up through wooded landscape with small meadow openings. Wildflowers are abundant even in mid-July. Best of all, you can sample this small creek or cross the highway and fish the Gallatin River.

**MM 31:** You are now exiting Yellowstone Park, and you will need a Montana State Fishing License.

**MM 34: Taylor Creek**
Taylor Creek is good fishing for fair-sized cutthroats. The campsites are primitive (open meadow camping), but they are shaded, and a number of them are located next to the creek. The road, however, is quite bumpy and rutted, but high-clearance passenger vehicles will reach the camping areas just a few miles from the highway. Although I found the road

restricted to 20 mph, I was amazed by the progress a UPS truck was making on his return to the highway from the Nine-Quarter Circle Guest Ranch. Follow the Taylor Creek Road (#134) 5.9 miles to reach Wapiti Creek turn-off. Wapiti Creek is fair fishing for small trout, but this creek is very small. Wapiti Creek Road is closed just a mile or so from the junction, just short of the Wapiti Ranger Station. The Taylor Creek road continues to another

Upper Taylor Creek

fork in the road. Make a left and follow the creek until you reach a private bridge and the trailhead to Lightning Creek. Lightning Creek is a small tributary of Taylor Creek. (The trailhead is across the creek from the private bridge.) Near the private bridge are a couple of primitive campsites along Taylor Creek. Upper Taylor Creek may be reached by following the USFS trail through a canyon to a small meadow section, which holds a few nice cutthroats. The upper section fishes well for 8- to 10-inch trout, but the view is lost to clear-cutting, and the upper creek is difficult to maneuver due to down-fall and tight quarters.

Taylor Creek gently runs its course through sage-brush meadows below the road closure. Although more heavily fished in the first few miles, the creek supports healthy populations of rainbows and cutthroats. Some larger trout may be taken during the late summer spruce moth hatch. From the highway to the road closure is 10.7 miles. If you are camping along Taylor Creek and you don't feel like cooking, I recommend the Cinnamon Lodge Restaurant, which offers great Mexican food. The restaurant is just a few miles north of the Taylor Creek turn-off at mileage marker 37 on Highway 191.

I fished the Taylor's Fork of the Gallatin River about a mile up from Highway 191, where I camped with my donkey. I fished for about a half-hour when I arrived and then again the next morning. It was still running high and dirty after a number of days of hard rain. I didn't catch a thing! I drove up the road and then hiked up to the headwaters and caught some nice cuts from 12 to 14-inches. I have yet to fish Lightning Creek, which is another fork of Taylor's Creek. The Gallatin River outside the park had lots of fishermen, but the reports were slow. I did fish the Gallatin River inside the park near Specimen Creek. I caught some nice rainbows, but I had to flee for my life (or my sanity), as the flies were so thick and aggressive that I couldn't concentrate and missed a couple of fish in the 12- to 14-inch bracket. The worst of it was that I had purchased a mosquito net and had left it in my truck. Later I fished Fan Creek and Specimen Creek. Both of fered great creek fishing and wonderful scenery, along with fewer flies and mosquitoes.

Since the next day was July 15, the opener on the Yellowstone River in the park, I decided to pack up Buddy for this heralded event. The water was high that year so the hordes stayed away. No one was having any luck fishing with drys. When I finally arrived, the only place to park was along the side channel at Buffalo Ford. I walked up to the head of the island, as the side channel is closed to fishing. A lure fisherman was standing next to the closed sign letting his lure drift down into the no-fishing zone. The old rascal caught six big fish in the "slough" on a big green and white lure. I went upstream of him and fished for an hour without a bump. Finally, the gray-haired reprobate left. I moved down a bit so nobody could get between me and the fishing closure sign.

Lower Taylor's Fork of the Gallatin River

I waited for over an hour until I watched a big cutthroat slowly feed on the surface, albeit just below the sign. Oh, how I wanted to drift a bead-head prince down to him. He was only two feet behind the imaginary line that cut from the sign to the tip of the island. I waited another half-hour. Finally, he was legal. I fished him for an hour with just about everything I had. Finally I tied on a size 20 PMD on a 6X leader. Meanwhile, a chatty Texan crowded me asking for advice on what to use. He had been next to me for hours, and he had observed that I had not had a single take. Perhaps he just thought that misery loves company. I was in no mood to chitchat. Suddenly the big cutthroat

hit while the Texan was at my shoulder showing me his box of flies. I could have landed this big cutthroat with a 7X tippet; he offered no struggle. I didn't measure him, but he was over 18 inches. The next one I caught was slightly smaller. Four hours of fishing for two fish, and all the while poor Buddy was cooped up in the trailer. Although it was not hot, I was feeling guilty about his confinement and the fact that I had told myself I was just going to make a few casts and take some pictures of opening day on the Yellowstone.

## The Gallatin River Below Taylor's Fork

### MM 41.5: Red Cliff Campground

Located 48 miles south of Bozeman on Highway 191, the campground offers 68 camping sites and four picnic sites. Just below Red Cliff, the highway enters the Porcupine Wildlife Management Area that ends just short of the West Fork of the Gallatin. The West Fork of the Gallatin is a small stream, and it parallels the road leading to Big Sky Resort. The stream fishes well for 7- to 9-inch trout, if you care to fish in a commercially-developed playground.

### MM 45.2: Porcupine Creek

If you are traveling with small children and would like to picnic along a beautiful little creek, follow Road #653 a half-mile to the Porcupine Creek trailhead, which is restricted to hikers and horse riders. Although the creek holds fish in its small pools, for the most part they will be very small.

### MM 53.2: Portal Creek

Portal Creek rushes down a tight canyon and offers good fishing for young people willing to scramble over deadfall and dab in the pools. The road follows the creek a hundred yards above. At three miles the road crosses the creek. Just past the bridge on the left is a small spur road that comes to a dead-end. For tent campers looking for seclusion along a tumbling canyon creek, this is it. From the highway to the bridge is approximately three miles.

### MM 56.8 Moose Creek Flat Campground

Located 32 miles south of Bozeman, the campground has 14 camping sites and very small brookies.

### MM 57: Swan Creek Campground and Greek Creek Campground

Greek Creek Campground is on Highway 191, 31 miles south of Bozeman and has 14 campsites. Swan Creek Campground is one mile east of Highway 191 on Swan Creek Road with 11 camping sites.

### MM 61.3: Lava Lake

A small 20-acre lake in steep timbered mountains, Lava Lake produces 10- to 12-inch rainbows. The distance from the trailhead to the lake is approximately 3.5 miles.

### MM 65.3: Squaw Creek, Rat Lake and Spire Rock Campground

Spire Rock Campground is located 26 miles south of Bozeman off Highway 191, crossing Squaw Creek Bridge. From the highway take Squaw Creek Road two miles. The campground has 20 camping sites and is a non-fee campground. Squaw Creek is a fast, tumbling creek. It provides good fishing for rainbows, cutthroats and brookies. From the highway to Rat Lake is seven miles. For the first mile and a half, the road parallels the Gallatin River and offers many pullouts and picnic spots. Spire Creek Campground is a fee campground offering tables and outhouses. The road is suitable for passenger vehicles all the way to the trailhead to Rat Lake, if the road is dry. At 5.5 miles from the highway, the road forks down to the creek to a beautiful non-fee, primitive campground. This is a great spot for children to play in a shallow creek. The road passes this spot and crosses a small white bridge. From the bridge to the trailhead is exactly one mile. The trailhead to the lake is open to ATVs (40-inch restriction), hikers and horse riders. This is not a wilderness area, and it is very popular during the early spring when the Gallatin River is running high and muddy. The 18-acre lake is shallow with grassy, gentle slopes meeting the water on one side and surrounded by timber on the other side. The lake holds some large rainbows for float tubers who want to spend a full day. The trailhead is not marked, but it is easy to recognize as the road makes a sweeping turn up the mountain, and the trail is easily seen on the other side of some large boulders.

### MM 68: Spanish Creek and Campground

Spanish Peaks Campground and trailhead is reached 9.2 miles from the highway. The lower reaches are on private property and closed to the public. Deviating from the norm, the last 3.5 miles of the road are paved. The road trip offers spectacular scenery as it crosses one of Ted Turner's ranch holdings. The campground is a horse-camping trailhead right on Spanish Creek. The trailhead leads to many lakes in the Spanish Lakes Wilderness area. The south fork of Spanish Creek offers good fishing for small size trout in a lush setting.

Highway 191 junction with Interstate 90

# Interstate 90 – Bozeman

## Side Trip – Hyalite Reservoir and Drainage

**Directions:** Take Highway 84 right down the main street of Bozeman to 19th Street. Follow 19th Street past the university for seven miles.

Hyalite Reservoir

Turn left at the USFS sign and follow the paved Hyalite Road 10.3 miles to the dam and boat launch. Hyalite Reservoir, with its rugged and towering peaks in the background, offers beautiful shoreline camping and fishing, albeit for stocked trout. The lake is open to boats, but it is restricted to a no-wake rule. The southern section of the creek is most popular with fly fishers plying their belly boats and pontoon boats for good-sized cutthroats. Emerald and Heather Lakes offer good fishing for those willing to hike into the backcountry. The following mileage marker postings begin from the junction of 19th Street and Highway 84 in Bozeman.

### Hyalite Creek

This small, brushy creek holds lots of pocket water for good creek fishing using attractor patterns.

### MM 13.2: Langhor Trail Campground

A beautiful campground along Hyalite Creek. A few primitive camping sites exist as well along the road.

**MM 17.3:** Blackmore Recreation Area, Gallatin National Forest.

**MM 18:** Hood Creek boat ramp and group picnic site.

### MM 19.1: Bridge crossing over the East Fork

The East Fork and the West Fork offer good, brushy creek fishing. The opening date for fishing both forks is the third Saturday in July.

**MM 19.2: Turn-off for Heather Lake and Emerald Lake Trailhead**

Emerald Lake, a shallow 25-acre lake resting in an open basin at 7,750 feet elevation, is 4.5 miles from the trailhead and a half-mile below Heather Lake at elevation 9,000 feet. Both lakes offer good fishing for 10- to 12-inch cutthroats.

**MM 20.5:** A beautiful, primitive campsite along upper Hyalite Creek.

**MM 21: Grotto Falls Trail**

Wheelchair-accessible trail to Grotto Falls

# 7

# YELLOWSTONE RIVER DRAINAGE

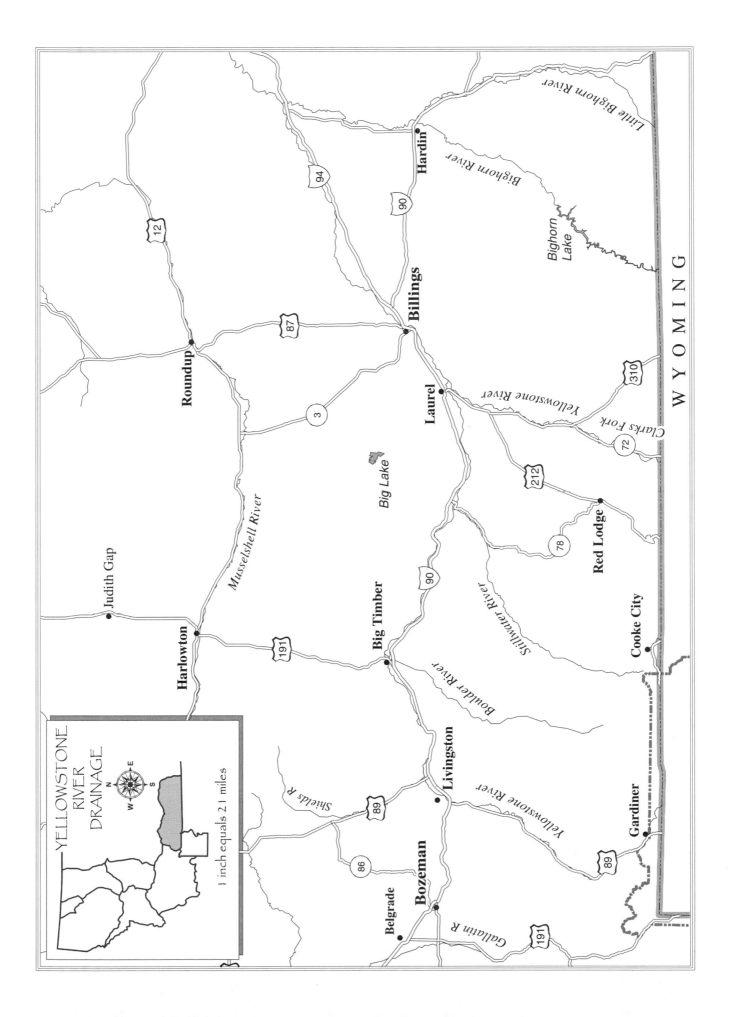

# Highway 89 –
# The Yellowstone River from Livingston to Gardiner

**Exit 333:** Livingston, Montana, route to Yellowstone National Park

## The Yellowstone River

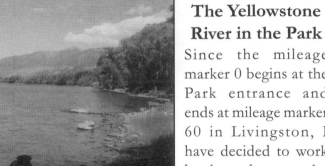
Yellowstone River

The legendary Yellow-stone River inspires awe and reverence. From its source waters high in the Absaroka Mountains to its rendezvous with the Missouri River in North Dakota, the great Yellowstone River remains an uninterrupted, free-flowing river for over 600 miles.

Outside the Park, the river affords excellent fishing opportunities for both wade fishers and float fishers from Livingston to Gardiner. Below Livingston, the Yellowstone River offers excellent fishing to Big Timber. One disadvantage of this section is that the float fishing access points are further apart and access to the river is more restricted. For the most part, the Yellowstone River is an easily navigated river.

However, the three-mile section of water from Gardner to McConnell Landing is a whitewater section, as is the section from Joe Brown to Yankee Jim Canyon. This section requires an experienced whitewater oarsman. From the East River Road to Livingston is relatively easier to float, although braided channels, sharp turns and sweepers require the usual vigilance. Mayor's Landing on Eighth Street is the last Livingston take-out.

## The Yellowstone River in the Park

Since the mileage marker 0 begins at the Park entrance and ends at mileage marker 60 in Livingston, I have decided to work backwards on the chance that you may be traveling to the park from Livingston. Shuttles may be arranged through the fly shops.

**MM 60:** Livingston, Montana

**MM 51:** East River Road fishing access

**MM 50: Carter Bridge**
Carter Bridge has a good boat take-out and is a good spot for wade fishermen.

**MM 45:** Trail Creek fishing access

**MM 43.3: Pine Creek** Take the Pine Creek road 1.4 miles to the bridge fishing access and boat launch.

## MM 41.4: Mallards Rest Campground

The campground is a fee campground and offers 20 sites on a "pack it in – pack it out" basis. It also offers a boat launch and good access for wade fishers.

**Note:** From Carter Bridge to just above Point of Rocks, the East River Road parallels the river. The East River Road has Loch Levin Campground, which is nine miles south of Livingston. Take the Pine Creek Road and head south again to the campground. Loch Levin Campground has 30 campsites, water, toilets and a boat launch.

 ## MM 37.2:

### Mill Creek Bridge

Mill Creek Bridge has a private boat launch that is not posted. The gate is open, but I would skip this access unless you have a four-wheel drive vehicle. The launch is steep and rocky with little room to maneuver. Take the Mill Creek Road 11 miles to Snowbank Campground, which has 12 camping sites.

### Mill Creek

Cross the bridge and follow the paved road

for six miles and then a dirt road for another 7.4 miles to a private meadow. Although the meadow is on private property, this section may be accessed later in the summer from the highway about a hundred yards downstream. Look for a pullout. Follow

Yellowstone River below Livingston

Yellowstone River below Gardiner

the fence line to public access to the water on National Forest land. However, be sure you stay under the high water mark at all times. The meadow gets fished heavily. Snowbank Campground is a fee campground with plenty of shade and garbage removal. Above the campground are some primitive camp-

Fishermen fillet walleye at Dailey Lake.

sites. The water is icy cold above the meadow section and interspersed with a lot of private property. Late in the summer small parachute hoppers work best.

### East Fork of Mill Creek

Although the East Fork is small and shallow, small pockets and riffles offer up good catches of 8- to 10-inch cutthroats. It is a great creek for kids. The

access road ends a mile and a half at a locked gate to a private ranch. The ranch can be bypassed by trail, but I did not have time to explore it.

### West Fork of Mill Creek

The West Fork road cuts right through a Bible camp and climbs high up into a steep canyon. The creek is fast moving, but it does hold some nice pools and pockets in the canyon section. The road ends 5.8 miles at the trailhead. I walked down into the canyon, but the going is tough due to downed trees from the 1988 fire. The creek is loaded with 5- to 9-inch cutthroats, but it is also loaded with mosquitoes.

**MM 33.4:** Fishing access.

### MM 31: Emigrant, Montana

Take the road to the river and cross the bridge. On the other side of the bridge is a day-use site with a good boat launch, as well as good access for wade fishers.

### Dailey Lake

Dailey Lake may be reached from the Mill Creek Road or from Emigrant. From Emigrant to the lake is eight miles. The lake is shaped like a silver dollar, and it is shallow all around the shoreline. Although the lake holds some trout, most of the locals fish for perch and walleye.

**MM 25.5:** Fishing access.

### MM 24: Big Creek

Don't judge this creek when you pass over it on the highway. Big Creek fishing access is 5.5 miles from the highway and six miles to the trailhead. The road is bumpy, but the creek is charming and host to 7- to 9-inch cutthroats, which are plentiful.

**◈ 🅰 MM 23.8: Meditation Point**

Here is a rest area and picnic site large enough for the largest RVs with good fishing access to the river.

**MM 21:** Tom Miner Creek provides a nice campground 11 miles from the highway, but it is too small to be worth fishing. The scenic drive is beautiful as the road winds through open parks and aspen shaded hillsides.

**◈ ◿ MM 21: Point of Rocks**

Point of Rocks has a boat launch.

**MM 19.7:** East River Road.

**🅰 MM 18: Carbella Campground**

Carbella is an unimproved campground one mile west of the Tom Miner Bridge. It has five campsites.

**◈ ◿ MM 13: Yankee Jim fishing access**

Just upstream from Yankee Jim is the Slip and Slide access, but you will need to carry your boat to the water's edge.

**◈ ◿ MM 7.1: Corwin Springs Boat Launch**

From the boat launch, visitors may take the dirt road that parallels the Yellowstone River on the western side. The road winds above the river for eight miles. It provides a few access points down to the river and passes a few primitive campsites.

**◈ MM 6.3:** LaDuke Spring picnic site.

**◈ MM 3:** McConnell Landing.

**MM 0:** Gardiner, Montana.

# Interstate 90 – Livingston (Shields River)

The Shields River begins in the Crazy Mountains, flowing past the small town of Wilsall and Clyde

**Big Creek**

Park on Highway 89. This small bottomland river joins the Yellowstone River east of Livingston, Montana. Although the river holds some hefty browns, it is impacted by irrigation drawdowns and thermal heating during the summer months. It is best fished in the spring and fall. Most of the land is posted, affording few access points. Even the headwaters are mostly posted, and by the time public land is reached, the river is nothing more than a rivulet and home to very small cutthroats. One worthy side trip out of Livingston is Fairy Lake.

## Fairy Lake

Fairy Lake is reached from Highway 89 near the town of Clyde Park or north of the town of Wilsall. The lake may also be easily reached 37 miles from Bozeman. The lake is 12 acres and sheltered in a

Fairy Lake

bowl. Access to the lake is less than a quarter of a mile straight down a trail from the campground. Popular with weekend visitors from the Bozeman area, surprisingly few visitors fished this little gem on the Saturday that I visited the lake with Max, my young Labrador retriever. Expect to catch 9- to 12-inch cutthroats on small bead-head nymphs.

# Interstate 90 – Livingston to Hardin

## The Boulder River

A twelve-and-a-half foot pram, even with a seven-inch rocker bottom, quickly becomes a liability in Class III whitewater. The Boulder River during run-off is the playground of kayakers and whitewater rafters. Having checked the river in three locations the evening before, I convinced myself that I could safely drift the river seeking out sheltered nooks to fish. My last river mistake had taken place almost 20 years ago during spring run-off on the upper Bitterroot River. The memory of trying to save a custom-made fly rod that had been wrenched out of a man's hands and the ensuing nightmare served me well for those 20 years. My passengers were thrown out in relatively safe water. They were wearing life jackets so they quickly scrambled to shore. As the oarsman and owner of the raft, I was in trouble. At the tail end of the rapid, a pulsing logjam roared, gap-toothed like an evil jack-o-lantern ready to swallow up my life. My life jacket lay on the floor of the raft – I had mistakenly grabbed a child's vest for myself that morning. I was wearing chest waders without a belt. As the raft slowly rolled over in the trough and flipped for the second time, I grabbed the rope that ran the length of the tubes. When I saw the logjam, I instinctually reached out and snatched a willow branch. Later I would discover that it was the last willow tree that I could have snagged. The light straps holding the frame had broken, which sent the frame and all of my equipment to the bottom of the river.

My filled waders pulled me down like a sea anchor. My left hand held a branch no bigger than my thumb. My right hand grasped one of the rings on the raft. With both arms stretched out, and my head barely above water, I realized I had no choice but to let go of the raft and offer it up to the logjam. As soon as I released the raft, I plowed under the water. I slowly inched my way to shore hand-over-hand on a thin willow branch. I was deeply ashamed of my poor judgement. I had tried to save a man's fly rod in swift water. My most serious error of judgment, however, was in thinking that I had the strength to row us out of harm's way. I was fearful that my mishap would be spread up and down the river, hurting my chances for employment as a river guide. From that day until a June 2001 day on the Boulder River, I had been an extremely cautious river boatman. How was it possible that I could have erred again?

I personally know of guides with 25 years of river floating experience who have never even had a close call. So, how could I have become complacent and careless?

Driving seven hours increased my anticipation for fishing this new water. The Boulder River, a tributary entering the Yellowstone River at Big Timber, has an excellent reputation for healthy rainbows and browns. Secondly, I was eager to test my small river pram on a few Class III sections. Pride and impulsiveness are more fitting a man in his prime than at age 56. I rigged up with a bead-head pheasant tail nymph, a small twist of lead and a strike indica-

Boulder River during spring runoff

tor. My large cooler was in the front of the boat, and Max, my year-old Lab, quickly jumped on top of it so that he could better survey the river. I pulled the anchor into the boat. I wanted to take no unnecessary risks. My neophrene chest waders fit snug. I finished my preparation by buckling the cross straps on my life jacket.

I launched at the Boulder Forks Access near McLeod. The water was fast, faster than I had calculated standing on the shore. Dropping into the first set of waves my boat seemed to shrink in size. I knew I would slice through the curl at the top of the wave, but I was surprised on how much water I actually took into the boat. Max, too, was surprised by the unexpected blanket of ice-cold water that

drained off his coat. I had been surveying the water as a fisherman instead of a whitewater adventurer.

The Boulder River is well-named. Jagged rocks on both sides of the river forced me into the main chute, but it was not a clean run. A number of the rocks lie just inches under the splashing water. I was slow to react. When I quickly dodged the first obstacle, the boat's stern was caught in the chute, spinning me almost backwards. The quick maneuver caught Max off-guard, and he was straddling the cockpit rim halfway into the water. The two seconds that it took to drag Max back into the boat and move my fly rod out of the way almost led to the sinking of my boat.

When I attempted to spin around and line myself out, I was dropping into another chute, a position no boater wants to be. I knew I was in trouble when I saw the partially submerged boulder just in front of me. I slammed into it sideways. My next surprise was to see that Max had climbed back up on the cooler, and he was now plunging ass-backwards and head-first into the churning water. I instinctively threw myself to the highest side of the boat, which was straddling the boulder. Digging the right oar into the water, I spun the boat around backwards and slipped into the chute for the second time facing the wrong direction. Fortunately, I had coated the bottom of the boat with a coat of epoxy mixed with graphite. I wasted no time in spinning the boat around. All I could see of Max was the top of his head. The water was so white and bubbly I could not see his body, but I knew from the position of his head that he was in a vertical position and dog paddling for his life. After about 30 yards we were reunited.

For the next set of rapids I stood up to get a better view. When I sat down, hurriedly I might add, I cracked the ¾-inch plywood seat in half. I was stunned to find myself on the bottom of the boat barely peering over the cockpit rim. I got through this stretch with one knee on the bottom and one leg stretched out in front of me. I pulled over and set up the cooler as my new seat and took a fishing break to calm my nerves. For the first time in my life, I was truly scared on the oars. My self-confidence was shaken.

The good news is that I had good fishing, catching three trout, two 12-inch rainbows and a small brown. For the next seven miles I had to pull over and take rest breaks. Each time I caught two or three fish. A Good Samaritan caught up to me in a 14-foot cataraft. He and his wife were taking out at the Eightmile Bridge and asked me if I would like to join them rather than go on for another seven miles of equally rough water. I am sure that if I had been younger, my pride would have kept me from accepting the offer. As it was, I was exhausted and very intimidated by the water. I gushed with gratitude and honestly conveyed my apprehension about going any further. When I helped him drag his cataraft up an embankment, I noticed that he had a rod case strapped to the frame. Darn if he wasn't combining a whitewater run with fishing. Hmmm…

The Boulder River tumbles down three separate canyons of the Absaroka-Beartooth Wilderness, almost 50 miles to the town of Big Fork, where it enters the Yellowstone River. The water plummets down a fair gradient and averages 45 to 60 feet across. True to its name, the entire river is studded with large and small boulders. Wading can be difficult on the slippery rocks, but the rewards can be great. Both rainbows and browns move up from the Yellowstone to spawn, which provides some truly large lunkers for sure-footed waders who are smart enough to get out into the water. Resident trout in the lower river can reach 18 to 20-inches, while the rainbows and cutthroats in the National Forest section above the Natural Bridge State Monument typically run 10 to 14-inches. The Boulder River demands respect during spring run-off. It is not considered a float-fishing river. River runners should have a large raft or cataraft and be very experienced navigating white-water with little room for maneuverability. When the water drops in late July, it is impractical if not impossible to float through the miles of rock gardens.

Regardless of where you fish, the pocket water, fast chutes, short runs and broken riffles provide excellent fishing. Fish the river just as you would a large creek. Keep in mind that the fast riffles provide excellent lies and feeding zones for good-sized trout. The turbulence breaks just above the trout so they can rest comfortably on the bottom waiting for fast food deliveries. These fish are not picky. They have learned to be fast, grabbing opportunists. Use bead-head nymphs, a pinch of lead and a strike indicator. Fish upstream with short casts working each side of the boulder seams, as well as the pocket behind the boulder. Don't forget to fish directly in front of the boulder for typically smaller trout. Spin fishers should fish the water just like fly fishers. Keep the rod tip up and just let the lure tumble without snagging the bottom. Popular lures for all streams in Montana include small Panther Martins, Thomas Cyclones, Mepps, Kastmasters and Roostertails.

Fly pattern selections are typical of most cold water streams in Montana. Although the Boulder River has a Salmon Fly hatch, it is difficult to fish during late June. When the water becomes fishable, typically the first week of July, use standard dry fly patterns, heavy nymphs and watch for heavy caddis hatches in the evening. The Goddard Caddis works very well because of its exceptional floating quality. Hopper action is outstanding during the heat of summer. Be sure to put on a split-shot piece of lead and sink those hoppers in the pools, under bank cover and behind the boulders. Another effective technique is to use a greased Bailey's Muddler as a hopper pattern in the pocket water. If you don't catch a fish, let it sink and strip it in as a streamer. Although it is true that much of the Boulder River is not accessible due to private landowners, some of whom are very rich and famous, the river can be accessed at county bridges and state access points. Don't even bother drooling over the only section offer-

Upper Boulder River

ing large pools and long runs. This stretch of river is posted for miles, and conveniently for THEM, the river exits the canyon and the 70-foot falls. I looked for a trail down to the water, but it is an 80-foot straight drop to the tumbling water below. If you arrive during high water, be sure to fish above the falls in the National Forest section. Without the West Fork and the East Fork of the Boulder, the main stem above the falls fishes very well in late June using lures and weighted nymphs.

Don't waste your time with the **East Fork**. It is small and offers only a small campground and very active mine traffic. The primary source of platinum and palladium metals in the United States, the 28-mile long ore deposit is mined 18,500 feet be-

low the surface from the East Boulder River mine to the Stillwater River near Nye. Platinum is used in jewelry, electrical devices found in computers and in the catalysts on our cars and trucks. The Big Timber *Pioneer* in its 2001 summer edition reported that the price per ton of platinum "hovered around $570 per ounce while palladium prices were around $840 per ounce.... The East Fork mine expects to mine... 3,000 tons of ore per day to produce between 450,000 and 500,000 ounces of platinum and palladium a year." If you wonder where all the waste material goes, look at the remnant piles on both sides of the Stillwater River downstream from the trailhead.

The **West Fork of the Boulder River** is almost entirely posted until it enters National Forest lands in the canyon. The West Boulder Road is reached just short of McLeod and the Boulder Forks Access. Take the West Boulder Road for 7.5 miles and turn left at the West Fork Boulder River National Forest Access, which goes through private property for another seven miles before reaching the canyon and public fishing access. The total mileage from Big Timber is 30.5 miles. The campground is situated on 10 acres with 10 sites. Tents and trailers. RV limit: 20 feet. Firegrates. Picnic tables. Pit toilets. Potable water. The trailhead to the wilderness winds through a half-mile of private property before it reaches the wilderness. The fish are naturally smaller, and the creek is steep and not easy to fish.

West Boulder River in the wilderness area

## Access to the Boulder River

If you enter the town of Big Timber from Interstate 90 driving west, you will cross the Boulder River. Just across the bridge is the Old Boulder River Road, a dirt road that winds its way up the east side of the river for eight miles until it intersects with the county road at the Eightmile Bridge. Big Rock Fishing and Camping Access is 3.5 miles up Old Boulder Road. It offers great access to the river. It has no tables,

but it does have a pit toilet facility.

Those fishermen daring to float the lower river put in at Big Rock and float down to the city park or further on down to where the river enters the Yellowstone River. The takeout on the Yellowstone River is Otter Creek Access. From Big Timber take Highway 191 north to Harlowton. Turn right 1.4 miles on Howie Road. Go another 1.3 miles to the Otter Creek Access on the banks of the Yellowstone River. Otter Creek offers a boat launch, an outhouse and shade. If you plan on floating down to Otter Creek, the closest access is the Pelican Access (Grey Cliff Bridge) 11.3 miles upstream.

To reach the upper Boulder River from Big Timber, turn south on McLeod Street (pronounced McCloud). Follow Highway 298 south to public fishing on National Forest lands.

**8 miles:** The Eightmile County Bridge offers access as well as a 10-foot slide to the water's edge for rafters.

**16 miles:** West Boulder turnoff.

**16.5 miles: Boulder Forks State Fishing Access** This access offers a primitive camping spot with shade, a short run of the West Fork and an easy launch on the Boulder River.

**19.2 miles: East Boulder Road** Anglers can fish a small section of the East Fork and work their way down to the Boulder. Be sure to stay below the high water mark. I watched an angler land and release two nice trout not very far from the bridge during the fall.

**25 miles: Natural Bridge** Forest Service boundary. Picnic area with scenic overlooks and paved trails.

### 30 miles: Falls Creek Campground

Eight sites. Tent camping only. Tent pads provided. Potable water. Pit toilets. Firegrates.

### 33 miles: Big Beaver Campground

Five sites. Tents and trailers. No tent pads. RV limit 32 feet. Firegrates. Pit toilets. Picnic tables. No potable water.

### 33.5 miles: Aspen Campground

Eight sites. Tents and trailers. Tent pads provided. RV limit 32 feet. Firegrates. Handicapped access toilets. Picnic tables. Potable water.

### 35 miles: Shipping Corral Picnic Site

Toilets. Picnic tables. Firegrates. Intended for day use only!

### 40.5 miles: Hell's Canyon Campground

11 sites. Tents and trailers. Tent pads provided. RV limit 16 feet. Not on the river but in walking distance. No potable water. Pit toilets.

### 42 miles: Lower Fourmile Dispersed Site

No sign. Four sites. No potable water. Pit toilet.

**42.5 miles: Fourmile Guard Station** The cabin belongs to the Forest Service and is available for rent to the general public, 18 years of age or older, on a first-come, first-served basis. The Forest Service has priority use of the cabin at any time. Contact:

    Big Timber Ranger District
    P.O. Box 196
    Big Timber, MT 59011
    (406) 932-5155

### 46 miles: Hick's Park Campground

16 sites. Tents and trailers. Tent pads provided. RV limit 32 feet. In one area, two adjacent sites have three tables.

**48 miles: Box Canyon** End of maintained county road.

Big Beaver Campground

# Interstate 90 – Columbus, Montana

## The Stillwater River

Every reference to the source of the Stillwater's name offers the same conjecture – some early explorer left his sense of humor inked on some early map. Like its cousin river in the next drainage, the Stillwater too has boulders and can be treacherous during spring run-off. Wade fishing this river is not for the faint of heart or old guys short on breath with weak knees. Float fishers beware! From the Castle Rock Access down to Cliff Swallow Access, the Stillwater River garners respect and awe from veteran kayakers. Whitewater rafters float from Cliff Swallow to the town of Columbus. So what does this river have to offer visiting anglers? The answer is spectacular scenery, high trout populations, and relatively low angling pressure. Although most of

Upper Stillwater River

the river tumbles down through private property, public access is provided throughout its length.

The source of the Stillwater lies deep within the canyon walls of the Absaroka-Beartooth Wilderness at the northern edge of Yellowstone National Park. The trailhead is at Woodbine Campground. The wilderness section is not always easy to fish, but rainbows, cutthroats and brookies from 7 to 10-inches eagerly rise to large attractor patterns. Three and a half miles up the trail from Woodbine Campground, hikers will see a three-acre pond named Sioux Charley Lake. The "lake" is marshy in places, very shallow and is host to small brookies. In and around Woodbine Campground are a few protected spots

for smaller trout, but the river is scoured and offers poor fishing prospects for the next three miles down to the mine.

The first public access after the mine is a picnic site. Floaters in late June will discover clear but cold water from the picnic site below the mine down to Moraine Fishing Access. Even this section has some tricky water that could spoil a float trip. After the Moraine Fishing Access, rafters should exit the remainder of the river. Keep in mind that a number of commercial whitewater companies ply their trade on the Stillwater from the Johnson Bridge just outside the town of Absarokee down the river to Fireman's Point. By mid-summer the upper river and mid-section is too low to float. The advantage of this swift and tumbling river for the wade fisher is long stretches of fishing water without the intrusion of floaters, a rarity in Montana. The state of Montana offers a number of access sites beginning just outside the town of Columbus, where the Stillwater River enters the Yellowstone River.

Three tributaries increase the volume of water in the Stillwater River. The first is the West Fork of the Stillwater River near Nye. The second contributor is the West Rosebud Creek, which drains Mystic Lakes and enters the Stillwater, after first joining East Rosebud Creek, three miles south of Absarokee on Highway 78. During early summer both Rosebud Creeks are quite muddy. During this time, fishing is best above the Rosebud Creeks.

## Columbus, Montana

The town site is right on the banks of the Yellowstone River. The city provides a spacious campground and boat launch at Itch-Kep-Pe, next to the Highway 78 bridge, less than a mile and a half from Interstate 90. The campground is shaded. The small town of Absarokee is 14 miles south on Highway 78 after crossing the bridge over the Yellowstone River. For travelers heading to Yellowstone National Park who want fantastic scenery along the way, continue 47 miles through the town of Absarokee and follow the route to Red Lodge. From Red Lodge follow the spectacular Beartooth Highway to the Cooke City entrance to the Park.

## Side Trip –
## Highway 78: Columbus to Absarokee

### MM 3.3: Fireman's Point

Fireman's Point provides good access to a long stretch of river as well as a raft launch. The landing during high water is difficult, and rafts need to be dragged up a wood slide.

### MM 7.3: Swinging Bridge Access

Camping is allowed.

### MM7.8: White Bird Access

Camping is allowed.

### MM 14: Absarokee

From the town of Absarokee the traveler has four roads to choose from, which lead to three separate fisheries. Continuing on Highway 78 leads to East Rosebud Lake. Or from Highway 78 south of Absarokee take Highway 425 to **Rosebud Creek, Emerald Lake, and Mystic Lake**. The third choice is to take Highway 419 to the Buffalo Jump Bridge on the Stillwater River at the community of Nye. The fourth choice in roads is to take Highway 420, which parallels the Stillwater River to Nye. To think that Robert Frost struggled with only two choices in his poem, "The Road Not Taken"! Clearly, he was not a fly fisher, or he would surely have come back and taken the more traveled route as well!

Max surveys the Stillwater River above Rosebud Creeks.

### Absarokee to Nye Along Highway 420 along the Stillwater River

Just outside of Absarokee, make a right turn off Highway 420 to Absaroka Campground and the Johnson Bridge, which offers fishing access plus a raft launch. Continuing on Highway 420, the pavement peters out and the next access is Cliff Swallow Fishing Access, followed by Castle Rock Fishing Access and then Moraine Fishing Access. The Moraine Access is just a couple of miles from the Buffalo Jump Campground at the Nye Bridge. Just before you reach the junction of Highway 419 at the Nye Bridge, you will cross the West Fork of the Stillwater River. Most of the West Fork travels through private property and is posted. The upper reaches in the wilderness section reportedly fish well for small rainbows and cutthroats. I am sorry but I completely missed this one. The easiest access looks to be from the Stillwater Mine. The road winds up above the mine and then drops over to the trailhead.

A "stillwater" tributary during spring runoff

### Absarokee to Nye along Highway 419

Take Highway 78 heading south from Absarokee to the junction with Highway 419. The road is paved all the way to Nye, but just after the community of Dean there are many annual potholes and breaks. Three miles from the junction with Highway 78 is Fish Tail and Rosebud Isle Fishing Access. Before reaching the community of Nye, travelers may stop at Dean, which offers a fly shop, a restaurant and a saloon. The road then crosses the river at Buffalo Jump Campground. Less than a mile from the bridge, Highway 420 joins Highway 419 right across from a restaurant. The next fishing access is the Old Nye

East Rosebud Lake

Picnic Site just below the mine. The road then continues past the mine to the trailhead at **Woodbine Campground**. Woodbine Campground is beautiful and offers 43 campsites, all of which have paved entries. Trailer spaces are provided for trailers up to 30 feet. Concessionaire operated.

### Absarokee to Emerald Lake and Mystic Lake

From the town of Absarokee, take Highway 420 to Fish Tail and Rosebud Isle. Turn left on Highway 425 (West Rosebud Road) to Mystic Lake. After traveling 6.6 miles to where the pavement ends, a sign reads: Pine Grove Campground nine miles, Emerald Lake 13 miles and Mystic Lake Trailhead 14 miles, which is the end of the road. Pine Grove Campground has 46 sites, many of which are suitable for trailers up to 30 feet. Fishing access and unimproved camping sites are available just past the campground. Emerald Lake is a shallow 50-acre lake annually stocked with rainbows, most of which never see a second season. Mystic Lake is three miles from the trailhead. The lake is actually a Montana Power Company reservoir two miles long and a half-mile across. The lake offers good fishing at the inlet for 8- to 12-inch rainbows, a few lunkers and lots of smaller cutthroats. Island Lake is six miles from the trailhead, past Mystic Lake, and offers similar fishing. The Stillwater River above Island Lake reportedly fishes very well for rainbows and cutthroats.

### Absarokee to East Rosebud Lake

From the town of Absarokee, take Highway 78 south 14 miles to the small town of Roscoe. Exit Highway 78 at Roscoe and take the East Rosebud River Road. The road is a dirt road; then at 8.2 miles the pavement starts again as the roads enters the National Forest. The entire area was ravaged by fire in 1996, but the surrounding rugged vistas, in spite of the fire, awe first-time visitors. East Rosebud Creek runs through private property until it enters the National

Forest. The creek offers good fishing for small trout. The Lower Sand Dunes picnic site is at 9.2 miles and Upper Sand Dunes is at 9.5 miles from Roscoe. At 11.9 miles the pavement ends, and the road is extremely bumpy. Although it is posted at 25 mph, the natural speed bumps keep travelers creeping

Outlet of East Rosebud Lake

along at 10 mph. East Rosebud Lake and Campground is 14.2 miles from Roscoe.

The lake is surrounded by private property established in 1894. The property owners provide a courtesy boat launch site for the general public. Be sure to check in at the store. The lake fishes well for 10- to 15-inch rainbows.

The trailhead parking area provides an area for stock. Popular with trail riders and hikers, the

Absaroka-Beartooth Wilderness, established in 1978, covers 953,377 acres of pristine wilderness. For further information contact the Beartooth Ranger District Office in Red Lodge, Montana.

From the East Rosebud Trailhead the wilderness boundary is a half–mile, **Elk Lake** is 3.5 miles, **Rim Rock Lake** is six miles, **Rainbow Lake** is seven miles, and Lake of the Falls is nine miles. Elk Lake is a shallow 5-acre lake holding small

offers both good fishing and stunning views. The 68-mile drive winds its way up from lush forest, through countless switchbacks to sub-alpine plateaus. Twenty-nine mountains thrust their jagged peaks into the Big Sky at elevations exceeding 12,000 feet. The highway enters Wyoming near the summit and re-enters Montana about seven miles outside of Cooke City.

From the summit visitors scan hundreds of lakes

The Beartooth Highway to Yellowstone National Park

nestled in glacial carvings on the edges of plateaus and in hollowed amphitheaters. Many are barren, but surprising numbers hold hearty strains of golden trout and Yellowstone cutthroats. Summer does not linger in this country. Violent thunderstorms and plummeting temperatures can scurry visitors and photographers to the comfort of their vehicles anytime before the road closes for the winter.

brookies; Rim Rock Lake is eight acres and reportedly offers only fair fishing for 8- to 12-inch rainbows. Rainbow Lake is said to provide good fishing for 8- to 12-inch rainbows.

# Interstate 90 – Laurel to Red Lodge

## Side Trip – Rock Creek and the Beartooth Highway

Described as one of the most spectacular and scenic highways in America, the Beartooth Highway from Red Lodge to the northeast entrance of Yellowstone National Park in Cooke City, Montana,

Rock Creek, flowing past the town of Red Lodge, has its beginnings high up in the Absaroka-Beartooth Wilderness. Anglers and campers wishing to fish Rock Creek and Wyoming's waters on their way to Yellowstone National Park will find the easiest route off Interstate 90 at Laurel, Montana. Follow Highway 310 for 13.8 miles south to its junction with Highway 212 to Red Lodge. Highway 310 follows the general course of the Clarks Fork of the Yellowstone River, a river not worthy of fishing due to degradation, unless you are a local and have time to search out sections holding good-sized browns during the fall. From Laurel to Joliet the creek is without public access, but it is not considered a productive stretch. From Joliet we begin our journey into one of Montana's jewels. Keep in mind that the mileage markers begin in Cooke City and increase in numbers towards Joliet.

**MM 96:** Joliet, Montana.

 **MM 90: Cooney Reservoir**

Cooney Reservoir is a shallow lake best fished in the early morning hours. The lake offers a state fee campsite. The lake is 28,400 acre feet and provides fair fishing since its 1982 rehabilitation, but don't expect an alpine setting.

**MM 82:** Roberts, Montana.

**MM 84.5:** Rest area with public access to Rock Creek. Rock Creek suffers greatly during drought cycles and demands from irrigators. The creek is best fished during spring and fall.

**MM 79: White Birch Fishing Access and Campground**

**MM 76:** Fox/Bench Road Fishing Access.

**Red Lodge, Montana**

**MM 60.7: Ratine Campground**

Ratine Campground is eight miles south of Red Lodge. It has access to the creek and offers six sites, with a 16-feet trailer restriction.

**MM 60:** Pullout access to the creek.

**Parkside Campground**

Twelve miles south of Red Lodge, Parkside Campground has 28 campsites, a 32-feet trailer restriction. It is operated by a concessionaire, as is the neighboring campground Greenough Lake.

**Greenough Lake Campground**

Offering 18 sites with trailer spaces up to 30 feet, the campsite has easy access to the creek plus a small pond, which is planted with fingerling trout.

Upper Rock Creek

**Limber Pine Campground**

Limber Pine Campground abuts Greenough Lake Campground and has 13 campsites with a 32-feet trailer restriction. A bridge crosses Rock Creek to the Rock Creek Road, which continues a short distance to the M-K Campground.

**M-K Campground**

A mile or so from Limber Pine Campground, M-K

is a non-fee campground with no services. It offers 10 campsites with easy access to the creek. From the campground to the road's end at the trailhead to Glacier Lake, the going is slow and bumpy. For those of you who want secluded and primitive camping, a number of beautiful spots may be found ahead. However, the fishing high up in this canyon is only fair for small fry.

### Glacier Lake

The trailhead to Glacier Lake is at the end of the Rock Creek Road, another three or four miles past M-K Campground. Glacier Lake is a deep, 150-acre lake and offers both beauty and good fishing for good-sized cutthroats. Fair warning, however, the one-mile hike is straight up!

**MM 39.4: Wyoming Border, Shoshone National Forest** Heading down the highway to Cooke City, one will need a Wyoming fishing license. The first popular high-elevation lake is Long Lake, followed by Little Bear Lake and then Island Lake. Island Lake has a campground with a boat launch. It is stocked with rainbows and includes cutthroats and brookies that cruise the shoreline during late afternoon and evening. Just down from Island Lake is the Top of the World Store. The store sells Wyoming fishing licenses, gas, food, as well as renting some very rustic cabins. The next large lake accessible from the highway is Beartooth Lake, which offers camping, a boat launch and some very large lake trout in addition to rainbows and cutthroats. If you are heading for the Park or Cooke City, continue past the highway junction to Cody, Wyoming. Highway 212 goes right past the upper Clarks Fork of the Yellowstone, which is a good fishing stream, a small part of which lies in Montana. In and around Cooke City are a number of campgrounds and trailheads to secluded lakes. This is beautiful country!

Return to Interstate 90 from Billings to Hardin.

# Interstate 90 – The Big Horn River

Forty-two miles from Billings, Montana, the Bighorn River glides through the Crow Indian Reservation to the town of Hardin and then onwards to the Yellowstone River. From the Interstate 90 exit at Hardin to Fort Smith the two-lane country road winds another 48 miles through dry rolling hills and fertile ranch land to the Yellowtail Dam boat ramp. The breathtaking scenery of buttes and coulees compete with the jagged overthrust of snow-capped mountains, both in Wyoming and Montana. The tall prairie cottonwood trees line the river bottom, and the cold, pristine waters provide an aquatic underworld rich in plant life and insect life. Completed in 1965, the Yellowtail Dam transformed a slow prairie river into one of the finest trout streams in the United States; however, from 1975 to 1981 the Crow Indian government closed the river to non-tribal members.

In 1981 the United States Supreme Court affirmed both state and federal access rights to the waters of the Bighorn River up to the high water mark, which is defined as the "continuous area where vegetation ceases". The Bighorn River's reputation grew quickly. Splashed across the covers of outdoor magazines, the Bighorn River's fame inspired fly fishers from around the country to test its fabled waters. Renowned as one of the best tailwater fisheries in the world, legions of fly fishers arrive yearly to fish the 13-mile stretch of tailwater, and few go away disappointed.

Although the piscatorial wonders of this river are undisputed, paradise and solitude are two terms rarely joined together in describing this river. Fifty boats on the same 13-mile stretch is not an exaggeration, nor is the much-touted statistic of 5,000 to 6,000 fish per mile. Factor in browns that average 14 to-16 inches and rainbows averaging 16 to 18-inches, and it is no wonder so many visitors are willing to experience a circus-like atmosphere of multi-colored rafts and drift boats.

Another preeminent factor for the Bighorn River's reputation is the extended fishing season. The Yellowtail Dam, impounding almost 70 miles of canyon water, releases water from the bottom of Bighorn Lake. Although fluctuations may adversely impact fishing, water temperatures from the mid-40s to the mid-60s foster trout growth for most of the year, unlike some rivers where trout have a short growing season due to chilly water conditions throughout most of the year.

The river is open year-round, but practically speaking, the winter months of December through February can be grim, when one considers below-zero readings and the wind chill factor. Nonetheless, hearty locals and adventuresome out-of-towners ply the waters throughout these winter months fishing with tiny midge patterns

Side channel of the Big Horn River

tossed to lethargic fish in the more quiet pools. March and April welcome temperatures in the low to mid 50s and water temperatures in the low 40s. March anglers still predominately fish the midge hatches, but by late April Baetis begin to show up, which provides for some excellent nymphing opportunities. Standard patterns such as the Gold-ribbed, Hare's Ear and Pheasant Tail nymphs prevail, but be sure to stock up on specialty patterns from one of the local fly shops, especially for shrimp patterns, scuds and sow bugs. (I had great success with a San Juan Worm with a brass bead in the center.) May and June are less crowded as local fishermen and visitors alike measure the impact of spring run-off.

May temperatures range from the mid 60s to the low 70s with water temperatures slowly climbing above the mid 40s mark. The Baetis hatch comes into fruition, which offers both dry and nymph fishing possibilities. River flows increase from a low of 2,000 cfs to above 6,000 cfs. Ideal floating conditions diminish above 6,000 cfs. As the river grows in both volume and size, the fish become dispersed. Even when other Montana rivers are blown out, good fishing may still be experienced from the dam down to the three-mile access point. By late June some of the fishing pressure is reduced with the appearance of the Salmon Fly hatch on many other famous rivers in the region. Bead-head nymphs and San Juan worms are especially popular at this time.

July through August draws hordes of anglers, and for good reason. Daytime temperatures range from the high 70s to the high 80s, with the water temperatures gradually increasing from the low 50s to the high 60s. But the real draw is the fantastic dry fly fishing brought on by the small, yellow stonefly, the Pale Morning Dun hatch, the Baetis hatch and the ubiquitous arrival of the Grannom (black) Caddis. Adding to the enchantment of these hatches is the spinner fall in the evening and the beginning Trico hatch. It is no wonder that the river is so crowded. Surprisingly, the trout display great tolerance for this daily flotilla. Perhaps the trout, hidden in the undulating waves of plant life, are impervious to the blending shadows from passing boats. Given the size of the water, the available numbers of fish and the plethora of insect life, most people are pleasantly surprised with their success rate during these popular months.

September and October cool the hot days of summer with temperatures again in the mid 70s and water temperatures correspondingly settling back to the mid 50s. By October the Tricos are on the wane, but the Baetis hatch is still an important one, as is the evening caddis hatch. By November the waters are downright chilly again, dipping down to the mid-40s. Streamers such as Wooly Buggers, Zonkers, leech patterns and Matukas should be readily at hand.

I finally fished the fabled waters of the Bighorn River, and I am saddened when I reflect that it took me 19 years to finally fish it (testimony to the multitude of competing waters in this wonderful state). Getting off the river at 8 PM, on my first day on the river, I headed down the road for a nine-hour drive home. I had not gone 10 miles before planning my next trip. The next day I posted the following trip report on my web site.

# Saga: October 25, 2000 – The Bighorn River

I slept in the back of my truck near the launch site at the BLM campground near the dam. Pulling up to the launch site below the dam at 7:30 AM, I discovered that I was not the early bird. Within the next 20 minutes, guides and fishermen flew into the area. Gentlemen, start your engines! It was incredible how many boats arrived in waves,

like convoys crossing the Atlantic during World War II. No one seemed to have the time to be neighborly. Few hellos were exchanged. It was a race to the water with the guides projecting a no-nonsense demeanor reminiscent of Ward Bond in the old television series "Wagon Train". Ten boats launched while I was still climbing into my waders and rigging up. I could feel the excitement and anticipation. Three hours after launching, I was frustrated and irritated that I had not one strike. Although the fishing was slow due to water manipulation, I could see others fighting fish as they drifted past me.

I played leapfrog with some of the boats as we drifted down the river. Regretfully, I have to admit that I found solace in the fact that they too had not caught a thing. The number of boats in the 13-mile stretch that I floated easily numbered close to 50. We traveled in packs, breaking up and then re-assembling like mallards over a grain field. I resented the jubilant loudmouths who whooped and hollered when they hooked a fish. Their triumphant voices seemed to echo for miles, and there was no joy in this man's Mudville. Hearing their whoops of delight, I got out of the boat to fish a promising spot, only to have some party glide down and let out a holler directly in front of me. During the first three hours, I couldn't buy a fish. I had spent 50 bucks on flies and incidental supplies in a nearby shop. The proprietor drew a diagram on how to precisely set up the strike indicator, the split shot and the two flies. I followed his directions to the letter. When the water surface was broken by the morning's first rises, I strained to see if the fish were actually feeding on the surface for sporadic Baetis duns or whether they were just under the surface film capturing nymphs. I agonized over whether I should break out a small Parachute Adams or Blue-Wing Olive.

While I drifted in solitude, I searched for every possible reason why I wasn't catching anything. I finally concluded that I was conceivably casting too far out. Seated in my low profile boat, a combination duck boat and riverboat, I was unable to see the subtle takes of those browns hiding in the heavy weed cover as I manned the oars. My theory proved to be correct. I was not really staring intently at my strike indicator as I drifted my flies and navigated the river. Indeed, the takes were very subtle! I started flipping my rig right along side of the boat and stuck my first brown. Alas, I lost five weighty fish in a row. Two of them I had to break off when I had to grab the oars to maneuver around an anchored boat. It was heart-breaking because they were really close to the boat. I tried holding the rod between my knees while I rowed, but it didn't work.

I anchored the boat too soon on one large fish and couldn't pull up the anchor in time when he made a run downstream. The fifth fish I lost when I jumped out of the boat and forgot my net. These are all actions that are taken for granted by clients. When a client or a partner hooks a fish, the rower takes on a number of responsible actions. I reflected on the night before when I had squeezed in two hours of fishing before dark and had caught only one 15-inch brown on a dry – not much to brag about. I was feeling defeated until I landed a 17-inch brown at mid-day.

After that fish was landed and safely released, I could do no wrong. I went on to land at least 10 more browns, only one of which was under 14 inches. With that lone exception, all of the trout were in the 14- to 16-inch range. I savored every moment of the 13-mile float from the dam down to the Bighorn access. As the sun began to sink, the evening caddis hatch triggered action on the top, but I didn't stop to change my rig. I was quite satisfied with the action I was having casting into small pods of rising trout with a bead-head nymph and a trailing scud. I even ended the day with a great "one-that-got-away" story. I humbly submit that I have not had a Montana or a Wyoming or an Idaho fish ever take me down to my backing. I have always

been amazed at this expression so freely added for dramatic effect. Through the years I have caught a number of trout in the 20-inch range, but I have never had this experience until that day.

I won't bore you with the details. Suffice to say that this hog took me down to my backing two times. Jumping out of my boat, I moved down through a crotch-high riffle, working him in for my moment of triumph. I lost him in 12 inches of rocky, weed-infested water when my line caught on a rock. My mother's Irish creed of "Hope for the best, but expect the worse" bubbled up to my consciousness as I reeled in the slack line and advanced toward the fish. On my approach, the resting rainbow snapped the 5X tippet and escaped. I saw his tail and back. He was huge, but I had no regrets over losing him.

An hour and a half from Billings, fishing the Bighorn takes a lot of planning, as it is really out of the way. Hardin has a number of hotels. For those that can afford to stay at a nice lodge on the river, I recommend the Bighorn River Resort (800) 665-3799 or the Bighorn River Lodge (800) 235-5450. Public campsites are located at Mallard's Landing and the Bighorn access. Operated by the Montana Department of Fish, Wildlife and Parks, each site offers a couple of campsites, an outhouse and a boat ramp. The next public campground is just outside of Fort Smith and is a Bureau of Land Management campground. It is the nicest of the public campgrounds.

The first campground out of Hardin is at Mallard's Landing. The Bighorn access, which is 13 miles from the launch site at Yellowtail Dam, offers two separate ramps, a bit of shade and a seven-day camping limit. During the summer of 2000 the fee schedule was $10 per night, per camper if no one in the party held a Montana fishing license. With a Montana fishing license from at least one member in the group, the fee was $5 dollars per camper. The only private campground is a half-mile from the Three-Mile Access. Cottonwood Camp tonwood Camp is a complete and full-service campground and lodging facility for sportsmen and families. The camp is located less than a mile off Highway 31, just off the Three-Mile access road at the second left and only three miles from Fort Smith. (Cottonwood Camp, P.O. Box 7667, Fort Smith, Montana 59035 (406) 666-2391) Fort Smith offers a number of fly shops, a café, a motel, a market, shuttle services and boat rentals, but BYOB as Fort Smith is a dry town.

Don't expect solitude, and keep your expectations from getting the better of you as you race to get on the water, which is, of course, easier said than done. I can still hear my Hardy Princess reel screaming and the sound of the deep wallop that only a big rainbow can make. At the take out a number of men were regaling in the story of a guide, fishing on his day off with a friend on this same day and same stretch of water. He landed a 27 incher. Oh, Montana...

# 8

# YELLOWSTONE
# NATIONAL PARK

Unlike the state of Montana, Yellowstone National Park does not use mileage marker signposts (MM). Mileage estimates within the Park are based on an odometer from a 1993 Chevy pickup truck with over-sized tires. I was often in conflict with the official signs so look upon these declarations of mileage with a jaundiced eye (M=mileage estimate).

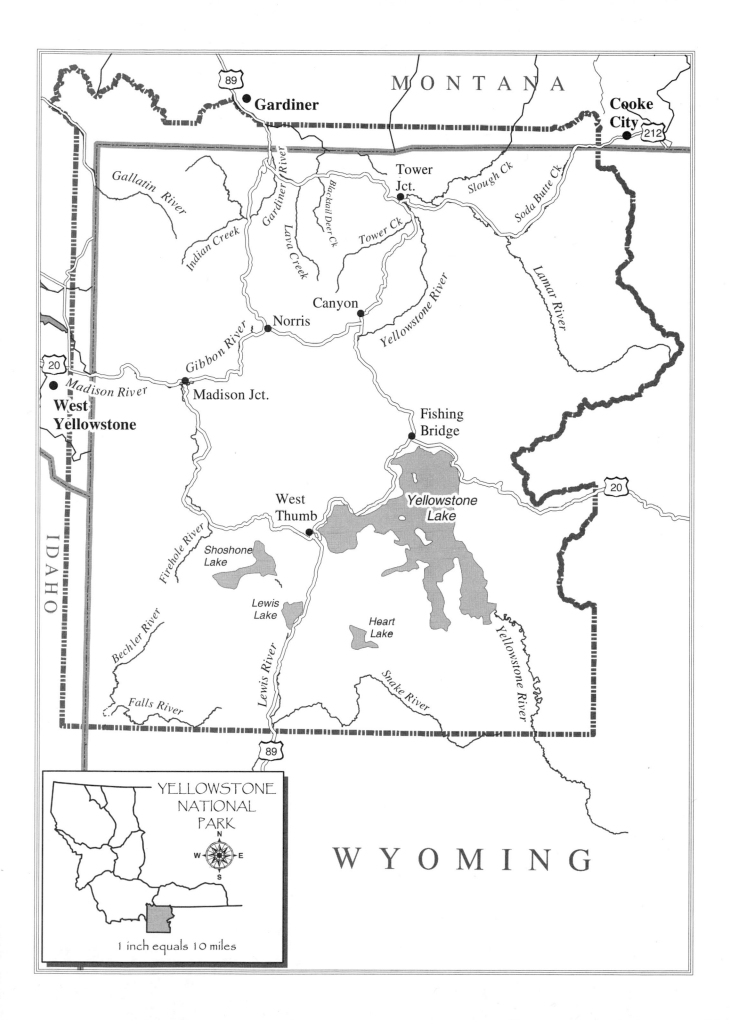

Fishing Fact: Larger than Rhode Island and Delaware combined, Yellowstone National Park is immense at 3,472 square miles. Yellowstone Lake alone covers 136 square miles. As the world's first national park, it no doubt vies for the title "World's Greatest Trout Park". If you are limited to less than a week to both explore and fish Yellowstone Park and you are mainly interested in driving to your destination or taking a day hike, this section of the book will serve

you well. However, if you have planned an extensive vacation in the Park to fully fish its riches, including the backcountry, then I would recommend purchasing *Fishing Yellowstone National Park* by Richard Parks (ISBN: 1-56044-625-0) or *The Yellowstone Fly-Fishing Guide* by Craig Mathews and Clayton Molinero (ISBN:1-55821-545-x).

## Campground Information

"Campsite availability is first-come, first-served at the following campgrounds: Mammoth, Norris, Indian Creek, Pebble Creek, Slough Creek and Tower Fall. During peak camping season (late June to mid-August) all campgrounds may be filled by 11:00 AM; arrive early to obtain a site. [Slough Creek often has vacated campsites filled by 9 AM.] Reservations can be made for Canyon, Bridge Bay, Madison, Grant Village, and the Fishing Bridge RV Park by calling (307) 344-7311. Overnight camping of any type (tent, vehicle, or RV) outside designated campgrounds is not permitted.

"Hookups are available at the concession-operated Fishing Bridge RV Park, which is open from late May to early October. The RV Park provides water, sewer, and electrical hookups. The RV Park is restricted to hard-sided camping units; tents and trailers are not allowed.

"Showers and laundry facilities are provided by a concession service for an additional fee. They are located adjacent to the campgrounds at Canyon, Grant Village, and Fishing Bridge RV Park (showers and laundry are located within four miles of Bridge Bay campground)." –Park hand-out: Yell 361, 1998

The park entrances are the South Entrance above Jackson, Wyoming, the West Entrance in the town of West Yellowstone, the North Entrance below the town of Gardiner, Montana, the northeast entrance a few miles from Cooke City, Montana, and the East Entrance leading to Cody, Wyoming. All entrances lead to Yellowstone Lake, and a loop connects all the entrances. In keeping with the spirit of this fishing guide, I have included only those rivers, streams and lakes that can be reached by vehicle or in a short day hike. Since the Park does not employ mileage marker signs like the state of Montana, I have concentrated on the park entrance roads and the Grand Loop Road.

## West Yellowstone Entrance

Park Entrance to Madison Campground: 14 miles
Madison Campground to Old Faithful: 16 miles
Old Faithful to West Thumb: 17 miles
West Thumb to South Entrance: 22 miles

**Note:** The information covering the Park section of the Gallatin River and its tributaries along Highway 191 is covered in the Southwestern Montana section, Highway 191. Highway 191 is the western border of the park to the Gallatin Canyon, where the Park boundary ends.

## North Entrance: Gardiner

### From Mammoth to Tower to Cooke City

**Gardner River**

A special bait section for children provides excellent fishing for small brookies above Osprey Falls close to the Indian Creek campground. Below the falls, the Gardner plunges down a canyon on its course to the Yellowstone River. The next access is the Mammoth-Tower Bridge a few miles east of Mammoth. Upstream from the bridge the canyon impedes progress, but this short section holds numerous 6- to 10-inch rainbows and brookies. Below the bridge the Gardner River is joined by Lava Creek. Standing on the Mammoth side of the bridge, you can look down to where Lava Creek joins the river. Hiking down below this section provides good fishing for cutthroats and brook trout, although be prepared, for some of the choice waters do come up empty. Rather than turn

the corner and head upstream to the bridge again, take the time to fish the first half-mile of Lava Creek. Lava Creek is strictly dabbing your fly in small pockets, but when I last fished it during August of 1998, the rainbows were averaging 10 inches, and they were fat. This section of the Gardner River, extending for three miles, can be hot during August so tie on a beadhead Prince as a dropper.

Access to the Gardner River and Lava Creek

**Yellowstone River in the Black Canyon**

Cross-country trail access. The Black Canyon may be reached by hiking across sagebrush, bench land and down to the river. From the bridge above Tower, near the confluence with the Lamar River, down to Blacktail Deer Creek, the distance to the river may vary from two to four miles. I especially enjoy fishing this rugged canyon with its big water. Concentrated nymph fishing is so much easier than training my trifocals on a size 18 dry at Buffalo Ford. But hiking in and out unnerves me, even with my pepper spray, as I generally fish alone. Somehow I never remember to make noise. I huff and puff up the slope, furtively glancing behind me.

## Mammoth to Tower

Mileage is estimated beginning at the junction in Mammoth.

To Tower Junction: 18 miles
To Canyon Village: 37 miles
To the Northeast Entrance: 47 miles

### M 1.7: Mammoth-Tower Bridge (High Bridge)

Blacktail Ponds

### M 4.7: Lava Creek Picnic Site

The fishing is somewhat difficult both upstream and downstream of Undine Falls due to brush and downed trees, but the fishing is good for small trout.

### M 6.3: Blacktail Ponds

A small pond a short distance from the road, Blacktail Ponds is void of shrubbery or brush, although it is very boggy for most of the shoreline. It is rare to pass by this pond at dusk without seeing at least one nymph fisherman working the pond for 10- to 14-inch cutthroats and brook trout.

### M 6.9: Blacktail Deer Creek

Blacktail Deer Creek crosses the Mammoth-Tower Road above Lava Creek crossing. The creek cascades down the mountain four miles to meet the Yellowstone River. The creek offers good fishing for brook trout above and below the road.

### M 15.3: Floating Island Lake Fishless.

### M 18.5: Conoco Gas Station, Roosevelt Lodge
Showers available.

### M 20.8: Tower Falls, Hamilton Store and snack bar

### Tower Creek

Tower Creek may be reached from the Tower Creek Campground. Fishing is good for small rainbows and brookies. From the Hamilton Store next to the falls, a trail leads down the canyon to the Yellowstone River and a short section of Tower Creek. This trail is the only easy access to the Grand Canyon of the Yellowstone. Pack a lunch.

## Tower Junction to Cooke City (Lamar River)

### M .7: Yellowstone River above Tower

The confluence with the Lamar River is a mile downstream. Just as you cross the bridge leaving Tower Junction, there is a picnic site and parking area. A trail leads down to the confluence of the

Lamar River and the Yellowstone River. The Lamar section consists of heavily silted pools and steep banks, but from the Lamar upstream for a half-mile, the Yellowstone River offers rough and tumble nymph water. It is too small of a section to share, but I have always been pleased with the results.

cated sites were full!

During that first day, I returned to fish the Gardner again. Returning to the campground, the sky clouded up and in no time at all, my windshield wipers were on high, smearing and skipping across bug splats. The next day I fished the Lamar for the

**M 5.1: Access to the Lamar River**

**M 5.9: Slough Creek**

Years ago when I lived and taught in Wyoming, I heard near-reverent praising of Slough Creek. As I recall at that time, only trailers were allowed in the camp-ground so I passed it up for more favorable fish-ing in other areas of the park. In finalizing the Park, I headed for Slough Creek as soon as I entered the Park. Pull-ing a 15-foot 1984 Komfort camp trailer, I was prepared. I arrived at a gala of colorful tents at the campground at 9 AM and watched two families depart. Slough Creek Campground is off the beaten track, actually only 2.3 miles of washboard road from the Cooke City Road, but it is a long ways from the Interstate for travelers heading home. By 9:30 the three va-

Tower Creek access trail to the Yellowstone River

A gust of wind blows a tent into Slough Creek.

first time. Because of a heat spell, it had been fishing very slowly. When I arrived at a secluded spot, the water was somewhat roiled, but the off color was not enough to concern me. I fished for an hour and a half, to no avail. Having been skunked, I headed for the confluence of the Lamar and the Yellowstone

Lamar River

determined to catch a fish on the Lamar – nothing. Catching a few hefty cutthroats on the Yellowstone River, I headed back to Slough Creek for an early dinner. After dinner I hiked up the trail to the first meadow.

The trail to the three meadows of Slough Creek does not begin in the campground, as a narrow canyon impedes progress. The first meadow is notoriously difficult to fish, from what I had read and from what I heard in camp. Everyone advised me to pass

up the first meadow and fish the second meadow, which is about five miles up from the trailhead. By the time I had hiked in to the first meadow, I realized that I had only about two hours to fish. I walked up to the first bank and peered into the softly flowing creek. I put on my Polaroid glasses, and in doing so I looked down to see a 16-inch cutthroat slurping midges, oblivious to my presence.

I crawled through the grass to the next run and spotted a 17- or 18-inch cutthroat gently fanning his tail and sipping bugs right next to the bank less than 10 feet in front of me. Ten offerings later, I stood up. The cutthroat moved one foot over and two feet up and continued slurping size 22 white midges. Slough Creek cutthroats are like the elk and buffalo. If you don't get too close, they just ignore you and go on chewing their cud, or in this case sipping midges. For the second time in one day I had been skunked!

Most of the fishermen I spoke to that evening said they had poor to fair fishing at the second meadow and excellent fishing for smaller trout at the third meadow, which is eight miles from the trailhead. Next time I am going right back to that first meadow with 7X tippet and an assortment of midge patterns.

Slough Creek offers excellent fishing from the campground to its meeting with the Lamar River, but it is similar to a spring creek and requires skill and patience. Surprisingly, few people actually fish this section, while upwards of a hundred fishermen a day hike up to the meadow sections.

## M 8: Lamar River

Another day! Regardless of my dismal experiences on the Lamar, the river offers excellent fishing for cutthroats and rainbows once the river has cleared (later than most). Craig Mathew in his book *The Yellowstone Fly-Fishing Guide* mentions the proclivity for Lamar cutthroats to migrate up and down the stream, which in turn keeps anglers covering a lot of ground.

Gliding through open meadows with towering mountain ranges in the background and sparse clusters of cottonwoods, it is easy to visualize what the entire region looked like prior to settlements. From its confluence with Soda Butte Creek to the canyon, a distance of six or seven miles, the Lamar receives lots of fishing attention. The expansive grassland, home to buffalo and antelope, hosts large grasshoppers and other terrestrials, which find their way into the Lamar. The canyon, although more difficult to fish, offers slightly larger trout in the pools and pockets.

### M 18.3: Trout Lake

How could an angler pass up a body of water named Trout Lake? Nor should you, if you have the time to fish this little gem nestled in the mountains a mere half-mile from the unsigned pull-out. If you are coming from Cooke City, the pullout is 1.3 miles from Pebble Creek Campground. What Trout Lake lacks in fast action, it more than makes up for in the size of fat rainbows in the 14- to 17-inch range. An excellent lake for a float tube, head for the left side of the lake if the wind comes up.

### M 19.3: Pebble Creek and Campground

Pebble Creek has a small volume of water, but up in the canyon section the creek has many pools which hold small cutthroats, although passage becomes difficult. The upper section above the canyon may be reached by crossing the footbridge in the campground and hiking a little over a mile.

### Soda Butte Creek

Gliding down a beautifully timbered canyon from Cooke City down to the Lamar flood plain, Soda Butte Creek offers quiet solitude and good fishing for cutthroats.

# Gardiner Entrance: Mammoth to Norris to Madison Junction

Mammoth to Norris: 21 miles
Norris to Madison Campground: 14 miles

A young man fishes a quiet pool on Pebble Creek.

### Gardner River

From the Gardiner Entrance to Mammoth, the road parallels the Gardner River and offers a number of pull-outs, but this section is swift water and not for neophytes. The Gardner River may also be accessed at the mouth from Park Street in Gardiner. Take the trail past the pump house down to the river.

## Boiling River

If you want to take a break from fishing and soak in a hot-pool on the Gardiner River, follow the Boiling River Trail one mile to this popular swimming hole. Look for the trailhead 2.6 miles from the Gardiner Entrance.

Soda Butte Creek

## Mammoth Campground and visitor center

The Mammoth Campground is just below Mammoth. The campground is popular.

## Joffe Lake

More aptly described as a one and a half-acre pond, Joffe Lake is an old reservoir a couple of miles south of Mammoth. Take the Mammoth-Norris Grand Loop Road. At 1.3 miles south of Mammoth, turn south onto a dirt road. The lake is great fishing for youngsters, who will be thrilled catching 6- to 8-inch brook trout.

## Swan Lake

The lake is exceedingly shallow and fishless.

## Indian Creek

Sitting on a small rise eight miles south of Mammoth, Indian Creek Campground is surrounded by verdurous meadows and winding streams. Indian Creek joins the Gardner River near the campground and offers special bait fishing opportunities for children fishing for small brookies. **Obsidian Creek** joins the Gardner River in the vicinity of the campground and also offers good fishing for brookies with special regulations for children. By following the Bighorn Pass Trail near the campground, families may also fish **Panther Creek**, a small tributary of the Gardner River. For children and novice anglers, this campground offers wonderful fishing opportunities and good wildlife viewing prospects.

## Gardner River, Sheepeater Canyon

After the Gardner River picks up the tributary creeks, the river takes a sweeping turn and heads back north, where it is crossed by the Mammoth-Tower Road and then joined by Lava Creek. Leaving the meadow section by the Indian Creek Campground, the river plunges down Sheepeater Canyon and drops over the 100-foot Osprey Falls. Access is difficult above and below the falls, and the fishing is considered to be not really worth the effort or the risk. One such access, however, is from the Sheepeater Picnic site.

## Grizzly Lake and Straight Creek

The trailhead to Grizzly Lake is reached 15 miles from Mammoth or 6.5 miles north of the Norris Junction. Look for the pullout and a trail sign for the Grizzly Lake Trail. It is easy to miss. Grizzly Lake is a 1.8-mile hike up a series of switchbacks to the lake. The 136-acre lake offers good fishing for 7- to 10-inch brook trout. Straight Creek both feeds and empties the lake. An alternate route to the lake is to fish up Straight Creek from the meadow section next to the road. Look for the parking area for the Mount Holmes Trail, which is three miles south of Indian Creek Campground. The trail follows Obsidian Creek for a mile, but do not waste your time fishing it. From Straight Creek the trail gradually climbs another three miles up the canyon to meet the lake.

Straight Creek provides excellent fishing for small brook trout. However, for every 8-inch brook trout that you land, you will have to release 10 dinks from 4 to 6-inches. The canyon was burned badly in the 1988 fire, and the gray husks of mature trees litter the creek bed and hillside. I do not disdain fishing small creeks for small fish, but this creek seems to promise more than it delivers. This is another great creek for kids, as it provides lots of action from hungry little brook trout that will hit any fly thrown their way.

## Beaver Lake, Lake of the Woods

Beaver Lake is located just over seven miles south of Mammoth. It is basically fishless, as is Lake of the Woods.

Joffe Lake

Straight Creek with a reminder of the 1988 firestorm.

**Twin Lakes**

Although you will see people fishing these two shallow lakes, they are considered to be almost barren.

**Norris Campground, Solfatara Creek**

Entering the Gibbon River at Norris Junction and the campground, Solfatara offers fair to good fish-

Norris Campground

ing for smaller trout.

## Canyon to Norris (Upper Gibbon River)

From its source waters, Grebe and Wolf Lakes, the Gibbon River flows through timbered terrain until it crosses the Norris-Canyon Road and enters Virginia Meadows on its way to the Norris Campground area. Anglers can expect to fish for browns, rainbows and brook trout. Joining Solfatara Creek at Norris Junction, the Gibbon gradually gains stature along with wary browns. Down further lies the Gib-

bon Meadow followed by a nice fishing section before Gibbons Falls. From Gibbon Falls, the Gibbon resembles more of a freestone creek until it reaches the meadow section and the confluence with the Firehole at Madison Campground. The best fishing period is the latter part of June and fall, but the fish also respond to a well-placed hopper during the heat of summer. The following information begins at Grebe Lake on the Canyon to Norris section of the Grand Loop Road. The Gibbon River flows down to Norris Campground, circles around Norris Geyser Basin, then follows a southerly course to the point where the Gibbon joins the Firehole to form the Madison River.

**Grebe Lake (headwaters of the Gibbon River)**

The trail is an easy three-mile hike on a level trail, which no doubt adds to this lake's popularity for scenery and good fishing. The trailhead parking lot is 3.6 miles from Canyon Junction or 8.4 miles from Norris Junction. Grebe Lake is good fishing for both rainbows and arctic grayling. The rainbows generally run in the 10- to 12-inch range. Anglers also have the opportunity to catch native arctic grayling. Generally the trail is passable by mid-June. A float tube is recommended, although wading is best accomplished on the northern and eastern shoreline.

**Cygnet Lake**

Fishless.

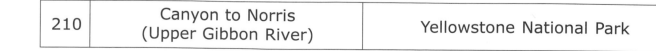

## Wolf Lake

Wolf Lake is downstream from Grebe Lake. Wolf Lake is generally described as good fishing for both rainbows and grayling. A small lake a little over 50 acres in grizzly country, the lake may be accessed from Grebe Lake or from Ice Lake, which is reached three and a half miles east of Norris Junction. Follow the trail for a half-mile to its junction with the Howard Eaton Trail at Ice Lake (fishless) and continue east. The trail continues on the Wolf Lake Trail, a total of four miles from the trailhead.

## Ice Lake
Fishless.

## Virginia Cascade Drive Access

The access road is available for hikers who would like to get close to the Gibbon River. This section of road is 1.7 miles east of the Norris Junction and provides access to **Virginia Meadows**.

## Norris Campground, Norris Meadow

The meadow section around the campground is heavily fished, and during the heat of summer with increased numbers of campers the trout learn to be wary after a couple of months of bombardment.

# Norris Junction to Madison Junction
## Gibbon River

For the next 15 miles, the Gibbon rushes to meet the Firehole. For the most part the road parallels the river through a series of meadows before dropping down into the Gibbon Canyon to Gibbon Falls. During the heat of summer the meadow sections can present some challenging fishing. In lieu of a good hatch, the best bet here is if the sky is overcast, the wind is blowing and the hoppers are popping. Below the meadows the river picks up speed and flows over small cascades. Pocket water and some pools are available as the river narrows and picks up speed before plunging over Gibbon Falls. Just below the falls is the Gibbon Falls Picnic Area. Anglers may hike upriver a few hundred yards to access Canyon Creek, which joins the Gibbon River on the east bank. Canyon Creek offers good fishing for small brook trout in the 6- to 8-inch range, as well as a few resident grayling. Below the falls is a popular gathering spot for anglers fishing the fall brown trout spawning run. During the heat of summer, this section of the Gibbon River draws savvy anglers. The river offers riffles and long runs, and the road is high up on the mountain, which provides some sense of solitude. This last section flows through carved bench land until it meets the meadow section at Madison Junction.

# Madison Junction to Yellowstone Lake
## Madison Campground, Madison River

Centrally located, the campground borders the confluence of the Gibbon River and the Firehole. West Yellowstone is 14 miles. This 14-mile section of the Madison River offers numerous access points, but during the heat of summer it only offers fair fishing.

## Firehole River

Offering a mix of geological wonders, the Firehole offers a classic mixture of brook trout, brown trout and rainbow trout in this nutrient-rich stream that draws anglers from around the world to match their skills with some picky and educated trout. From its headwaters at Madison Lake, the Firehole resembles a mountain creek as it courses downward to Old Faithful and the Geyser Basin. The river is closed to fishing starting at the bridge a mile and a half east of Old Faithful to the bridge at Biscuit Basin. With the discharge of water in the Geyser Basin and the infusion of water from the Little Firehole, the Firehole reaches its maturity. Above Old Faithful the Firehole runs cooler throughout the summer and provides anglers with good opportunities for catching smaller brook trout.

With the discharge of thermally-heated water from the closed section, fishing in the Little Firehole provides cooler water and larger fish in the lower reaches and smaller fish in the canyon pocket water.

From Biscuit Basin to Cascades, a distance of approximately 12 miles, the Firehole glides through a classic meadow with spring creek-type water. Here dry fly fishermen present their match-the-hatch offerings in early summer and fall. The Cascades change the nature of the river as the water spills and tumbles. The Firehole, joining with the Gibbon River, begins the Madison River. Shallow wading water in an idyllic setting promise more than what the river will produce during the summer months when thermal heating drives the fish to cooler sanctuaries. The best time to fish the Firehole is during the spring and again in the fall. The season opens on the Saturday of Memorial Day weekend. Many sections of the Firehole are easily accessed along the road from the Madison Campground to Old Faithful and beyond.

Upper Firehole River

### Shoshone Lake

The second largest lake in Yellowstone Park with over 8,000 acres, Shoshone Lake is huge, remote and accessed only by trail. When I taught in Jackson, Wyoming, my first fishing outfitter was Roberta Knapp. Roberta was one of the first woman outfitters in Wyoming. A tall, strong woman, this lady could fish and row a boat under any conditions. I learned a great deal from her, as she was a generous person and a passionate fly fisher. Driving out of the Gros Ventre one summer day, she shared with me all of her great fishing stories about fishing big browns and lake trout on the channel between Shoshone Lake and Lewis Lake. If you are fishing the Park during the fall, be sure to take the Lewis Channel Trail, a seven-mile hike, or the trail just above it, which takes a straight line through the woods directly to Shoshone Lake, a distance of 4.5 miles. Fishing heavy fall streamer patterns for big browns and lake trout in the fall has to be a wonderful experience, and I am sad to say I never made it.

Shoshone Lake fishing is rated excellent during early summer with drys, nymphs, scuds and leech patterns. Later in the summer the trout retreat to deeper waters, which can be reached by canoe paddling from Lewis Lake, through the channel, and into Shoshone Lake (with a one-mile portage at the end of the channel).

## Lewis Lake

Lewis Lake allows motorized boats. Boat fishermen both spin and troll for large lake trout and browns. The lake's east shore parallels the road leading to the South Entrance. Fly fishermen fare well at both the inlet and the outlet to **Lewis River**.

# West Thumb to Fishing Bridge Junction

## Yellowstone Lake

Looking at a map of Yellowstone National Park, Yellowstone Lake draws center attention at 87,450 acres. Famous for its staggering numbers of Yellowstone cutthroat, the lake is presently under siege from the unauthorized introduction of nefarious lake trout. Thanks to some stupid bucket biologist, lake trout are expanding rapidly and preying on cutthroats. Regulations now require killing all lake trout caught.

Excellent fishing may be experienced right along the shoreline using small drys and nymphs. Anglers may keep two fish under 13 inches, but this is not always easy since most Yellowstone cutthroat measure between 14 and 16 inches. Boating is allowed, but it requires a special permit along with special regulations for fishing in the arms of the lake. The most popular fishing from shore is between the Sand Point picnic site and the Gull Point area, which is on the Grand Loop Road between West Thumb and the Fishing Bridge Junction. Be sure to walk across the Fishing Bridge and gaze at all the fish.

### Yellowstone Lake Outlet to Gardiner

The river gathers her source water down through the meadows of the Thorofare to empty into the Southeast Arm of Yellowstone Lake. Only hikers with long strides and heavy packs reach the pristine fishing of the Thorofare for 16-inch hungry cutthroats that snatch offerings rejected anywhere else. Only experienced hikers conditioned to arduous terrain, hordes of early summer mosquitoes, and the ominous presence of bears should contemplate planning a trip to the Thorofare.

Although the outlet of Yellowstone Lake is closed the first mile, the next six miles of catch and release draw fly fisherman from around the world to test their skills against 16- and 18-inch Yellowstone cutthroats. But into this zone of packed fishermen and multitudes of hefty cutthroats, Mother Nature levels the playing field with prodigious hatches. For the uninitiated, wading knee-deep into the broad Yellowstone amidst what appears to be hundreds of sippers can be awe-inspiring. After a fly fisher has changed flies a half a dozen times and added a section of 6X or 7X tippet to no avail, the river suddenly becomes daunting, more challenging than a spring creek. On my last visit to Buffalo Ford, I wandered the banks with only a Canon AE-1 intent on catching a big one on film. My photographic experience, with the camera set on automatic, matched the expertise of the majority of young fly fishers eagerly casting over the water. After an hour of observing five or six casters, I realized that the light was fading fast and with it the prospects of photographing a landed fish.

I moved up the road to the next pullout and spotted my man. Ten feet from the bank, I saw the flash of line, splaying droplets of water across the darkening water. The rod arced and the pumping action told me he was about to land a nice cutthroat. Parking my truck, I quickly crossed the road and sat down on the bank behind him. Two friends were fishing below him with the same success, and their banter and jubilation frayed the nerves, I'm sure, of those frustrated fishermen in the general area who never did land a fish as long as I sat observing. Sunglasses were off, and the men strained their eyes across the water skewing their heads to negate the water's glare in the closing hour of dusk. Suddenly a rod flew up again, and the same man landed a hog which he guessed, and I quietly concurred, was in excess of 18 inches. He quietly advised the two other men to switch to a rusty spinner, as that was the only fly the bigger fish were keying on in the middle of a smorgasbord of aquatic offerings.

A rusty spinner, I thought to myself. Do I have one in my box? And then I remembered my first enthusiastic foray into the waters of Buffalo Ford

over twenty years ago. I was teaching in Jackson, Wyoming, and joined two high school students on our first Yellowstone River initiation. The river was crowded that day, and it appeared that everyone was landing 14 to 16-inch fish all around me. I was so eager my hands were shaking in anticipation.

After 40 minutes of chasing rises like a dog chasing his tail, I was dejected. My two young companions, fortunately, had moved far down the river and were not witness to my dejection. Wading over to

the bank humbled, I asked another fisherman what he had been using. He was leaving and looked on me in kindness. I had no idea what the fly pattern was that he handed me, but I caught fish for the next hour before it broke off. When I lost that fly, I went to my fly box and found a similar colored fly and trimmed it down to size. Although not as efficient as the first, it, too, caught fish. I joined my two young companions with a sigh of relief and a feeling of wonder having caught so many beautiful fish in a relatively short period of time.

From Sulfur Caldron to Alum Creek the river is designated as a bird sanctuary and wildlife study area. Just above the falls lies a short section open to fishing, but the water speeds up in this section so wading is risky.

From there the river gathers speed and plunges 300 feet over Yellowstone Falls, coursing its way through the Grand Canyon where angels fear to tread. Anglers seeking solitude need to have stamina in order to reach this section. Anglers may once again ply the waters of the Yellowstone at the confluence with the Lamar River and in the Black Canyon region east of Gardiner.

## Saga: Yellowstone

On my very first trip to Yellowstone Park in the early '70s, I stopped at Bud Lilly's Fly Shop in West Yellowstone. My two fly boxes in those days held mostly my own attractor abominations. I was eager to gain some good advice, as I was camped at Madison Campground. My first day fishing produced pretty slim pickings. As a young man in my 20s, I was mostly familiar with creek fishing for rainbows and brookies on the eastern slopes of the Sierras. I had "novice" written across my forehead.

Bud Lilly assisted me and never gave me the bum's rush when he found out that I was near broke and planned only to purchase three or four flies. He dropped three huge Bitch Creek nymphs into the palm of my hand and told me how to fish them. I had never seen such leviathan monsters. I was incredulous. I wasn't even sure how well I could cast one. But oh, how sweet it was when I landed a 19-inch brown out of a meadow pool on the Gibbon River, a short hike from the campground. Later that evening I cast to the same trailing piece of grass, the exact same spot, and pulled in an 18-inch rainbow.

One of my sons was horrified a few years ago when he found the photographs of me holding up those bloody corpses. I explained to him the mentality of those days and quickly shared with him my conversion during that same year. I suppose as a final act of contrition I should burn the photographs, but I have put off that decision for later. Ten years later I moved to Jackson, Wyoming, and I had another great Yellowstone fishing experience, which I will always treasure. I backpacked to the outlet of Heart Lake as a fishing guide and leader of five teenage boys.

The last trail hike I had made was as a Boy Scout. My pack was an old hand-me-down from my father, and it didn't have a padded hip belt. We had reserved the last campground at the outlet of Heart Lake. Getting a late start, we arrived at the ranger station on the lake and made arrangements to sleep at a midway campsite. One of my attendees had just leaned over the lake to scoop up a handful of water, and his sleeping bag fell into the lake. It slowly expanded with water like a graham cracker in milk.

It was mid-June and cold. During the day I had already lightened the load of one boy's pack, and I was exhausted. That night I lay in a small tent with

Calling home from a phone booth near Buffalo Ford on the Yellowstone River. "Hi, Honey, I took a short-cut home through the park after the conference..."

nothing to keep me warm but my clothes. I was shivering. Giving up my sleeping bag to the youth was my responsibility, and I had no bitterness until early in the morning when I was shaking terribly from the cold. This homophobic young man in my warm sleeping bag wouldn't let me get near him!

The next day four of the boys pulled off the trail a mile from the campsite to fish the rising sippers on the lake. I was stuck with the frail young man who by this time had passed on the remaining heavy items from his pack to mine. Arriving at the camp we were so exhausted that all we could do was collapse to the ground. The youth was so exhausted that he didn't bother extricating himself from his nearly empty pack. We were just a few feet away from the outlet creek. The boy turned to me and said, "I'll never do this again for the rest of my life. I'm sorry you had to carry all my stuff."

"It's ok," I said. "And just for the record, I've decided that I'll never backpack again for the rest of my life! My feet are killing me, but I'm too pooped to take off my boots."

Suddenly, a cannonball dropped into the small

creek beside us. Thinking the troop was behind us up the slope, I yelled out, "Knock it off!" When the next rock slammed the water, we waited, but there was no response.

The young man, struggling out of his pack, looked up the slope and then gazed at the water. "Dave, those aren't rocks. They're fish. They're huge fish. They're feeding right in front of us, Dave."

"Go ahead, sport. They're all yours," I said.

"Maybe later," the lad replied. Within two seconds of this arcane conversation, we were both energized and racing to present the first cast. Within the next hour or two, we had both landed seven or eight spawners returning to the lake. All of these fish ranged in size from 18 to 20 inches, and all of them were caught on size 12 attractor patterns. At the outlet, I caught and measured a 24-inch male that I landed on a small Muddler. All of the fish were caught along a quarter-mile, flat stretch of water before the creek plummeted down the canyon. The remaining young men boisterously appeared a few hours later bragging about catching a ton of 16-inch cuts along the shoreline. We nonchalantly told our tale, which earned nothing but hoots of derision.

For the next two days we caught the same fish and more. Each time one of us stalked the water's edge, we had to scale back our offerings until the last fish landed was caught on a size 20 Adams. I will never forget those two days.

# TIPS FOR HIRING A FLY FISHING GUIDE

Let me begin by saying that after 15 years of being a fly-fishing guide in western Montana, I offended a party of fly fishermen on my first spring outing of the season. They had come to fish the Blackfoot River, a little early, I might add. After three days with this very large party, their complaint against me was awkwardly relayed to me by the guide in charge. I was shocked. I must be honest in telling you I was hurt and angry, but then I had to realistically appraise my guiding skills and etiquette.

Had I become complacent and sloppy through the years? After much reflection, I had to shoulder most of the blame. We were fishing in coffee-colored water. Our Woolly Buggers, shackled and weighted down with lead, resembled some primordial serpent. The runoff was late and especially heavy. As a schoolteacher, I was unaccustomed to fishing in the manner that all of us were forced to fish; generally the runoff is usually over by the time school is out. Although my clients caught about the same numbers of fish as the clients in the other boats, I failed to be assertive and take charge, according to one of the clients.

On one of the days, I was encouraged into a friendly conversation on incompetent teachers and tenure laws. I threw caution to the wind and laid the blame on the shoulders of lazy administrators who fail to follow due-process procedures and document.

This conversation followed a request by the client to exchange political views with a Democrat. The man had promised his wife he would yearly hold at least one civil conversation with a Democrat, and I was his man.

I thought to myself, don't get pulled into a political debate. In spite of the slow fishing, everyone seemed in jovial spirits, so I threw caution to the wind, again! I had broken another rule: Don't discuss your personal life, your politics or your religion. Apparently my behavior and views were brought up at the round table that night. On the third day I broke from the pack (nine guides) and headed for the upper Clark Fork. That was the day the fishing improved dramatically on the Blackfoot, and you can guess the rest of the story.

My worst offense, however, was reserved for the last day when I gave casting advice to an elderly gentlemen who had been fly fishing for 40 years and loved to either encroach on his partner's water or cast out in the middle of the river. I had become critical. I heard it in my voice. I drove home from the Blackfoot that fourth morning reflecting on the qualities that I admired in the top guides who I worked with through the years, and I took stock of myself as a guide.

The following year, at age 52, I retired myself as a guide, knowing that I could no longer keep up with the younger, more passionate guides. Let me share with you the responsibilities of both the guide and the client. Hopefully, this will help you communicate with your outfitter in selecting a guide who is best suited for you.

## Guide Responsibilities

1. Be an accomplished fly fisher, a cautious rower and an enthusiastic teacher.
2. Hold a state guide license and be trained in first aid and CPR.
3. Work hard to help your client catch fish. Never give up or become discouraged.
4. Be friendly and honest. Never inflate the fishing prospects, and allow a client to cancel a trip due to inclement weather or poor fishing conditions.
5. Be punctual. Be organized, and carry extra equipment and supplies.
6. Provide a classy lunch!
7. If you are with a large group and you are having good luck on a particular pattern, share with your fellow guides.
8. Know when to join in conversations and when to withdraw and allow privacy or just quiet time.
9. Ask the clients how much instruction they want. Gauge their response. Many clients find themselves invited on trips, and yet they are really not interested in learning a new skill, not to mention feeling the pressure from a guide. Many of these clients are content to enjoy the float trip in the company of their friends.
10. Never take for granted the natural beauty that surrounds us. Share in the wonders of nature and the catching and releasing of wild Montana trout.

## Responsibilities of the Client

Be realistic in your expectations and as well as your fishing skills. As a guide of many years, I would just cringe when I had a client who booked a trip in the heat of August, had little or no rudimentary casting skills and fully expected to catch a trophy trout that day. A few years back I heard a guide good-naturally say to a client who was denigrating the river, "Well, the fish are here all right, but like a lot of folks, they're not hungry all the time. That's why they call it fishing, not catching."

If a guide tells you he wants you to cast no more than six inches from the shore, he's serious! If you didn't have the skills to do so he wouldn't ask you. A client who spends a fortune to come to fish in Montana and then winces when he looses a few bucks' worth of flies always puzzles me. If you're not losing flies, you're not fishing hard.

Also, dress appropriately. If you do not have waders, wear an old pair of pants and a pair of tennis shoes. At least once a year I would have a client who would show up in dress pants and Gucci loafers. Realistically, this limits the guide's opportunities to stop the boat and let clients wade fish favorite hot spots.

Speaking of flies… Please ask the guide ahead of time if you are expected to pay for the flies. Some shop guides merely add the flies onto your total bill and deduct any flies you didn't use that day. Some outfitters and guides make it a policy to provide the flies free in the hopes that the tip they receive will compensate their loss of flies for the day. Other outfitters and guides bill the client for each fly and leader used. I have worked under both systems. I will tell you honestly that many times I will have given up $20 worth of flies and leaders. As an independent guide, I paid retail prices for flies and leaders most of the time.

Regarding tips (no objectivity here!). Did you enjoy your day? Did the guide work hard at getting you over fish? Did you have a gourmet or lavish lunch? Was the trip well organized? I won't share trade secrets about how much the outfitter pays the guides, but I will tell you that the guide is responsible for all of his equipment and insurance. With few exceptions, the lunches are made by the guide or paid for by the guide. Shuttling the guide's rig usually costs

costs $25 a trip. Boats and rafts are usually replaced within six or seven years at around $2,000-$4,000. Trailers are forever breaking down. The season is very short. Up-front yearly start-up costs translate to three guide trips before the guide makes a profit. OK – guides do have a great job, but tips are greatly appreciated.

What type of guide do you want? Most people rarely make requests of the outfitter in selecting a guide. Are you new to the sport? Do you really want a day's worth of concentrated instruction? Some guides do poorly with beginners; others never know when to let up. Good communication between the guide and client easily resolves this dilemma. I generally push and demand a great deal up until lunch. After lunch I let my beginners just have fun. When they need instruction, I wait for them to ask for it. Ask your outfitter for the best instructor for a beginner.

Do you want a young guide who bursts with enthusiasm, rows the boat with a fierce macho pride, and jumps up and down like a cheerleader? Your outfitter has them. (God, I am getting old.) Be open with the outfitter regarding what you want in a guide. And finally, I would like to close with some advice to novices. Take a class before you book a trip. Check out a fly casting VCR tape. I recommend Doug Swisher's instructional tape on casting, as well as his book. But if you want to learn on your vacation, ask for a walk-in trip instead of a float trip. Trust me, you will learn more in one day of instruction on a creek catching dozens of seven-inch trout than you would spending a couple of days casting from a boat with no previous experience.

# ACCOMMODATIONS AND SERVICES

I have included accommodations and services that are close to good fishing areas. The following businesses have been added to my web site under Accommodations and Services. Each of the following businesses is a retail outlet for this book. For more information about these businesses, visit www.glaciertoyellowstone.com. For Travel Montana Internet Information, go to http://travel.mt.gov. For a complete regional listing of accommodations and services, request a free travel planner from:

Travel Montana
Department of Commerce
P.O. Box 200533
Helena, Montana 59620-0533
(800) 847-4868

---

## Northwestern Montana
## Fly Shops • Sporting Goods

**Crown Enterprises, Inc.**
40 East Idaho Street
**Kalispell**, MT 59901
(406) 755-6484

**Kootenai Angler**
13546 Highway 37
**Libby**, MT 59923
(406) 293-7578

**High Basin Sports**
Box 1110
**Seeley Lake**, MT 59868
(406) 677-3605

**Lakestream Fly Fishing Shop**
15 Central Avenue
**Whitefish**, MT 59937
(406) 862-1298

**Libby Sport Center**
204 West 9th Street
**Libby**, MT 59923
(406) 293-4641

**Snappy Sport Center**
1400 Hwy. 2 East
**Kalispell**, MT 59901

**Sportsman & Ski Haus**
40 East Idaho
**Kalispell**, MT 59901
(406) 755-6484or (406) 257-7525

# Northwestern Montana
# Lodges • B&Bs

**Alpine Adventures at Spotted Bear Ranch**
115 Lake Blaine Drive
**Kalispell**, MT 59901
(406) 755-7337 or (800) 223-4333
www.spottedbear.com
sbr@montana.com

**Candlewycke Inn Bed & Breakfast**
311 Aero Lane
**Big Fork**, MT 59911
(406) 837-6406
www.candlewyckeinn.com
candle@digisys.net

**Laughing Horse Lodge & Restaurant**
71284 Hwy. 83
**Swan Lake**, MT 59911
(406) 886-2080
www.laughinghorselodge.com
laughinghorsemontana@yahoo.com

**Tamaracks Resort**
P.O. Box 812
**Seeley Lake**, MT 59868
(406) 677-2433
www.tamaracksresort.com

# Northwestern Montana
# Campgrounds • RV Parks

**Glacier Peaks RV Park**
3185 Highway 40 W.
**Columbia Falls**, MT 59912
(406) 892-2133 or (800) 268-4849
www.digisys.net/rvs

**Mountain Meadow RV Park**
9125 Hwy. 2 East
**Hungry Horse**, MT 59919
(406) 387-9125
www.mmrvpark.com
camp@mmrvpark.com

**West Glacier KOA**
355 Half Moon Flats Road
**West Glacier**, MT 59936
(406) 387-5341 or (800) 562-3313
wgkoa@netrix.net

# Western Montana
# Fly Shops • Sporting Goods

**Angler's Roost**
815 Hwy 93. S.
**Hamilton**, MT 59840
(406) 363-1268

**Blackbird's Fly Shop and Lodge**
1754 Highway 93
**Victor**, MT
(406) 642-6375 or (800) 210-8648
www.blackbirds.com

**Bob Ward and Sons**
1120 North 1st Street
**Hamilton**, MT 59840
(406) 363-6204

**Bob Ward and Sons**
3015 Paxson
**Missoula**, MT 59801
(406) 728-3221

**Fishaus Tackle**
702 N 1
**Hamilton**, MT 59840
(406) 363-6158
www.montana.com/fishaus
fishaus@montana.com

**Grizzly Hackle Intl.**
215 W. Front Street
**Missoula,** MT 59802
(406) 721-8996

**Kesel's Four Rivers Fly Shop**
501 S. Higgins
**Missoula,** MT 59801
(406) 721-4796
www.fourrivers.net
keselg@fourrivers.net

**The King Fisher**
926 East Broadway
**Missoula,** MT 59802
(406) 721-6141 or (888) 542-4911

**Missoulian Angler**
420 N. Higgins
**Missoula,** MT 59802
(406) 728-7766

**Rock Creek Mercantile Fly Shop and Motel**
15995 Rock Creek Road
**Clinton,** MT 59825
(406) 825-6440
www.rcmerc.com
rcmerc@blackfoot.net

**Sportsman Surplus**
Tremper's Shopping Center
Brooks Street
**Missoula,** MT 59801
(406) 721-5500

# Western Montana
# Lodges • B&Bs

**Alpine Meadows Ranch**
469 Bunkhouse Road
**Darby,** MT
Fax: (619) 755-4194
www.alpinemeadowsranch.com
info@alpinemeadowsranch.net

**Bear Creek Lodge**
1184 Bear Creek Trail
**Victor,** MT 59875
(406) 642-3750
Fax: (406) 642-6847
www.bear-creek-lodge.com
info@bear-creek-lodge.com

**Big Horn Bed and Breakfast**
31 Lower Rock Creek Road
**Phillipsburg,** MT
(406) 859-3109
www.bighornmontana.com
bighornbnb@blackfoot.net

**Blackbird's Fly Shop and Lodge**
1754 Highway 93
**Victor,** MT
(800) 210-8648
www.blackbirds.com
blackbrd@bitterroot.net

**Blue Damsel Bed & Breakfast**
1081 Rock Creek Rd.
**Clinton,** MT 59825
(406) 825-3077
www.Thebluedamsel.com
nki@thebluedamsel.com

**The Mountain Motel B&B**
P.O. Box 423
**Alberton,** MT 59820
(406) 722-4990
Montanahotel@blackfoot.net

**Rock Creek Cabins**
2237 Hillside Drive
**Missoula,** MT 59803
(406) 251-6611
www.bigsky.net/fishing
rockcrk@bigsky.net

**Rock Creek Mercantile Fly Shop and Motel**
15995 Rock Creek Road
**Clinton**, MT 59825
(406) 825-6440
www.rcmerc.com
rcmerc@blackfoot.net

**Rye Creek Lodge**
P.O. Box 877
**Darby**, MT 59829
(406) 821-3366
www.ryecreeklodge.com

# Western Montana
# Campgrounds • RV Parks

**KOA El-Mar Kampground**
3450 Tina Avenue
**Missoula**, MT 59802
(406) 549-0881 or (800) 562-5366
mslakoa@bigsky.net

## Rocky Mountain Front

**Montana Ranch Adventures**
RR HC72 Noffsinger Road
**Browning**, MT
(888) 338-3054
mracompt@northerntel.net

**Montana River Outfitters**
923 10th Avenue N.
**Great Falls**, MT 59401
(406) 761-1677 or (800) 800-8218
www.montanariveroutfitters.com

**Wolverton's Fly Shop**
210 5th Street
**Great Falls**, MT 59405
(406) 454-0254

# Upper Missouri River Basin

**Missouri River Trout Shop and Lodge**
110 Bridge St.
**Craig**, MT 59648
(406) 235-4474 or 800-337-8528

**Montana Fly Goods Company**
2125 Euclid Ave.
**Helena**, MT 59601
(406) 442-2630 or (800) 466-9589

# Southwestern Montana
# Fly Shops • Sporting Goods

**Beartooth Flyfishing**
2975 Hwy. 287 N.
**Cameron**, MT 59720
(406) 682-7525

**Blue Ribbon Flies**
P.O. Box 1037
**West Yellowstone**, MT 59758
(406) 646-7642

**Bob Ward & Sons**
1925 Dewey
**Butte**, MT
(406) 494-3445

**Bud Lilly's Trout Shop**
39 Madison Avenue
**West Yellowstone**, MT 59758
(406) 646-780 or (800) 854-9559

**Complete Fly Fisher**
P.O. Box 127
Hwy. 43
**Wise River**, MT 59762
(406) 832-3175

**East Slope Anglers**
Box 160249
**Big Sky**, MT 59716
(406) 995-4369 or (888) 359-3974

**Fish-On Fly & Tackle**
3346 Harrison Avenue
**Butte**, MT 59701
(406) 494-4218

**Four Rivers Fishing Co.**
205 S. Main
**Twin Bridges**, MT 59754
(406) 684-5651

**Frontier Anglers**
680 N. Montana Street
**Dillon**, MT 59725
(406) 683-5276 or (800) 228-5263

**Gallatin River Fishing Headquarters**
610 N. Montana Street
**Dillon**, MT 59725
(406) 683-6660

**Gallatin Riverguides**
Box 160212
**Big Sky,** MT 59716
(406) 995-2290
www.montanaflyfishing.com

**Harman's Fly Shop**
310 S. Main
**Sheridan**, MT 59749
(406) 842-5868

**Headwaters Angling**
Box 964
**Ennis**, MT 59729
(406) 682-4263

**Jacklin's Fly Shop**
105 Yellowstone
**West Yellowstone**, MT 59758
(406) 646-7336

**Madison River Fishing Co.**
P.O. Box 627
**Ennis**, MT 59729
(406) 682-4293 (800) 227-7127

**Madison River Outfitters**
117 Canyon St.
**West Yellowstone**, MT 59758
(406) 646-9644

**Montana Fly Co.**
P.O. Box 29
**Melrose**, MT 59743
(406) 835-2621

**Montana Troutfitters Orvis**
1716 W. Main
**Bozeman**, MT 59715
(406) 587-4707
www.troutfitters.com

**Powder Horn Outfitters**
35 East Main
**Bozeman**, MT 59715
(406) 587-7373

**The Rivers Edge**
2012 N. 7th Avenue
**Bozeman**, MT 59715
(406) 586-5373

**RJ Cain & Co.**
204 E. Main Street
**Bozeman**, MT 59715
(800) 886-9111

**Sunrise Fly Shop**
P.O. Box 85
**Melrose**, MT 59743
(406) 835-3474

**The Tackle Shop**
127 Main
**Ennis**, MT 59729
(406) 682-4263

## Southwestern Montana
## Lodges • B&Bs

**Best Western Buck's T-4 Lodge**
P.O. Box 160279
**Big Sky**, MT 59716
(406) 995-2191 or (800) 822-4484
Fax: (406) 995-2191
www.buckst4.com
buckst4@mcn.net

**Gallatin River Lodge**
9105 Thorpe Road
**Bozeman**, MT 59718
(406) 388-0148
www.grlodge.com
info@grlodge.com

**Iron Wheel Guest Ranch (B&B)**
40 Cedar Hills Road
**Whitehall**, MT 59759
(406) 494-2960

**King's Motel Flatline Outfitters**
307 S. Main Street
**Twin Bridges**, MT 59754
(800) 222-5510
www.kingsflatline.com
kingsflatline@yahoo.com

## Southwestern Montana
## Campgrounds • RV Parks

**Butte KOA**
1601 Kent
**Butte**, MT 59701
(406) 782-0663

**Dillon KOA**
735 West Park
**Dillon**, MT 59725
(800) KOA-2751

**Yellowstone Grizzly RV Park**
210 S. Electric Street
**West Yellowstone**, MT 59758
(406) 646-4466

**Yellowstone Holiday RV Campground
& Marina**
P.O. Box 759
16990 Hebgen Lake Road
**West Yellowstone**, MT 59758
(406) 646-4242 or toll-free (877) 646-4242
www.yellowstoneholiday.com
yhr@wyellowstone.com

**Yellowstone Park KOA**
6 miles west on Hwy. 20
**West Yellowstone**, MT
(800) 562-7591

## Yellowstone River Drainage
## Fly Goods Shops • Sporting Goods

**Bighorn Fly and Tackle Shop**
485 South 24th Street West
**Billings**, MT 59102
(406) 656-8257

**Bighorn Fly and Tackle Shop**
1426 N. Crawford
**Hardin**, MT 59034
(406) 665-1321

**Bighorn Fly and Tackle Shop**
1 Main Street
**Fort Smith**, MT 59035
(406) 666-2253

**Big Horn Trout Shop, Inc.**
Box 477
**Fort Smith**, MT 59035
(406) 666-2357

**Dan Bailey's Fly Shop**
209 West Park Street
**Livingston**, MT 59047
(406) 222-1673

**George Anderson's Yellowstone Angler**
P.O. Box 660
**Livingston**, MT 59047
(406) 222-7130

**Greater Yellowstone Flyfishers**
211 N. Main
**Cooke City**, MT 59020
(406) 838-2468

**Knoll's Yellowstone Hackle and Flyshop**
P.O. Box 76
**Pray**, MT 59065
(406) 333-4848
http://www.avicom.net/knoll/
knoll@avicom.net

**Quill Gordon Fly Fisher**
P.O. Box 7597
**Fort Smith**, MT 59035
(406) 666-2253

**Montana Master Angler**
107 South Main
**Livingston**, MT 59047
(406) 222-7437

**Rainbow Run Fly Shop**
2244 Grand Avenue
**Billings**, MT 59102
(406) 656-3455

**Yellowstone Angler**
P.O. Box 660
**Livingston**, MT 59047
(406) 222-7130

## Yellowstone River Drainage Lodges • B&Bs

**Carriage House Ranch**
P.O. Box 1249
**Big Timber**, MT 59011-1249
(406) 932-5339
www.carriagehouseranch.com
chr@carriagehouseranch.com

**The River Inn Yellowstone Cabins**
4950 Hwy 89
**South Livingston**, MT 59047
(406) 222-2429
www.wtp.net/go/riverinn
riverinn@wtp.net

**Yellowstone Country Bed and Breakfast**
30 minutes from the north entrance to Yellowstone National Park
**Emigrant, MT**
(406) 333-4917, (406) 333-4640 or (800) 459-8347
www.yellowstonebb.com
yellowstonebb@int.net

# Yellowstone National Park

### Amfac Parks and Resorts
(307) 344-7311
Bridge Bay Campground: 420 sites
Canyon Campground: 280 camping sites
Fishing Bridge RV Park: 345 RV sites
Grant Village Campground: 414 sites
Madison : 292 sites

## Government Agencies

### Montana Department of Fish, Wildlife & Parks
Region 1 FWP Headquarters
490 N. Meridian Rd
Kalispell, MT 59901
(406) 752-5501

Region 2 FWP Headquarters
3201 Spurgin Rd.
Missoula, MT 59801
(406) 542-5500

Region 3 FWP Headquarters
1400 South 19th
Bozeman, MT 59715
(406) 994-4042

Region 4 FWP Headquarters
P.O. Box 6609
Great Falls, MT 59406
(406) 454-3441

Region 5 FWP Headquarters
2300 Lake Elmo Drive
Billings, MT 59105
(406) 252-4654

Region 8 FWP Headquarters
1404 8th Ave.
Helena, MT 59620
(406) 444-4720

## National Forest Ranger Districts
Beartooth Ranger District (406) 446-2103
Big Timber Ranger District (406) 932-5155
Bozeman Ranger District (406) 587-6920
Bureau of Land Management /
  Lee Metcalf Wilderness (406) 683-2337
Cabinet Ranger District (406) 827-3533
Darby Ranger District (406) 821-3913
Deer Lodge Ranger District (406) 846-1770
Dillon Ranger District (406) 683-3900
Gardiner Ranger District (406) 848-7375
Hamilton Ranger District (406) 363-3131
Helena Ranger District (406) 449-5490
Hungry Horse Ranger District (406) 387-5243
Libby Ranger District (406) 293-7773
Lincoln Ranger District (406) 362-4265
Livingston Ranger District (406) 222-1892
Madison Ranger District (406) 777-5461
Phillipsburg Ranger District (406) 859-3211
Missoula Ranger District (406) 329-3750
Plains / Thompson Falls Ranger District
  (406) 826-3821
Kootenai National Forest Supervisor's Office
  (406) 293-6211
Rexford Ranger District (406) 296-2536
Rocky Mountain Ranger District
  (Rocky Mountain Front) (406) 466-5341
Seeley Lake Ranger District (406) 677-2233
Spotted Bear Ranger District (406) 758-5376
Stevensville Ranger District (406) 777-5461
Sula Ranger District (406) 777-5461
Swan Lake Ranger District (406) 837-5081
Tally Lake Ranger District (406) 862-2508
West Fork of the Bitterroot Ranger District
  (406) 821-3269

Wise River Ranger District (406) 832-3178
Wisdom Ranger District (406) 689-3243

## Chambers of Commerce
Beaverhead Chamber of Commerce
(406) 683-5511
Big Fork Chamber of Commerce (406) 837-5888
Big Sky Chamber of Commerce (406) 995-3000
Bitterroot Chamber of Commerce
(406) 363-2400
Bozeman Chamber of Commerce (406) 586-5421
Butte-Silver Bow Chamber of Commerce
(800) 735-6814
Columbia Falls Chamber of Commerce
(406) 892-2072
Cooke City Chamber of Commerce
(406) 838-2495
Ennis Chamber of Commerce (406) 682-4388
Gardiner Chamber of Commerce
(406) 848-7971
Helena Area Chamber of Commerce
(800) 743-5362

Kalispell Chamber of Commerce (406) 758-2800
Libby Chamber of Commerce (406) 293-4167
Livingston Chamber of Commerce
(406) 222-0850
Missoula Chamber of Commerce
(800) 526-3465
Polson Chamber of Commerce (406) 883-5969
Red Lodge Chamber of Commerce
(406) 446-1718
Seeley Lake Chamber of Commerce
(406) 677-2880
West Yellowstone Chamber of Commerce
(406) 646-7701
Whitefish Chamber of Commerce
(406) 862-3501

Upper Hyalite Creek (Southwestern Montana)

# NOTES